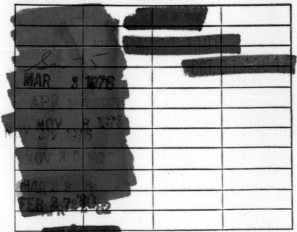

THE CHAMELEON AND THE DREAM

SLAVISTIC PRINTINGS AND REPRINTINGS

edited by

C. H. VAN SCHOONEVELD

Indiana University

78

1970

MOUTON

THE HAGUE · PARIS

THE CHAMELEON AND THE DREAM

THE IMAGE OF REALITY IN ČEXOV'S STORIES

by

KARL D. KRAMER

University of Michigan

1970

MOUTON

THE HAGUE · PARIS

LIBRARY OF CONGRESS CATALOG CARD NUMBER: 76-106463

Printed in The Netherlands by Mouton & Co., Printers, The Hague.

To Doreen

FOREWORD

To write about Čexov has its pitfalls, not the least of which is an awareness of how Čexov himself regarded critics: he accused them of being leeches, of employing an obtuse vocabulary which neither aids nor hinders one's understanding of a literary work because it is irrelevant to it, and of acting as though they understood the fundamental laws governing art – laws which, though they may exist, have never been helpfully expounded by critics. He made fun of one student of his art who divided his work into three periods, and claimed that only one critical opinion on his own work had ever stuck in his mind: the prediction by a now forgotten critic – were it not that Čexov remembered him – the prediction that Čexov would end in the gutter.

But in writing to Suvorin about Tolstoj's essay on art in early January 1898, he offered by implication an 'out' for the critic: "To say of art that it has grown decrepit, that it's entered a blind alley, that it's not what it ought to be, and so forth, and so forth – all this amounts to the same thing as saying that the desire to eat and drink has grown old, become obsolete, and is not what it needs to be. Of course hunger is an old story, and in our desire to eat we've entered a blind alley, but eating, nevertheless, is a necessity and we shall go on doing it whatever nonsense philosophers and angry old men may utter." If to go on writing is a necessity, then to continue trying to understand what has been written is equally necessary. This book is primarily devoted to such an effort. The initial impulse to study Čexov was a desire to come to grips with the meaning of particular stories. Hopefully, that impulse has been at least partially realized in the following pages.

All the same, it would be idle to claim that Čexov is a neglected figure in literary criticism. Be that as it may, I do not believe there has been any sustained study of the process by which he came to capture his own image of reality in his stories. Less than a dozen years ago Edmund Wilson in a preface to a Čexov collection complained of the garbling of

Čexov's development in most anthologies. Though paperback anthologies of Čexov stories in the United States today are scrupulous in their attention to chronology, little attention has yet been given to the continuity in his development from the early comic sketches to the late, subdued, more full-bodied, and more complex comic sketches. This book is also an attempt to analyze this development.

I wish to thank Victor Erlich, George Ivask, and Frank Jones for their reading of the original manuscript and for their provocative suggestions and judicious criticism. That these suggestions and criticisms may not have borne full fruit is of course my responsibility and not theirs.

Funds making this publication possible were derived from income on the endowment of the Horace H. Rackham School of Graduate Studies at the University of Michigan; for this aid I extend my gratitude.

An essay, published previously in *Slavic and East-European Studies*, included most of the material to be found in Chapter VI of this book.

Ann Arbor, Michigan, April 1967   K. D. K.

CONTENTS

Foreword 7

   I.   Short Story: The Art of Moral Revelation 11

  II.   Literary Parodies 28

 III.   Chameleons 49

 IV.   Pathos and the Failure of Feeling 60

  V.   Dreams 76

 VI.   The Question of Identity 93

 VII.   The Dialogue with Melodrama 113

VIII.   Stories of Time 134

 IX.   Stories of Ambiguity 153

Selected Bibliography 174

Index 177

I

SHORT STORY: THE ART OF MORAL REVELATION

One of the most representative practitioners of the short story, Anton Čexov appeared at a point in the history of the genre when its fundamental qualities were undergoing refinement. Before looking at the process of Čexov's individual literary development, one needs to isolate these qualities of the genre and to indicate some of the ways in which Čexov's own refinements mark him as one of the first of modern short story writers. Like the elegiac poem, the short story is a form which shows us what a thing or person is or has been; but typically it is not concerned with showing us the process of becoming or going from. It is a literary type which has the extraordinary advantage of dispensing with time. It depicts things and beings in a state of stasis, and up to the present moment this is what it has best been able to do.

Often writers on the short story have sought its origins in Roman tales such as those of Apuleius, or at the very latest in Boccaccio's *Decameron*. While it is true that short works of narrative fiction have been written since Roman times, these relatively early pieces bear only the most superficial resemblances to the work done by nineteenth- and twentieth-century writers. Those who go back to Boccaccio, for instance, to seek the first great short story writer leave a great deal unexplained: where is the line of development from the fifteenth century to the nineteenth? Between Boccaccio and the modern period there had been isolated instances of short narrative fictions, such as those of Cervantes, but a tradition of such works never really became established during this four-hundred-year period.

When German, French, Russian, and American writers at the beginning of the last century began developing a tradition of such short works, they rarely turned to their purported forebear for inspiration. In a very practical sense they were making a new beginning in the short story, which was much more indebted to its bulkier companion, the eighteenth-century novel, than to Boccaccio. Viktor Šklovskij [1] has indicated a basic discontinuity between Boccaccio and the early nineteenth-century writers: the stories in *The Decameron* were based on previously formulated and distinctly formal plots which have circulated through the Western world for centuries, and therefore one can trace analogues for them. The interest these stories arouse and the measure of their success lie in the manipulation of the *donnée* – the basic framework of incidents which had been handed down; the writer's achievement depends on what he sees in the basic framework and is able to express.

One does not ordinarily seek or find analogues for the stories of Maupassant, Čexov, or Joyce. The short story writers of the nineteenth and twentieth centuries have not as a rule taken their basic plot structures, or series of related events, from previously existing models. Ordinarily, as Šklovskij points out, the modern short story writer takes his basic material, including situation, from observed experience. This marks an extremely important break between Boccaccio and Cervantes and the modern period. The break is so basic that in effect the later writers are beginning all over again. The short story as we know it today goes back no further than the early nineteenth century. When one attempts to relate earlier work in short narrative prose to the short story of the past century and a half, he finds that the essential nature of the mode eludes him.

If one seeks the derivation of the genre, he may find considerably more fruitful connections between the lyric poem and the short story. Both the short story and the novel are products of extremely recent times. It has often been suggested that elements of the epic poem and of tragedy have found their way into the modern novel; by the same token, it might well be suggested that elements of the lyric poem have found their way into the short story. Irene Hendry, discussing specifically James Joyce's *Dubliners*, has noted that ". . . in poetry the isolated moment of revelation dates at least from Wordsworth's experiences in the presence of mountains, leech-gatherers, and the lights about Westminster Bridge".[2] Although the mode of operation in the two forms is vastly different, they arrive at much the same goal. The lyric poem proceeds by way of manipulation of words, largely through images, but its

---

[1] Viktor Šklovskij, *Xudožestvennaja proza: Razmyšlenija i razbory* (Moskva, 1959), p. 484.
[2] Irene Hendry, "Joyce's Epiphanies", in *James Joyce: Two Decades of Criticism*, ed. Seon Givens (New York, 1948), p. 33.

shortness dictates that what it is centrally concerned with is delineating the revelations of an isolated moment in time. The short story proceeds primarily through situation and incident towards the same goal – a state of temporal stasis, in which a thing or person is defined and revealed. This similarity can be seen also through contrast: the epic poem, the tragic drama, and the novel deal with continuity, change, development, movement; the lyric poem and the short story deal with a separate moment, the revelation of a state of being; death often figures importantly in these two modes because it represents a standstill, a final halt to all movement. The longer forms can deal with past, present, and future; the shorter forms are limited to past and present, usually one or the other, and almost never deal with the future. In this connection it is interesting how often Čexov's short stories are written entirely in the present tense, as if he wished to freeze all action, to separate it from time, movement, and change; "A Dreary Story" (*Skučnaja istorija*) is the most obvious example.

Searching for the first appearance of something which can be identified as short story, one finds recognizable shapes at the end of the eighteenth and the beginning of the nineteenth centuries. Some remarks by Northrup Frye, addressed primarily to the novel and the romance, are helpful in defining connections between this early work and the modern short story:

The essential difference between novel and romance lies in the conception of characterization. The romance does not attempt to create "real people" so much as stylized figures which expand into psychological archetypes. It is in the romance that we find Jung's libido, anima, and shadow reflected in the hero, heroine, and villain respectively. That is why the romance so often radiates a glow of subjective intensity that the novel lacks, and why a suggestion of allegory is constantly creeping in around its fringes. Certain elements of character are released in the romance which make it naturally a more revolutionary form than the novel. The novelist deals with personality, with character wearing the *personae* or social masks. He needs the framework of a stable society, and many of our best novelists have been conventional to the verge of fussiness. The romancer deals with individuality, with characters *in vacuo* idealized by revery, and, however conservative he may be, something nihilistic and untamable is likely to keep breaking out of his pages.[3]

Frye's distinctions between novel and romance are well founded; but rather curiously they resemble Frank O'Connor's attempt to distinguish

[3] Northrup Frye, *Anatomy of Criticism* (Princeton, New Jersey, 1957), pp. 304-305.

between novel and short story. He claims that "the novel is bound to be a process of identification between the reader and the character. . . . One character at least in any novel must represent the reader in some aspect of his own conception of himself . . . and this process of identification invariably leads to some concept of normality and to some relationship – hostile or friendly – with society as a whole." But in the short story, he continues, "there is this sense of outlawed figures wandering about the fringes of society, superimposed sometimes on symbolic figures whom they caricature and echo – Christ, Socrates, Moses. . . . As a result there is in the short story at its most characteristic something we do not often find in the novel – an intense awareness of human loneliness." [4] O'Connor's idea of 'loneliness' and Frye's of 'individuality' and 'characters *in vacuo* idealized by revery' very nearly coincide. In short, Frye's distinction between novel and romance seems much to the point in discussing novel versus short story. However, when he goes on to apply his own generic distinctions to the latter, he confuses essential characteristics with historical accident:

The prose romance, then, is an independent form of fiction to be distinguished from the novel and extracted from the miscellaneous heap of prose works now covered by that term. Even in the other heap known as short stories one can isolate the tale form used by Poe, which bears the same relation to the full romance that the stories of Chekhov or Katherine Mansfield do to the novel. "Pure" examples of either form are never found; there is hardly any modern romance that could not be made out to be a novel, and vice versa. The forms of prose fiction are mixed, like racial strains in human beings, not separable like the sexes.[5]

His choice of illustration for tale and short story is revealing: there is not only an obvious difference in theme, treatment, and approach in the 'tales' of Poe and the 'short stories' of Čexov and Katherine Mansfield; there is also an important time lag. It is my contention that more lines of connection between Poe and Katherine Mansfield can be established than differences. When we speak of short prose narratives, the forms are not only 'mixed'; they indicate a steady pattern of evolution within the form.

Even the development of the terms 'tale' and 'short story' can be traced to historical usage. Throughout the nineteenth century the short story in England and America was referred to as tale. Poe's collection

---

[4] Frank O'Connor, *The Lonely Voice: A Study of the Short Story* (New York, 1962), pp. 17-19.
[5] Northrup Frye, *Anatomy of Criticism*, p. 305.

was called *Tales of the Grotesque and Arabesque*; Hawthorne entitled one of his books *Twice-Told Tales*; there is Irving's *Tales of a Traveller*, Melville's *The Piazza Tales*, and Ambrose Bierce's *Tales of Soldiers and Civilians*. These writers intended no distinction between 'tale' and 'short story': the first use of the expression 'short story' is recorded by the *Oxford English Dictionary* as dating from 1898. Modern editors usually refer to the short stories of Poe, Hawthorne, Melville, rather than to their tales. Apparently the basic distinction between the two labels is simply a matter of historical usage. To associate the tale with romance and the short story with realism is an historical rather than generic division.

Much the same situation has existed in the Russian language. In Russian there are two terms which refer to short narrative prose fictions: p*ovest'* and *rasskaz* (roughly, 'tale' and 'short story'). Today the word *povest'* is reserved for works somewhat longer than the *rasskaz*. Thus, in modern usage "The Death of Ivan Il'ič" or "Notes from Underground" would be referred to as *povesti*, while the term *rasskaz* would be reserved for such shorter works as Čexov's "Lady with the Dog" (*Dama s sobačkoj*) and "The Darling" (*Dušečka*). During the first half of the nineteenth century, however, only the term *povest'* was in current usage to refer to a short prose narrative. Thus, Puškin and Gogol' called their stories *povesti* regardless of length: Gogol's "Tale (*Povest'*) of How Ivan Ivanovič Quarreled with Ivan Nikiforovič" is considerably shorter than many pieces which Čexov wrote and called *rasskazy*. Puškin entitled his collection *Tales (Povesti) of Ivan Belkin*, though by modern standards – that is, the test of length – the Belkin series consists of *rasskazy*. According to Dal's *Dictionary of the Russian Language,* as late as 1882 the term *rasskaz* was not in general use to refer to a short narrative fiction.

Čexov's own attitude toward these two terms is revealing; he appears in Russian literary history during the transitional period when *rasskaz* was first being used to refer to a legitimate literary genre. He associates *povest'* not only with greater length, but also with greater formal complexity; the two qualities no doubt should go hand in hand, but unfortunately they do not always. Here is an interesting example of an historical distinction: the editor of the Soviet edition of Čexov's *Complete Collected Works and Letters* invariably refers to "The Duel" (*Duèl'*) as a *povest'*, apparently because of its length. However, Čexov calls it both *povest'* and *rasskaz* on different occasions. How does he decide which to use? It may be simply that he considered the terms interchangeable, but at least one reference to "The Duel" as *rasskaz* seems to indicate a real distinction: "At last I have finished my long, wearisome *rasskaz* . . .".[6] If it were a *povest'* it would be long but 'wearisome' would not be an adjunct to length. The length, then, does not by itself make "The Duel" a *povest'*; it is too long for a *rasskaz*, but because its length does not result in greater formal or thematic complexity it remains a *rasskaz* by default.

Excluding some very early pieces, the first relatively long work produced by Čexov was "The Steppe" (*Step'*). This was to be his debut in the thick journals of the day, an important literary event for him. Describing "The Steppe" to Korolenko, he wrote: "On your friendly advice I have begun a little *povestuška* . . ." (XIV, 11). This diminutive, derived from *povest'*, could signify either affection or contempt. It is safe to say that the word indicates at least great modesty in regard to his undertaking, and perhaps that he expects at best barely to achieve the large form, for he goes on in the same letter to complain that he is writing so compactly that every page turns out like a little '*rasskaz*'. One suspects that Čexov tended to associate *rasskaz* with the kind of work he produced for the newspaper press and *povest'* with work of the quality demanded by the thick journals.

Ralph Matlaw maintains that Čexov "distinguished the *rasskaz* from the *povest'* according to the point of view taken in the work, subtitling first person narrations *rasskazy* regardless of their length ('My Life', 'House with Mezzanine')".[7] This is not entirely accurate, for he also referred to third person narratives as *rasskazy*, particularly "Three Years" (*Tri goda*), one of his very longest pieces from the same general period as "My Life" and "a House with The Mezzanine". Of the stories written after 1890, he consistently called only two *povesti* – "Ward No. 6" (*Palata No. 6*) and "In the Ravine" (*V ovrage*). Concerning the former, he wrote: "It has plot, complication, and resolution (*fabula, zavjazka i razvjazka*)" (XV, 358). This would once again seem to indicate that length alone is not sufficient, that the narrative complexity associated with length is his basis for the distinction.[8]

At any rate, historically the term *povest'* bears the same relation to

<hr/>

[6] A. P. Čexov, *Polnoe sobranie sočinenij i pisem* (Moskva, 1944-51), XV, 233. All subsequent references to Čexov's work, unless otherwise indicated, will be cited by volume and page number within the text.

[7] Ralph Matlaw, "Čechov and the Novel" in *Anton Čechov, 1860-1960: Some Essays*, ed. Thomas Eekman (Leiden, 1960), p. 149.

[8] It is, of course, also entirely possible that when he uses the term *povest'* he has in mind simply the kind of traditional story which Puškin wrote.

the term *rasskaz* as the English word 'tale' bears to 'short story'. Both *rasskaz* and 'short story' acquired specifically literary meanings very late in the nineteenth century. That which had been written earlier was called tale or *povest'* by default, as it were, simply because no other terms were available. We shall assume that the word 'tale' refers to short prose narratives written during the nineteenth century – that it is to be distinguished from the short story only in this one respect.

What is more important here is to indicate the lines of connection between the nineteenth-century tale and the twentieth-century short story. The first notable practitioners of the genre belonged to the Romantic Movement or were highly indebted to its literary emphases. It is important in the history of the short story that it was achieving its first major successes during a period when the Romantic Movement held sway throughout Europe. E. T. A. Hoffmann in Germany, Poe and Hawthorne in America and Puškin and Gogol' in Russia were to varying degrees under the influence of Romanticism. Many of the characteristic features of their stories were derived from it. Perhaps the most essential of these is the dominant role of mood, atmosphere, and tone. Though part of this influence was certainly the Gothic revival, another more important aspect was the example offered by the Romantic poets. On the one hand, the mysterious, otherworldly atmospheric effects of a poet like Coleridge, and on the other, the close identification of setting with theme, as in Wordsworth's poetry, may well have led the way for the early short-story writers. It is almost always tone that holds their work together and the discovery of this ordering principle appears to have been made by the Romantics. The first analysis of the short story as a literary mode is usually attributed to Poe, whose often quoted phrase, 'the single effect', certainly seems relevant to the problem of tone. The principle thus discovered has endured long after the Romantic Movement ceased to dominate the literary scene. Tone is just as basic to the short story of Čexov and Katherine Mansfield as it was in the early nineteenth century, although the range of effects which can be achieved has been considerably increased.

One element of the early short story which has not persisted is the emphasis on elaborate plot construction. If one thinks of Poe and James Joyce together the differences seem far greater than the similarities. But it may well be that the plots of Poe and Hoffmann are simply part of the historical trappings which have lost their effectiveness; Poe employed suspense, the unexpected, and the violent turn of events as a means of achieving tone – a single effect in his terms. The romantic predilection for the exotic, the fantastic, and the mysterious found an outlet in these relatively elaborate plots. A mystery ordinarily involves a complex series of related events and a concept of change and development which are alien to the short story. However, the chain of events in such stories as Poe's "Fall of the House of Usher" or Puškin's "Queen of Spades" subordinates movement and change to the one dominant note, strangeness or fantasy. If one takes a sufficiently unusual chain of events, what is apt to lay hold of the reader is not so much the impression of movement and change as the note of unity emerging from the very singularity of the events. Plot in "The Fall of the House of Usher" and "The Queen of Spades" becomes as important a device for achieving tone as setting or character.

With the steady growth of realism as a trend in European literature writers became less interested in the mysterious and exotic. Because the elaborate suspense plot was no help at all in depicting the day-to-day existence of ordinary people, it had outworn its usefulness in the short story. The particular tone or atmosphere which the Romantics sought was no longer in vogue. As a consequence, elaborate plots were rejected in favor of the ever more bare narrative constructions of Maupassant, Čexov, Joyce, and Katherine Mansfield. Today the only types of short story in which elaborate plot still prevails are the ghost story, the tale of terror, the detective story, and science fiction, where the unusual and the mysterious are the chief attractions.

If the Romantic Movement had an impact on the evolution of the short story, it also can account for some of the differences between story and novel. Historically, the great difference between the two is the fact that the novel largely escaped the influences of the Romantic Movement. It had already established itself prior to the Romantic age, as the short story had not. Thus Lionel Trilling could say, "The novel, then, is a perpetual quest for reality, the field of its research being always the social world, the material of its analysis being always manners as the indication of the direction of man's soul." [9] Mr. Trilling was able to qualify his statement by adding: ". . . the novel as I have described it has never really established itself in America." [10] Perhaps it is possible to generalize about the function of the novel, and at the same time to ignore its development in America. However, the development of the short story in America has been so central in the mainstream of the whole genre that it is impossible to ignore it here. Trilling's generaliza-

[9]   Lionel Trilling, *The Liberal Imagination* (New York, 1950), p. 205.
[10]   Lionel Trilling, *The Liberal Imagination*, p. 206.

tion might well apply to the short stories of Maupassant and Čexov, but it will hold true neither for the short story in America, nor for the developments in the genre throughout Europe under the influence of Romanticism.

Thus, the short story was necessarily influenced by the historical situation at the time of its emergence on the literary scene. There remain, still, basic characteristics of the genre which lie outside the historical context. Commentators and anthologists often discuss the short story when they really wish to talk about the novel. Space limitations in anthologies make it easier to print short stories, and the commentator directs his attention to the common characteristics of both modes. To be sure, the two share many characteristics. Character, situation, plot, point of view, the discovery-complication-resolution-peripety formula, and symbolism are all exploited in the short story as well as in the novel. However, the relative importance of some of these devices varies enormously from one mode to the other: character is a much more central concern of the novelist, while tonal unity can be considerably more crucial in the short story. Nevertheless, there is no denying that this body of fictional techniques is common to both literary modes. The great insurmountable gap between them is length, and though there are many similarities between the long and short forms, the question here is how does one distinguish the short story from the novel? What are the implications of the former's shortness as to theme, structure, technique?

One implication is that technique itself assumes a more crucial role in the short story. By the sheer bulk of the novel the writer can afford passages which bear only a tenuous connection with his central themes, while each part of the short story seems magnified by the very littleness of its totality. At least two contemporary short story writers have attested to the relatively greater technical demands of their genre.[11] Though it does not always hold true, there have been cases of novelists who were unable to write short stories and short story writers who tried but failed to produce novels. Undeniably a great novelist, Dickens, like his English contemporaries, apparently had very little inclination towards the short story. The fact that Dickens is noted for studies of character and that Thackeray seems to have been at his best when dealing with panoramic scenes may well be signs of an anti-short-story

---

[11] See Sean O'Faolain, *The Short Story* (New York, 1951) and Ray B. West, Jr., *The Short Story in America* (New York, 1952).

bias in these writers: detailed characterization and panoramic description, while often major virtues in the novel, are largely superfluous
in the short story. Čexov was the opposite type of writer; he often
confessed to an inclination – a compulsion even – to cut off his
stories at the point where development enters. Ray West, Jr. has noted
that the short story "... does demand a certain conscious awareness.
In any case, we can point to the fact that those authors who have
excelled in the short story have all indicated a deliberate awareness of
the problems of their craft: Nathaniel Hawthorne, Herman Melville,
Henry James, Ernest Hemingway, and William Faulkner; those who
have not had this awareness – Mark Twain, Theodore Dreiser, and
Thomas Wolfe – are best known for their longer fiction." [12] One might
easily draw up a similar list for any other national literature. This
relative lack of awareness may account for the small number of good
short stories in nineteenth-century English literature. In Russia, on the
other hand, nearly every major novelist can lay claim to a solid group
of works in the genre, and many Russian poets, who never tried their
hand at a novel, have written first-rate short stories.

Another result derived from the difference in length is that the short-
story writer simply has no room for any kind of development.[13] How,
then, can he elude or exploit the restrictions imposed on him? One
method has been the devices of allegory and parable, whereby the writer
can telescope a great deal of human experience into an ideal situation
in which the reader is more than usually willing to sacrifice his credulity
for the sake of the device's charm. The short story writer has always
sought means of telescoping; it is therefore not surprising that one often
finds parable and allegory scattered through the works of many short-
story writers; they feel a kind of kindred spirit in these devices. Čexov
occasionally resorted to them, notably in "The Bet" (*Pari*). In his
shortest pieces Tolstoj too often resorted to parable. In the main, however, allegory and parable have not proven entirely successful techniques in the short story. Particularly as realism came to dominate the
literary scene in the second half of the nineteenth century, the demand
for verisimilitude seemed to deny their validity.

[12]   Ray B. West, Jr., *The Short Story in America*, p. 22.
[13]   It should be pointed out, of course, that length alone does not make a short
story into a novel. In this sense Čexov was right in refusing to call many of his
longer works anything but *rasskazy*. We see in the detective 'novel' how greater
length does not in itself form a generic distinction. In spite of its greater length,
it is a type which focuses on revelation rather than on an evolutionary process;
the solution was there from the beginning had we only seen it.

A more fruitful solution has been the writer's ready admission and acceptance of the limitations imposed by the short story. He has tried to turn them into virtues by ignoring time or freezing it into a sudden moment of revelation in which the mode of existence of a thing or being is illuminated. Mark Schorer calls attention to a difference in kind between the short story and the novel when he observes: "If we can pin down the difference between the short story and the novellette and novel at all, it would seem to be in this distinction, that the short story is an art of moral revelation, the novel an art of moral evolution." [14] Boris Èjxenbaum calls attention to much the same distinction when he writes that the short story saves its punch until the final moment, while the end of a novel is a point of relaxation where the accumulated tensions are dispersed: "The short story is like a riddle; the novel something like a charade or rebus, in which the delight is in the doing rather than the solution of the puzzle." [15] The short story writer has very frequently seized upon the suddenness and shock effect inherent in a momentary realization of a thing's 'whatness', to use Joyce's term, and has made a dramatic virtue of the swiftness of the discovery. A classic instance of this is Henry James' somewhat belabored treatment of John Marcher's discovery of his fate in "The Beast in the Jungle". Unfortunately, it loses much of its dramatic punch because James insists on extracting the last ounce of irony from the discovery. Later writers have further refined the device by underplaying their hand, as it were.

The conception of moral revelation affects the relative importance of plot, character, and setting in novel and story. For one thing, suspense plays a far more crucial role in the shorter form. One reads on to find out what will finally happen, what the actual state of affairs is, or what kind of person the central character really is. "What is going to happen?" is ordinarily a fundamental question in the novel, though not necessarily a crucial one; our interest focuses primarily on: "how or why does it happen?" Wellek and Warren have in mind this distinctive interest of the novel when they write: "To tell a story, one has to be concerned about the happening, not merely the outcome. There is or was a kind of reader who must look ahead to see how a story 'comes out'; but one who reads only the 'concluding chapter' of a nineteenth-century novel would be somebody incapable of interest in story, which

[14] *The Story: A Critical Anthology*, ed. Mark Schorer (Englewood Cliffs, New Jersey, 1950), p. 433.
[15] B. M. Èjxenbaum, "O. Genri i teorija novelly", *Literatura: Teorija, kritika, polemika* (Leningrad, 1927), p. 172.

is process – even though process toward an end." [16] Thus, to read *The Brothers Karamazov* as a detective novel – simply to find out who was physically responsible for the murder – would be a bore; nine-tenths of the book would then become superfluous.

If the short story, lacking this fundamental interest in process, lays greater stress on suspense, on the ultimate revelation, then its balance of interest between plot and character also shifts. Henry James in "The Art of Fiction" addresses himself to the art of the novel when he stresses the primacy of character over plot or incident: "What is character but the determination of incident? What is incident but the illustration of character?" [17] The rhetorical form of the questions seems to indicate their mutual dependence, though actually both formulations imply a subservience of plot to character. If we are speaking of the novel, this dominant interest in character is accurate, but the short story is never so consistently interested in it. At least one gifted writer in the genre, Sean O'Faolain, has pointed to the back-seat role which character must assume in the short story:

... in short story writing there can be no development of character. The most that can be done is to peel off an outer skin or mask, by means of an incident or two, in order to reveal that which is – as each writer sees this "is." The character will not change his spots; there is no time; if he seems likely to do so in the future, the story can but glance at that future; if he seems likely to change at once, like Kolpakov in "The Chorus Girl," we will have small reason to believe the change permanent.[18]

With its greater emphasis on development and change the novel is ideally suited to focus on character. The short story must reduce character to type for the most part; first, simply because there is no time for development; secondly, because its central concern with suspense dictates an interest in incident rather than character. Marvin Mudrick has produced a formulation directly opposed to James' in regard to character and incident, and he states the case for the short story better than James can when he writes: "... the shorter the work of fiction, the more likely are its characters to be simply functions and typical manifestations of a precise and inevitable sequence of events." [19] This is easy

---

[16] René Wellek and Austin Warren, *Theory of Literature* (New York, 1956), p. 205.
[17] Henry James, "The Art of Fiction", *The Future of the Novel*, ed. Leon Edel (New York, 1956), pp. 15-16.
[18] Sean O'Faolain, *The Short Story*, p. 191.
[19] Marvin Mudrick, "Character and Event in Fiction", *The Yale Review*, L (Winter 1961), 205.

enough to see in a work like Robert Louis Stevenson's "Sire de Malé-troit's Door" where our interest focuses on a series of mysteries: will Denis escape his pursuers? What is the secret of the house into which he stumbles? And finally, how will he escape from Sire de Malétroit's clutches? The answer to the final mystery hinges on the conception of character in the story. The hero, Denis, is a proud, handsome, gallant, young officer. The heroine is well-mannered, beautiful, and modest. Character is reduced completely to type, and therefore incident is not dependent on it in any meaningful sense. Our expectation is that the hero will somehow escape through his wit and valor; but the actual outcome simply substitutes another possible solution based on the types: the handsome young man marries the beautiful young lady. Stevenson employs a standard technique in the manipulation of suspense: the creation of an illusory pattern which the reader follows, thus overlooking the possibility of another equally valid resolution.

In this kind of story everything depends on the final event. In a rather more sophisticated type the interest focuses on the implications of an event – its meaning – rather than on the event itself. In Hemingway's "The Killers" we are intrigued first by the mystery: who are the killers and what do they want? However, these questions have been resolved prior to the end of the story. It is only after the mystery has been cleared up that we see the real point: a world has been revealed in which men must lie on their beds awaiting an unavoidable but arbitrary death. Once again, however, the story never focuses on the characters, Oley Anderson or Nick Adams, but rather on the nature of the world in which they play a part. The story in which loss of innocence is the main theme usually follows this pattern. Even in stories where the revelation concerns the nature of the hero the writer is restricted to the discovery of a single deviation from the pattern-type, or the discovery that there can be no deviation, as in Čexov's "The Man in a Case" (*Čelovek v futljare*), where the suspense hangs on the question, will Belikov marry? The resolution simply denies the question: such a type can never marry. Thus, the short story frequently places a burden on incident to the neglect of character just because it is an art of revelation and depends on the manipulation of suspense.

If we refer back to "Sire de Malétroit's Door" the importance of suspense is obvious enough, but what then are we to say of "The Killers", which seemingly dissipates all its mysteries before the end? "The Killers" is a typical modern short story in this regard. The story which depends on revelation of event for its suspense is a limited form, but given the reader's expectation of this form, the writer is free to manipulate expectation. Upon finishing a typical modern short story one senses that he has missed the point somewhere. The end was not only unexpected, but somehow irrelevant to the questions apparently raised by the story. When this happens the writer has usually forced the reader to focus his interest on the wrong questions. This is the way Hemingway works in "The Killers". It is only after one realizes that a shift of focus has occurred that the story can release its full impact, and the reader's own sense of discovery magnifies that impact. Another common variation on this pattern occurs in James Joyce's "Araby". Together with the narrator the reader expects to comprehend the mystery and romance of Araby. The revelation is simply a denial of the mystery — a revelation which insinuates itself through a snatch of trivial, flirtatious conversation overheard by the narrator. Here the expectation is so neatly dissipated that the revelation may be missed completely. It is this kind of manipulation of suspense which characterizes the modern short story, and easily identifies Čexov as one of the moderns, though one suspects his manipulations are born primarily of an effort to restore a more direct connection between literature and life: the traditional story — "Sire de Malétroit's Door", for instance — spells literary artificiality for Čexov.

An adjunct to these implications regarding the relative importance of plot and character in the short story concerns the role which time plays. Because change and growth are essentially foreign to this genre, the conception of time passing is itself largely irrelevant. As I have said previously, the short story writer can ignore the concept of time; he does this in exchange for a revelation which makes a virtue of temporal stasis. In view of these distinctions, I would like to look in some detail at one of Čexov's longer pieces "Ionyč". This is something of a test case since although the story covers a time span of at least eight years in a man's life, it is essentially a short story because its method is revelation rather than evolution. Although externally a period of eight years is covered, it might be said that time is irrelevant to the internal life of the character depicted. "Ionyč" is divided into five sections, each presenting a variation on a single revelation: that the hero has stepped into a living death when he sets up medical practice in a provincial town. The hero, Starcev, does not actually change during the course of these eight years; rather, he becomes more completely that which he was from the very first page. Thus, the story presents the revelation of a single state.

The first section introduces the reader to a provincial town in which the chief characteristic is the absolute monotony of life. Čexov refers frequently to this one characteristic; I would suggest that there is only one state which is perfectly monotonous – death. The most interesting family in this town and the most complete personification of its flavor is the Turkins. There are suggestions everywhere in this first section that they are in fact spiritually dead. Either their actions are utterly divorced from life, or else these actions are symbolic of death; both characteristics obviously point in the same direction. Mrs. Turkin, Vera Iosifovna, writes novels which she reads to her guests at parties. On the occasion of Starcev's first visit to the Turkins she reads her latest effort: "She read of that which never happens in life..." (IX, 288). The implication is that her own experience never impinges on actuality; she is in fact outside of life. Mr. Turkin has taught one of the servants, Pava, to perform a scene which is symptomatic of the state of mind not only of the Turkins, but the entire town. "Pava took a pose, raised his hands upward and uttered in a tragic tone: 'Die, unhappy woman!' " (IX, 290). This action is repeated again at another of Turkin's parties later in the story, and one realizes that its performance is one of Mr. Turkin's favorite amusements.

The business of the first section of the story is to show Starcev falling under the spell of the Turkins and their way of life. The revelation of Starcev's living death is summed up in fragments from two songs: as he goes to their house for the first time, he sings: " 'When I had not yet drunk the tears from the cup of life...' " (IX, 287); on his way home later that evening he hums: " 'Your voice for me so tender, so languorous ...' " (IX, 290). He is innocent before he meets the Turkins, but by the end of the evening he has fallen under their deadly spell. It might be said that the rest of the story simply completes this revelation of Starcev's new identity. But the essence of the revelation is contained in the first section.

Section two is mainly concerned with Starcev's partial awareness of what has happened to him in this town. A year has passed and he has called upon the Turkins for a second time. He is attracted by their daughter, Ekaterina Ivanovna, and arranges a midnight meeting with her in the cemetery. She does not come to the meeting, and the scene in the cemetery shows the reader that Starcev realizes what he is becoming. The setting, the cemetery, is of course an obvious symbol. As he enters it, he reads a sign: " 'The hour cometh ...' " (IX, 293). Alone in the cemetery, "... he imagined himself dead, buried there forever, he felt as though someone were looking at him, and for a moment he thought it was not peace and tranquility, but stifled despair, the dumb dreariness of non-existence..." (IX, 293). In desperation at the thought of all those around him who were once alive, "... he felt like shouting that he wanted, that he was waiting for, love at whatever price" (IX, 294). But he does not shout, and this is as close as he will come to resisting the kind of death which has overtaken him.

In the third section Ekaterina Ivanovna becomes aware of the revelation – she senses that Starcev has become like everyone else in the town, while she still hopes to escape. He proposes to her, but she refuses: " 'Dmitrij Ionyč, I am very grateful for the honor, I respect you, but... but I am sorry, I cannot be your wife. Let's speak seriously. Dmitrij Ionyč, you know I love art more than anything in life, I love, I worship music terribly, I have dedicated my life to it. I want to be an artist, I want honor, success, freedom, but you want me to go on living in this town, to go on with this empty, useless life that has become unendurable for me' " (IX, 296). Thus she realizes that she would condemn herself to the same life if she married him.

In the fourth section four years have passed, and Starcev sees Ekaterina again at a party given by the Turkins, at which Vera Iosifovna reads aloud from her latest novel and Pava gives the same performance described in section one. Ekaterina tells Starcev: " 'How much stouter you are! You look sunburnt and more manly, but on the whole you have changed very little' " (IX, 299). He has changed very little because, of course, the passage of time has only contributed to the process of perfecting what was almost evident from the very beginning. Starcev himself can no longer understand why he thought he loved this girl four years earlier. This is because his resistance to the revelation has completely disappeared.

Several more years have passed before the final section, which is really anticlimactic. Avram Derman has noted that Čexov indicates the passage of time and the rise in Starcev's fortunes through the laconic device of describing his changing means of transportation: in section one he has no horse; in section two he owns a pair; in the fourth he drives around in a troika with bells on it; and in the final section he has added a liveried servant.[20] But not only is this a cryptic means of expressing the passage of time, it also serves as a symbol of the entire theme with variations: the apparent changes are actually

---

[20]   Avram Derman, *Tvorčeskij portret Čexova* (Moskva, 1929), pp. 262-264.

stages in the realization of a single state. Until the final section the reader sees the action from Starcev's point of view. But now the point of view has shifted to the outside; the reader sees the hero from the sidewalk as he passes down the street: "... one might think it was not a mortal, but some heathen deity in his chariot" (IX, 302). The explanation is obvious: the process has been completed, there is no longer a living being here; there is no longer a point of view from which to see the action. 'Heathen deity', with its suggestion of a being that never actually existed is an extremely apt image for Starcev at this point.

Thus, in each section of "Ionyč" the central revelation is acted out in an ever more fully realized form, and in spite of the story's lengthy time span, the notion of change and development is illusory. The story plays with suspense in two ways: the reader is first led to expect a romance between Starcev and Ekaterina, and then, as this line of development collapses, he resists the notion that Starcev cannot in any way escape his living death. The actual pattern is like that which a hammer makes while striking metal; it never changes pitch, but it may become louder and more overbearing. The ending seems irrelevant because the revelation has occurred previously, without the reader's full awareness of it. Čexov may not have been the first writer to use this device, but he is probably the first who is noted for it.

The short story writer, then, has evolved a variety of techniques for overcoming the limitations of his genre. But it is chiefly the attempt to reveal the inner essence of a thing or being, frozen, as it were, and divorced from time, change, and development, which has become the function of the short story at its most characteristic. The dramatic shock of sudden recognition has become the writer's central device for overcoming the lack of drama inherent in the genre, and the muffled ending has become a device for reinforcing its dramatic impact.

II

LITERARY PARODIES

It took an enormous number of trial stories before Čexov could produce so finished a piece as "Ionyč". During his first four years of literary activity he published roughly three hundred sketches, feuilletons, and stories. Most of these were of only trifling length, but several run to a hundred pages each in modern editions. One is struck by the number of occasions upon which the young writer rather self-consciously resorts to the literary craft for his subject. But he reveals a more significant kind of self-consciousness when he parodies numerous types of currently popular fiction. What is important here is that he demonstrates an early and lasting distaste for what he apparently feels is the literary artificiality of the traditional novella and novel. On several occasions he attempts unsuccessfully to escape this artificiality from within the traditional forms. It is natural to find such a tendency in a beginning writer, but what is remarkable in Čexov's case is that he persists in these attempts long after the apprenticeship years, during the period when he had most certainly discovered his personal form of expression. These later efforts are essentially as futile as the early ones; only in one story, "On Official Business" (*Po delam služby*), did he successfully combine his own brand of inner action with a popular type of fiction, and in this case he managed it by superimposing a detective story over his own form.

In the early years the plight of the professional writer was among the many phenomena of the modern world suitable for debunking. Thus, in a very early piece, "My Anniversary" (*Moj jubilej*), which appeared in fact during Čexov's first year in the writing game, the reader encounters a portrait of the frustrated literary man. "Three years ago I felt the presence of the holy flame for which Prometheus had been chained to a rock... And so for three years with a generous hand I have been sending round to all the ends of my vast fatherland my works, which have passed through the purgatory of the above-mentioned flame. I wrote in prose, I wrote in verse. I wrote in every measure, manner and meter, for free and for money, I wrote to all the magazines, but alas! !!... those who envy me found it necessary to reject my work. ..." (I, 77). The unsuccessful writer proceeds to describe the fortune which he has invested in postage stamps during the course of these three years. On this day he is celebrating the fact that he has received two thousand rejection slips. "... I raise a glass to the conclusion of my literary activity and retire to rest on my laurels. Either show me another person who in three years has received as many 'no's,' or put me on a solid pedestal!" (I, 78). Whenever in these early years Čexov chooses to lampoon a writer, the butt of his jokes is a rather stock figure – a third or fourth-rate scribbler for the comic weeklies – perhaps the only kind of writer toward whom he feels justified in expressing contempt. In spite of his apparent readiness to tackle any and all literary types he displays a certain ambivalence toward his craft in the early years, for he also, naturally enough, has some qualms about the extent of his talent. This ambivalence – bravura and shyness – reveals itself blatantly in his reply to a letter of 1886 from Grigorovič, who had congratulated the young writer on having 'real talent'. Suffice it to point out here that in this letter Čexov responds as though he had anxiously been awaiting confirmation of his own hopes for becoming a serious writer, while in the same breath he almost boasts of the ease with which he had been able to turn out the six hundred pieces written between 1880 and 1886.

But to see this cocky young man attacking every popular literary genre in sight, it is necessary to examine the early work in greater detail. A by no means complete list of his parodies would include the following: "What Is Most Often Met in Novels, Stories, and So Forth?" (*Čto čašče vsego vstrečaetsja v romanax, povestjax i t. p.*); "A Sinner from Toledo" (*Grešnik iz Toledo*), a parody of novels based on subject matter taken from medieval life; "The Unnecessary Victory" (*Nenužnaja pobeda*), a parody of the then popular Hungarian novelist Mor Jokaj; "The Swedish Match" (*Švedskaja spička*) and "The Shooting Party" (*Drama na oxote*), parodies on the detective story; "The Flying Islands" (*Letajuščie ostrova*) and "A Thousand and One Passions, or the Terrible Night" (*Tysjača odna strast', ili strašnaja noč'*), parodies of Jules Verne and Victor Hugo respectively.

In addition to the parodies of purely literary models, Čexov frequently took for the butt of his satire all kinds of sub-literary experiment. One regular target for his attacks was the various official reports with which

Russian society has always been especially burdened. One such document is his "Questionnaire to Be Filled Out for the Census, Composed by Antoša Čexonte" (*Dopolnitel'nye voprosy k ličnym kartam statističeskoj perepisi, predlagaemye Antošej Čexonte*). The document includes such items as "20) Is your wife a blonde? Brunette? Brown-haired? Redhead? 21) Does your wife beat you or not? Do you beat her or not? 22) How many pounds did you weigh when you were ten years old?" (I, 159). Another exercise in the parody of sub-literary genres is his "Letter to a Learned Neighbor (*Pis'mo k učënomu sosedu*) in which the ignorance of a landowner of the type satirized by Kantemir in the eighteenth century [1] is exposed not only through the man's opinions, but also through his literary style. He is unable to spell the commonest words; he attempts to use extremely formal phraseology, but constantly mixes colloquial terms with it.[2] Still another variety of these sub-literary parodies is his "Comic Advertisements and Announcements" (*Komičeskie reklamy i ob"javlenija*) and "Antoša Č's Office of Announcements" (*Kontora ob"javlenij Antoši Č ...*). The overall quality of these parodies is mediocre. However, this early work is important because it indicates how very often the young Čexov turned toward parody of literary or sub-literary types as he searched for material to feed the ever-hungry comic weeklies. This fact suggests several conclusions about the young Čexov. The attempts to work with established literary types, where the principal interest of the writer is not so much in the events represented as in different ways of treating the material, suggest that from the very beginning he was absorbed in problems of literary technique. In other words, the beginning writer, having come to the literary profession purportedly to earn money rather than to give vent to any deeply felt need to express himself, constantly exhibits an intense interest in mastering the techniques of his craft. The parodies also indicate a critical attitude toward formula plots which persists throughout his career. Čexov always felt a justifiable disgust with what is false in literature as well as in life. He constantly attacked writers he felt were 'literary'. In his late work he was to prove an innovator not only in literary technique, but in the very subject matter which a writer might treat. This dissatisfaction with literary clichés, his disgust with the

---

[1] See, for example, Antiox Kantemir, "Satira I, na xuljaščix učenija. K umu svoemu", *Sobranie stixotvorenij* (Leningrad, 1956), pp. 57-68.
[2] For an interesting analysis of the way Čexov uses style to satirize the landowner, see Thomas Winner, *Chekhov and His Prose* (New York, 1966), pp. 6-7.

currently popular exoticism of foreign literature – all this is implicit in his own critical treatment of the popular literary types.

In spite of the fact that the young Čexov was writing for the popular press and therefore, in effect, lampooning his own kind, one is struck by the amount of energy which he expended on these attacks: why should it be necessary to parody historical novels, tales of revenge, detective stories, fantasies of the future, or the rhetorical style of a Victor Hugo? In short, much of what he parodies hardly seems worth the effort. One possible answer to this question lies in the history of the short story itself and in the nature of Čexov's own contribution to the genre. The fact is that prior to the eighteen eighties the short story had not spawned a realistic tradition. It is something of an historical anachronism that even at this late date it was largely dominated by writers who were under the Romantic influence. Therefore, it was necessary for a writer to whom Romanticism was essentially alien to clear the air before he could virtually introduce many of the trappings of realism – ordinary people confronting ordinary situations – into the short story. Čexov's role in the development of the genre contains a further anachronism: if we view him as at least one of the fathers of the realistic short story, he nevertheless appears at the very end of the heyday of Russian realistic fiction and in many respects is more akin to the early symbolists than to the realists, as Dmitrij Čiževskij has suggested.[3]

One of his most successful experiments with plot construction, as well as one of the most fantastic stories Čexov ever wrote is "Live Merchandise" (*Živoj tovar*). A farce based on a love triangle, it appeared in serialized form in *The Alarm Clock* (*Budil'nik*) during August of 1882. It opens with a scene between Liza Bugrova and her lover Groxol'skij, who proposes that she leave her husband to live with him in the Crimea. They are discovered by Bugrov, the husband, so Groxol'skij offers to pay him a large sum of money for the privilege of stealing his wife. With very little fuss Bugrov accepts, and the lover and his mistress take a dacha in the Crimea. Groxol'skij, however, is bothered by twinges of conscience; the thought of the poor husband keeps coming back to him. Bugrov and his young son Miša eventually appear and take up residence next door, affording Liza an opportunity, with which she is naturally delighted, to see her son again. All goes well until one day Bugrov announces to his wife and Groxol'skij that his

---

[3]   Dmitrij Čiževskij, "Über die Stellung Čechovs innerhalb der russischen Literaturentwicklung" in *Anton Čechov, 1860-1960: Some Essays*, ed. Thomas Eekman (Leiden, 1960), p. 293.

father, a priest, is coming to visit, and that the father would neither understand nor sympathize with the arrangement. He asks that Liza keep out of sight while the elder Bugrov is visiting. The deceit is carried off successfully, and their life returns to its rather abnormal, routine flow. Bugrov, however, spends more and more time with Liza, who has become somewhat bored with the domestic life which she and her lover are leading. Husband and wife devise a scheme to run away together, but Groxol'skij gets wind of the plot and once again is forced to buy off the husband by giving him a very large estate, to which Bugrov and Miša promptly move. Eventually, Groxol'skij is financially ruined and therefore unable to hold Liza, who runs away to live with her husband on her lover's former estate. Out of kindness they agree to give food and lodging to the now destitute lover. The final scene is described by a narrator, supposedly an old friend of Groxol'skij, who has come to visit him. The lover now has his own quarters separate from those of Liza and Bugrov. Liza is pregnant, but Groxol'skij tells the narrator, the last laugh is on Liza's husband, for Groxol'skij will be the father rather than Bugrov.

David Magarshack calls "Live Merchandise" "one of his earlier realistic stories".[4] In this instance the term 'realistic' seems extremely inept. Čexov's treatment of the story runs counter to all standards of realistic fiction. The plot is utterly absurd, and Čexov carries it off with a nonchalant aplomb, as though such whimsical peregrinations were the most normal everyday occurrence. Perhaps it is this tone of acceptance which Magarshack takes for realism. Actually, it is the irony implicit in the writer's attitude which makes the story successful in its way. Čexov never attempts to justify or psychologize over Bugrov's ready agreement to exchange his wife for a large sum of money. There is no attempt to lend an air of inevitability to the many reversals in the story, whereby the lover plays the role of husband and the husband that of lover. The story would obviously fall to pieces if Čexov had tried to impart the verisimilitude of the realist to this inherently ridiculous chain of events. Though the story makes highly entertaining reading, in at least one sense it is purely a writer's story. The young Čexov is obviously experimenting; "Live Merchandise" is an exercise in bringing off a certain effect, in maintaining a certain tone.

Occasionally, Čexov wrote veiled attacks on the canonized masters of nineteenth-century Russian literature. One of these, "The Death of

---

[4]   David Magarshack, *Chekhov: A Life* (New York, 1955), p. 62.

a Government Clerk" (*Smert' činovnika*, 1883), reveals Čexov the realist criticizing Nikolaj Gogol' through gross understatement. In essence, it is the familiar story of how a government clerk sneezed on a higher official at the theater, and how, tormented by speculations on the possible consequences of his act, he died. Like Gogol's "The Over-coat", the core of the story comes from an anecdote, in the case of Gogol', apparently a series of them. "The Death of a Government Clerk" derives from an adventure related to Čexov by V. P. Begičev, director of the imperial theaters in Moscow.[5] Evidently, a government clerk attending a performance at the Bolshoi Theater had sneezed very loudly. The clerk's subsequent torments and eventual death were Čexov's elaboration on the incident. The development centers on the respect and concern for matters of form among the official ranks in the tsarist hierarchy. The satire is levelled at the grossly disproportionate impor-tance which such matters had assumed in tsarist officialdom. The general tone has an affinity with that of "The Overcoat", which abounds in such ironies as the following: "At the time when the foreheads of even those who occupy exalted posts ache with the frost, and tears come to their eyes, the poor titular councillors are sometimes utterly defenseless."[6] The sharp edge of such remarks lies almost hidden in the implication that it is surprising that 'those who occupy exalted posts' might be just as vulnerable to the climate as titular councillors. The same irony is present in such remarks as this one from Čexov's story: "To no one at any place is sneezing forbidden. Peasants sneeze, police officials sneeze and sometimes even privy councillors sneeze. Everybody sneezes" (I, 37). Čexov goes so far here as to employ Gogol's device: the word *daže* (even) is used with telling effect in both the examples just cited.[7]

There is at least one other stylistic device in "The Death of a Government Clerk" which suggests that Čexov had Gogol's story in mind as he wrote. This device is what might be called the false start. The narrator in "The Overcoat" finds it necessary to interrupt the ex-position to comment on or correct what he has just said. Thus, the story opens in this way: "In the department of ... but perhaps it is better not to mention in just which department."[8] It takes the narrator almost a

[5] N. I. Gitovič, *Letopis' žizni i tvorčestva A. P. Čexova* (Moskva, 1955), p. 67.
[6] N. V. Gogol', *Sobranie sočinenij* (Moskva, 1952), III, 135.
[7] For a perceptive discussion of a number of Gogol's devices, including his use of *daže*, see Dmitrij Čiževskij, "Gogol: Artist and Thinker", *Annals of the Ukrain-ian Academy of Arts and Sciences in the U. S.*, II (Summer 1952), 261-279.
[8] N. V. Gogol', *Sobranie sočinenij*, III, 129.

page to explain that officials are reluctant to have their departments mentioned in print, and so after serious discussion of the problem he compromises rather craftily by calling it '*a certain department*'. "The Death of a Government Clerk" opens with a similar tendency to interrupt the exposition with seeming irrelevancies. "On a certain fine evening a no less fine departmental clerk, Ivan Dmitrič Červjakov sat in the second row of armchairs and through his opera glasses watched *The Bells of Corneville*. He watched and felt as though he were in seventh heaven. But suddenly... In stories one often encounters this 'but suddenly'. Authors are right: life is full of such unexpected turns" (I, 37). At this point the narrator returns to his story proper. In Čexov the digression is considerably shorter, but it must be remembered that he was usually limited in his early pieces to one hundred lines. In its finale "The Death of a Government Clerk" can be seen as a travesty of "The Overcoat", when Červjakov dies with astonishing abruptness. He makes several attempts to see the official upon whom he sneezed. But the official is merely irritated by the clerk's bowing and scraping. After the second interview the sketch ends in this fashion: "Having mechanically made his way homeward, with his coat still on, he lay down on the divan and... died" (I, 39). Whether due to the restrictions of length or to a deliberate attempt to shock, or a little of each, Čexov gives his sketch a very unexpected turn in the final line. The net effect is an implied criticism of Gogol's story. If Čexov's ending is to be effective, the reader must recall the finale in "The Overcoat" where Akakij Akakevič's death is purportedly followed by the appearance of a ghost who stalks the streets of St. Petersburg removing the coats from the backs of important officials. Thus, the absence of any further action in "The Death of a Government Clerk" makes the story a jocose, corrective rewriting of "The Overcoat".

The longest of these early parodies are based on formulae of popular fiction and, when they are most interesting, involve an attempt to go beyond the limitations of the popular form. Viktor Šklovskij claims that Čexov mastered the development of the traditional plot before he rejected it and cites "The Swedish Match" (*Švedskaja spička*) as not only a parody of the detective story, but as an instance wherein Čexov demonstrated his mastery of relatively complex plot development.[9] "The Shooting Party" (*Drama na oxote*, 1884), is a considerably extended version of the traditional detective story. It is told within a narrative

---

[9]   Viktor Šklovskij, *Xudožestvennaja proza* (Moskva, 1959), p. 483.

framework which in its way is as elaborate as Henry James' in "The Turn of the Screw". The first narrator is the editor of a popular journal, who has received a manuscript from a rather perturbed young man. The narrative proper is told in the first person by the man who had given the manuscript to the editor. The reader is first introduced to the narrator, Kamyšev, and a Count Karneev, a very rich landowner. Both Karneev and Kamyšev greatly admire Ol'ga, the daughter of one of the landowner's employees. She is scheduled to marry Urbenin, Karneev's estate manager. However, on the wedding day she falls into a fit of uncontrollable tears. She leaves the wedding reception, and Kamyšev follows her out, purportedly to calm her. In the course of their meeting they declare their mutual love. After this first meeting Ol'ga sneaks away during the mornings to her lover. Soon, however, the Count himself develops an uncontrollable attraction toward her, and after a quarrel with her husband, she runs off to live with Karneev in his mansion. The climactic scene takes place on a hunting trip. The Count has neglected to tell the others, including Ol'ga, that he is married, and his wife unexpectedly turns up on the hunting expedition. Ol'ga, rather abashed at the sudden turn of events, has left the others to their picnic lunch. While walking in the forest, she is overtaken by someone who tries to murder her, though it is not until early the following morning that she finally dies. Kamyšev, the narrator, reports these events at second hand. He was not present at the picnic, but, as district police inspector, he is called into the case late that night. He questions Ol'ga, but she dies before giving him the name of her assailant. Her husband, Urbenin, is accused of the murder. Covered with blood, he had come upon the picnickers, claiming he had just discovered his wife's body. He has a proper motive – jealousy – and he admits that he was wandering in the forest on the afternoon of the murder. But as the evidence against Urbenin piles up, a servant on Karneev's staff suddenly becomes suspect. The servant had been caught washing bloodstains from his clothing. It develops that the servant, dead drunk, had been sleeping in the forest on the afternoon of the picnic. He vaguely recalls a gentleman coming up to him and wiping blood from his hands onto the servant's jacket, but he is not quite able to recall whose face he saw that afternoon. Kamyšev, who all along has been dubious of Urbenin's guilt, allows the husband freedom of the corridor in which he is confined both day and night. The following morning the servant is found dead. All are now convinced of Urbenin's guilt. He is subsequently tried and convicted of the murder of his wife. At this point Kamyšev's manuscript ends, and the editor, who is vaguely dissatisfied with the outcome, once again becomes the chief narrator. Some time later, when Kamyšev returns to learn the fate of his manuscript, the editor, as it were, delivers a double verdict, accusing the narrator himself of the murder. Kamyšev confesses and there follows a detailed account of how and why he killed Ol'ga, with the editor now in the role of investigator and Kamyšev as witness.

This is undoubtedly the longest piece Čexov ever wrote; in the edition of his complete works it occupies almost two hundred pages. It has been necessary to go over the plot in some detail in order to demonstrate the relative complexity of its construction. The reader knows that he is reading a detective story, and yet for over half the story no crime has been committed. Čexov successfully evokes the reader's own misgivings, doubts, and fears as to the identity of the victim and just what will happen. Once the murder is committed the narrative moves very rapidly and effectively. To a considerable extent Čexov relies on dialogue through the questioning of witnesses as a means of advancing the action from this point on. Such a method has now become a tried and tested device in detective fiction, as demonstrated by the huge quantity of novels by Erle Stanley Gardner which employ courtroom scenes. The surprise ending in which the narrator proves to have been the murderer has been used since with great success, notably in *The Murder of Roger Ackroyd*. Čexov predates Agatha Christie's solution by a good fifty years. "The Shooting Party" demonstrates a limited degree of mastery in using a highly complex mystery plot, though, admittedly, to compare Čexov with Erle Stanley Gardner and Agatha Christie represents a rather specialized success for him.

In an illuminating article on Čexov's longer fiction Ralph Matlaw has suggested that in "The Shooting Party" he tried to add another dimension to the detective novel – that he tried to escape the literary artificiality of the form.[10] In the first section one sees the attempt in the narrator's reiterated insistence that he is writing not fiction but a true story; in the second part it appears in the editor's moral revulsion at the way in which the narrator has counted on the stock response of his readers to avoid detection as the actual murderer. "They will thus have been seduced by the novel form into condoning the narrator's behavior, of which his crime is a logical result. Kamyšev will have employed the form to make a veiled confession and to rid himself of the oppressive

---

[10] Ralph Matlaw, "Čechov and the Novel" in *Anton Čechov, 1860-1960: Some Essays*, ed. Thomas Eekman (Leiden, 1960), pp. 148-168.

torture that for eight years people have been looking upon him without suspecting his crimes." [11] Undoubtedly, Čexov is attempting to use the detective story as a framework within which to explore problems more closely connected with real life than those ordinarily treated in this form. The difficulty he encounters emerges from the nature of his theme: the artificially of popular literature. His plot is in conflict with his theme; consequently, he can write neither an entirely effective detective story, nor a novel attacking the clichés of the novel. The two elements are mutually destructive.

In another long piece from this period, "Belated Blossoms" (*Cvety Zapozdalye*), a whole series of such elements are ranged against each other. The story contains undeveloped hints at themes which were to appear many years later in Čexov's work; the plot line follows several different characters whose relationships with one another are tenuous in the extreme; finally, the ending seems to deny once and for all every one of the more significant thematic strands. "Belated Blossoms" concerns principally a young Prince Priklonskij, his sister Marusja, and an ambitious young doctor, Toporkov. The prince, Egoruška, is the son of a once noble family now gone to seed. The story opposes him to Toporkov, the nephew of a servant in the Priklonskij household. Toporkov's fortune is on the rise; he has become a doctor. Several descriptions of his riding about town pompously in his carriage are reminiscent of the picture of Starcev at the end of "Ionyč", though in this earlier story Čexov does nothing to develop the significance of this behavior. At one point Toporkov is called in to treat Egoruška, who has had an accident on his way home from a debauch. The decline of the old family with the parallel rise of the new generation seems a fairly obvious theme here. The relationship between these two men closely resembles the relationships Čexov develops far more fully in *The Cherry Orchard*. The theme which they embody is underlined in their names: 'Priklonskij' is derived from a verb meaning to bend downwards, while 'topor' in Russian is an axe. The choice of names in itself would seem to suggest that Čexov was aware of the implications of the theme which he had set in motion, and yet the later development of the plot simply disregards these implications. Aside from these early hints at a conflict between the decadent old and the hardened new, there appears to be no reason for Čexov to have made Toporkov the son of a servant; he might just as well have been a doctor from the gentry.

---

[11]   Ralph Matlaw, "Čechov and the Novel", p. 156.

In fact, this line of development seems almost irrelevant to the story as a whole, for the main plot really has very little to do with Egoruška: the hero and heroine are Toporkov and Marusja. Later, another very suggestive line of development appears for a few pages and then is abruptly dropped. It centers around Marusja's experience, and for a short time it appears that "Belated Blossoms" may develop in a pattern similar to Čexov's last short story, "Betrothed" (*Nevesta*), through a series of disillusionments and bright new awakenings. At the beginning Marusja idolizes her brother. But when the young prince is carried home after his accident, the result of heavy drinking, and especially when Toporkov comes around on his medical visits, Marusja begins to see her brother as the weak drunkard he has become. As her disillusionment with Egoruška develops, Toporkov becomes for her the idol that her brother was incapable of representing. Marusja falls in love with Toporkov, and for a brief period there is some hope in the household that a match may be forthcoming. However, the pattern of disillusionment seems to be recurring as Toporkov, like Priklonskij, turns out to be something less than a perfect model for worship. Through a marriage broker he offers her his hand in exchange for sixty thousand rubles. It is apparent that Toporkov is merely interested in advancing his fortunes through marriage to a good family and the acquisition of a fortune. He is quite indifferent to the girl he marries so long as his conditions are met. Marusja, however, refuses to believe him capable of such a cold, practical attitude. At this point the second significant strand of development is abruptly broken off. The denouement belies all the important motifs which have crept into the story. Day after day Marusja waits, convinced that after his proposal Toporkov will come one day to carry her away. But he never comes. She decides to go to him in the guise of a patient and confess her love. She pays two visits to his office, but each time is so intimidated by his professional manner that she is unable to speak. Once again Marusja's experience parallels that of many another later Čexov hero or heroine who finds himself incapable of acting at the crucial moment. But Marusja goes back a third time and now, physically suffering from an advanced stage of tuberculosis, she breaks down, confesses her love, and collapses. Toporkov, who all through the story has been utterly indifferent to her existence, suddenly has a change of heart. All at once he falls in love with her and immediately gives up his practice to carry her off to a southern climate. But Toporkov's change of heart has come too late, and Marusja dies of consumption. Perhaps the most charitable thing that can be said of "Belated Blossoms" is that even when he worked with the tritest of sentimental materials Čexov could not help but infuse them with some hints at least of a real theme.

The relations between the three central characters further suggest that Čexov may have been experimenting with some typical elements from Turgenev's novels. As in "The Shooting Party" one of the themes at least hinted at here is the difference between literature and life. Marusja at the beginning of the story conceives of her brother as a Rudin type and attributes his drinking to a grief born of the blows of fate: "And Marusja (forgive her, reader) remembered Turgenev's Rudin and set to talking about him to Egoruška" (I, 432). The obvious purpose of this allusion is to expose later the absurdity of conceiving real life in literary terms: Egoruška is distinctly not a Rudin. When Marusja becomes aware of her passion for Toporkov, she conceives of him as her Insarov, the hero of Turgenev's *On the Eve*. She thinks about him: "I am free from all prejudices and will follow this serf to the ends of the earth" (I, 452). She thus imagines herself to be Insarov's Elena, a literary relationship which occurs to Čexov's characters in at least two stories from the mature period, as we shall see shortly. Given this equation for the relations between Marusja and Toporkov, it is conceivable that Čexov intended the ending of his story as a play on the Turgenev novel. In *On the Eve* Elena follows Insarov in his fight for the liberation of his native land. Toporkov leads Marusja to the south of France, but just who is following whom is a trifle confused in Čexov's version: the trip is made not in connection with any cause of Toporkov but rather for Marusja's health. Thus, the man is really following the woman 'to the ends of the earth' in "Belated Blossoms". The relationships are further confused in that here it is the woman rather than the man whose health is failing and who ultimately dies. In "An Anonymous Story" (*Rasskaz neizvestnogo čeloveka*) he creates a variation on the Elena-Insarov relationship which is a considerably more successful travesty than this one. If he intended this reference to *On the Eve* at the end of "Belated Blossoms", one is not sure just what point he is trying to make. All one can say is that it suggests real life does not turn out as fiction does. But he had already made this point with the allusion to Rudin, as well as in another of Marusja's fictionalizations of Toporkov's character: she decides at one point that he is marrying a merchant's daughter to spite her whom he really loves. She reasons this way because she "had read so many novels in which people take husbands or wives for spite against those they love, for spite to make them understand, be piqued, or to wound them" (I, 455). "Belated Blossoms" does reveal several interesting facets of Čexov's attitude toward a traditional plot. Whenever he uses it, he is unable to repress his instinct to attack it, as evidenced by the regular appearance of the theme, fiction versus reality. He further reveals an irrepressible urge toward literary parody in his longer works. In fact, the two stories from the mature period which are closest to the traditional novel in their construction both rely heavily on playful rewritings of plots from Turgenev, Lermontov, and others.

A prime example of the mature Čexov attempting once again to produce a meaningful representation of reality within the framework of a traditional literary structure is the 1891 story, "The Duel" (*Duèl'*). Several recent commentators have called attention to its various literary echoes.[12] The characters suggest such literary prototypes as Pečorin and Onegin (Laevskij), Maksim Maksimyč (Samojlenko), Bazarov (von Koren), and Anna Karenina (Nadežda Fëdorovna). The setting and situations call to mind "The Cossacks", *A Hero of Our Time*, *Fathers and Sons*, and "The Kreuzer Sonata". One may go a step further and note that literary models have permeated the very marrow of Laevskij's personality to the extent that he has become their victim; his humanity has been all but eclipsed by them so that he is at the beginning of the story virtually incapable of a real response. If I may call up one more literary reference, he is like Don Quixote, who has been blinded to reality by its literary misrepresentation; and he is himself a literary parody. Von Koren reports that Laevskij is continually comparing himself to Onegin, Pečorin, and Bazarov. Through direct observance the reader finds Laevskij comparing life in the Caucasus to a painting by Vereščagin of people condemned to death, languishing at the bottom of a deep well. When he looks at his mistress, Nadežda Fëdorovna, who he no longer loves, he is irritated by her "white open neck and the little curls of hair at the back of her head" (VII, 335). This reminds him that when Anna Karenina fell out of love with her husband, it was his ears she hated most. Whether his irritation aroused his literary recollection or whether the literary inclinations of his mind

---

[12] See Ralph Matlaw, "Čechov and the Novel" in *Anton Čechov, 1860-1960: Some Essays*, ed. Thomas Eekman (Leiden, 1960), pp. 160-161; Thomas Winner, *Chekhov and His Prose* (New York, 1966), pp. 100-101; Rufus Mathewson, "Afterword" in *Ward Six and Other Stories*, trans. Ann Dunnigan (New York, 1965), pp. 385-386.

aroused the feeling against Nadežda is a moot point here.[13] Shortly after this, Laevskij reflects: " 'In my indecision I am like Hamlet. ... How truly Shakespeare observed! Oh how truly!' " (VIII, 339).

"The Duel" opens as an outlandish parody of such literary types. There are so many of them flitting across its pages that Laevskij continually gets his types mixed. For one thing, he has come to the wrong place to do the wrong things: in the exposition the reader learns that he and Nadežda have left the big city to carry out a Tolstoyan program of tilling the soil. But to fulfill their purpose they have come to the Caucasus, the traditional literary center for Russian Romantics. The models have become confused in another way: in a characteristic reference to *On the Eve* Laevskij speaks of Nadežda as a woman "who has followed you to the ends of the earth" (VII, 329); however, the ends of the earth in this case turn out to be not a Bulgaria whose liberation is worth dying for, but simply the Caucasus.

If the portrayal of Laevskij is satirical, it is matched by the picture of his foil, von Koren. The initial description of him is devastating:

Having finished with the album, von Koren would take a pistol from the whatnot and, squinting through his right eye, carefully aim at the portrait of Prince Vorontsov, or else he would stand before the mirror and contemplate his swarthy face, large forehead, and black hair, which curled like a Negro's. ... Self-contemplation afforded him almost more satisfaction than looking at photographs or at the pistol in its expensive mounting. He was very satisfied with his face, his handsomely trimmed beard, and his broad shoulders which served as obvious proof of his good health and sturdy build. He was also satisfied with his dandyish costume, from the cravat, which matched the color of his shirt, down to his yellow boots (VII, 339-340).

Von Koren's casual play with a pistol becomes almost deadly by the end of the story, but in this first presentation of the man it is impossible to take him seriously.

The satirical note dominates the first half of the story: each of the two chief protagonists, for example, is utterly blind regarding himself, but possesses an uncanny ability to dissect the other's motives. Von Koren observes that Laevskij " 'if not today then tomorrow will grow

[13] See A. B. Derman, *Tvorčeskij portret Čexova* (Moskva, 1929), p. 258, where the author claims that in the passage cited "Čexov revitalized the old devices". I think here Derman has mistaken Čexov's purpose; taken in context the device does not reassert the effectiveness of a detail as Tolstoj had observed it, but rather points up the idea that Laevskij has no more reality than a character in a book, because he is constantly modelling himself on literary types.

tired of her [Nadežda] and run back to Petersburg, and this too for
his ideals' " (VII, 344). This reflection comes only moments after Laevskij had been privately mulling over precisely the same ideas. Later in
the story Laevskij analyzes von Koren: " 'He has appropriated everyone,
he meddles in others' affairs, he needs everything, and everyone fears
him. I am slipping out of his clutches, he senses it and hates me. Hasn't
he told you that I must be destroyed or sent to hard labor?' " (VII, 371).
This is, of course, exactly what von Koren had recommended earlier
in the evening. Čexov allows each to dissect skillfully the other's type,
but these analyses are so precisely accurate that one feels the author's
hand at work pulling the strings on his puppets. There is nothing wrong
with this in a satire or a parody; but when Čexov tries to take his
materials seriously the result is confusion.

As the story rises to its climax, Laevskij first performs a rather
amusing about-face: he suddenly overlooks the typical literary situations
to which he ought to respond and accidentally stumbles into honest
responses. Thus, his duel with von Koren grows out of a mistake. Actually, he insults Samojlenko with whom he is arguing, but von Koren
somewhat arbitrarily interprets his remarks as an insult to himself.
Later the same evening Laevskij finds Nadežda in another man's arms.
From the point of view of traditional literary duels this ought to be the
occasion for a challenge; however, Laevskij simply ignores it. In the
middle of the night, after Nadežda has returned home, she expects him
in the best tradition to throw her out into the storm. Instead, it is at
this moment that his attachment to her becomes all the more compelling in his own eyes.

But the treatment becomes blurred when Čexov tries simultaneously
to regard Laevskij seriously and as the prime target of his parody. This
is especially apparent during his hours of soul-searching just before the
duel: chapter seventeen opens with an epigraph from Puškin's "Remembrance" (*Vospominanie*, 1828). In one sense this epigraph underscores
the parody: it is typical of Laevskij that his reflections on his past
should closely parallel those already extant in a literary model. Indeed,
there are numerous elements of parody in this scene; as it opens, the
reader is informed: "On the eve of his death one ought to write to those
nearest him. Laevskij remembered this" (VII, 409-410). He then begins
a letter to his mother, apparently because he believes it is the correct
thing to do in this situation. The night is a stormy one, creating an
obvious parallel in nature to his own violent upheaval. One might consider the description of the storm another element of parody were it not

for the overwhelming number of stormy nights in Čexov's serious stories, during which the protagonist comes to grips with his own life. The difficulty with this whole scene is that the Puškinian torments to which Laevskij is subjected must be taken seriously as well, for it is in this chapter that he sees himself so wrapped up in literary projections that he has only one way out – to face life in practical terms.

The conflict between parody and serious treatment continues in the description of the duel the following morning. The scene unfolds from the deacon's point of view: "It would be nice to write a description of the duel in its comic aspect" (VII, 415), he reflects. To a large extent Čexov takes the deacon at his word in the description which follows, for in spite of its highly serious role as the turning point in the story, the duel becomes a burlesque in which all the principal characters are forced to consult their literary models to find out what they are supposed to be doing: " 'Gentlemen, who remembers how Lermontov described it?' asked von Koren, laughing. 'In Turgenev too Bazarov had a duel with somebody there . . .' " (VII, 421). Thus, from the point of view of parody, the finale would be hilariously absurd, if its absurdity were not to result in a senseless death. It is this latter aspect which asserts itself as the scene moves to its climax with von Koren intending to kill Laevskij. Reality interrupts literature at the penultimate moment as the deacon rises from his place of concealment to shout: " 'He's going to kill him!' " (VII, 422). From the literary point of view – what it is proper to do at a duel – the deacon's cry is just as absurd as the duel itself is from a realistic point of view.

The weakness of this story lies in Čexov's failure to control tone. He is again compelled to parody traditional literary elements – and it might have been an excellent parody if he had limited himself to this – but he feels that he must produce his own kind of serious truth out of this bundle of clichés. Within the traditional framework, however, his own confused strivings belie the effort.

Two years after "The Duel" he once again sets out to write within the confines of a more traditional plot in "An Anonymous Story" (*Rasskaz neizvestnogo čeloveka*, 1893). Like "Belated Blossoms", though more overtly, much of the action is a variation on Turgenev's *On the Eve*. One major aspect of the story revolves about the woman who wishes to follow the man she loves. Thus, the heroine, Zinaida Fëdorovna, is a reincarnation of Turgenev's Elena. Zinaida has become the mistress of a very wealthy and worthless member of the upper classes, Orlov. Čexov makes the parallel between Zinaida and Elena explicit when Orlov explains to friends at an evening party: " 'Turgenev teaches us in his works that every exalted, nobleminded girl should follow the man she loves to the ends of the earth, and should serve his idea. ... The ends of the earth are poetic license; the earth and all its ends can be reduced to the apartment of the man she loves' " (VIII, 192).[14] Zinaida, then, is a Elena searching for her Insarov. Orlov makes it clear that he has no intention of fulfilling such a role, however. " 'I am no Turgenev hero and if at some time it should become necessary for me to free Bulgaria, I won't need to do it in a lady's company' " (VIII, 192). When Orlov grows tired of his mistress, his complaint against her is once more in terms of refusing to play the part she has picked for him: " 'My whole life I have refused to have anything to do with a hero's role, I could never stand Turgenev's novels, and suddenly, as if to spite me, I've fallen into the part of a very real hero' " (VIII, 216).[15]

When Orlov deserts Zinaida, she is rescued by the narrator, the 'unknown man', a revolutionary who has disguised himself as Orlov's servant in order to learn details of the life of the latter's father, an

---

[14]   This remark is a distillation of a viewpoint which Čexov had apparently been mulling over for some time; in "The Duel" we have seen how Laevskij identifies Nadežda with Elena and the journey to the ends of the earth. Several pages after this remark Laevskij generalizes about woman's nature: " 'A woman needs first and foremost her bedroom' " (VII, 333). These notions are finally amalgamated at this point in "An Anonymous Story".

[15]   Čexov revised this story extensively when it appeared in the 1901 edition of his collected works. Among the changes was the elimination of several further references to Turgenev. The narrator, when he reveals to Zinaida Orlov's duplicity toward her, says: " '... but your fine feelings, purity, clear mind, honorable views – this is Turgenevitis [Turgenevščina], bad stories; it's dull and prevents you from living. You went to Orlov and thought you were fulfilling your duty ... but they laughed at you and joked about you from the very first day' " (VIII, 538). In another passage dropped from the 1901 revision Orlov says: " 'Writers like Turgenev have completely confused her. Now other writers and preachers have informed her of the sinfulness and abnormality of living with a man. The poor ladies [sic] have already grown tired of their husbands and the ends of the world, and they grasp at this news with both hands. How are they to live? Where are they to seek deliverance from the horrors of married life? And now the Turgenev ferment has saved them. Love saves them from every kind of misfortune and solves all problems. The way out is clear – leave their husbands for the men they love!' " (VIII, 543). In a reference to Rudin the narrator observes: "I looked around at my strange, senseless life and remembered somebody in Turgenev saying, 'And the Lord will help all the homeless wanderers' " (VIII, 550). It is also interesting to note that Čexov had been rereading Turgenev during this period. See his letter to Suvorin of 24 February 1893 (XVI, 30-32). Concerning On the Eve, he notes that he likes only Elena's father and the finale in Venice. He mentions specifically that he does not like Turgenev's portrayal of Elena.

important government official. The obvious parallel between the narrator and Insarov proves, however, illusory. In relation to *On the Eve* "An Anonymous Story" is a farce based on mistaken identity. The narrator does not tell Zinaida that he himself has become disillusioned with his revolutionary aims. Like Insarov he is a sick man and Zinaida follows him to Venice, the very location, curiously, of the final scenes in *On the Eve*. Zinaida feels that she has at last found her Insarov. Speaking of her life with Orlov and of her new views, she says: " 'All this love only clouds the conscience and confuses the mind. The meaning of life lies in one thing only – in fighting. To get one's heel on the vile serpent's head and to crush it!' " (VIII, 235-236). And again, " 'Good night. You must get well. As soon as you are well, we'll take up our work. ... It's time to begin' " (VIII, 236).

As time passes, however, Zinaida realizes that the narrator no longer holds his revolutionary convictions, that he is no more her Insarov than Orlov had been. She feels there is nothing to live for and while in confinement bearing Orlov's child she commits suicide. And now the farce of mistaken identities commences again. The narrator takes over the role of Elena, carrying on Zinaida's duties, as Elena does for Insarov at the end of *On the Eve*. Everything is appropriately reversed: Elena carried on a man's duties; therefore, the narrator must carry on a woman's. He returns to Russia with Zinaida's baby and becomes a mother to it. Thus, Čexov pursues his rather strange variations on the plots of other literary works.

The echo of Turgenev is not the only kind of literary play to be found here, however. One can also detect variations on the popular, sensational story of intrigue and suspense. The story opens with a description of the narrator's mission and his disguise. Briefly at the beginning it might seem that this will be a tale of espionage, rising to a climax with perhaps an assassination. But the plan to penetrate the private life of the high government official is a total failure: Orlov is utterly indifferent to his father's affairs. Instead, the narrator becomes increasingly absorbed by the sordidness of Orlov's own life of pleasure. Rather anticlimactically the father does come to his son's apartment one day; the narrator has an ideal opportunity to assassinate the man, but is unable to do it. The whole point of the plot thus far simply vanishes. There is no reason to remain at Orlov's; therefore, he leaves, carrying off Zinaida. In short, the action of the story has been tending in one direction, while the emotional inclinations of the narrator – his growing indifference to the revolutionary movement and his interest in Zinaida's personal plight – are moving in a contrary one. It is as though Čexov had deliberately misled the reader into a story very different from the typical tale of intrigue.

On the basis of the way he handles his plot devices, "An Anonymous Story" hangs together considerably better than "The Duel". However, here again there are signs that Čexov was far from adept at handling extended narrative. He introduces three of Orlov's companions purportedly to bring substance to the representation of Orlov's daily life. But actually, they perform no function in the plot. Instead of helping to embody his world, they seem to serve only as an audience for Orlov's observations on human nature. They take up more space than they deserve. In a story of this length they must have some integral role in the plot structure if they are to justify themselves. That Čexov could not so merge them in his narrative fabric is but one more sign of his lack of craftmanship when confronted with the problems of the novella or the novel.

Nearly all the stories discussed thus far share one feature: each has been an attempt to work within the framework of a more traditional plot and to exploit that framework so that it expresses a denial of the traditional character types and resolution. Because Čexov wishes to go beyond parody, his form constantly undermines his intention. He wrote one story "On Official Business" (*Po delam služby*, 1898), in which he efficaciously reverses this characteristic approach. In this story external action is reduced to the minimum, but he superimposes elements of the detective story over his bare plot. A deputy prosecutor, Lyžin, and the local doctor have been called out to investigate a suicide which could have been murder. In a literal sense no one takes the idea of murder very seriously, but as the story moves towards its revelation, a sense of moral guilt forces the central character to an awareness of responsibility for another man's suicide.

The night is the kind on which murders traditionally occur: the officials are forced by a blizzard to stop off at the hut in which the corpse lies. Outwardly, the situation seems sinister enough; however, Čexov constantly undercuts his apparent mystery story. Lyžin reflects: "If this man had killed himself in Moscow, or somewhere in the environs of Moscow, and it had been necessary to conduct an investigation, it would have been interesting, important, and perhaps even terrifying to sleep in the vicinity of the corpse" (IX, 348). But here in the provinces it is at best simply tiresome.

The inward movement of the story is toward Lyžin's momentary realization that his own rejection of all life outside the capital cities is the kind of attitude which produces suicides like that of Lesnickij. The story proceeds in the best detective story tradition through an examination of the witnesses. The first of them, Lošadin, a village police assistant, relates how the wealthy Lesnickij had become impoverished and was compelled to perform the same sort of routine village tasks as Lošadin himself. In the middle of the night the prosecutor and the doctor pay a visit to a local member of the nobility, von Taunic. On the way Lyžin recollects that he had once met Lesnickij, a man humbled by reduced circumstances. He recalls his gait, and feels that here in the storm someone is walking near him very much as Lesnickij had walked. This is one of the stages in Lyžin's discovery that he himself is not so very different from Lesnickij. It also casts Lyžin in a new role: the investigator has now become a witness.

At von Taunic's the host offers his testimony: " 'In every family such unhappiness can occur and this is terrible. It's hard to endure it, it's intolerable' " (IX, 353). This remark leads Lyžin to reflect that Lesnickij's fate could become his own if he were compelled to spend his life in the provinces. In the howling wind he seems to hear the voices of Lesnickij and Lošadin, moaning: " 'We go on, go on, go on . . .' " (IX, 355). The storm, through which they struggle as Lyžin sits comfortably in von Taunic's home, clearly symbolizes life. Lyžin realizes that only through the suffering of the Lošadins and Lesnickijs is it possible for him to dream of a bright future for himself in the capital: "And he felt that this suicide and peasant's misery lie on his own conscience" (IX, 355). Lyžin has been cast in the four major roles of the detective story: investigator, witness, potential victim, and murderer. The following day the storm continues, but Lyžin has forgotten his discovery. As he looks out the window, he thinks: " 'Well, what sort of moral can you draw here? A snow storm and nothing more . . .' " (IX, 356). His renewed indifference ironically confirms the verdict of his own guilt. Thus, Čexov enhances the drama of the moral discovery in "On Official Business" by imposing the pattern of a detective story over the structure. Without this pattern Lyžin's sense of moral guilt would have been considerably less compelling.

What do these experiments with the more traditional plot demonstrate? I think they show that Čexov was consistently unable to inject the inner action typical of his own stories into a plot where external action is expected. The attempt results invariably in a parody which undermines Čexov's serious effort. He was wholly successful in this kind of merger only when he reversed his procedure, as in "On Official Business", making the internal action central and imposing the pattern of a detective story over this. The limited number of these experiments testifies to Čexov's own awareness of a need to break away from the traditional story.

III

CHAMELEONS

However unsuccessful the extended parodies may have been and however useful for a writer who had first to clear away the Romantic trappings of the short story, the parodies do reveal a kinship with that great bulk of early stories in which Čexov displays a cheerful contempt for romantic love. One of the chief sources of comedy among the pieces written between 1880 and 1884 is the lover whose tender feeling evaporates as practical considerations overwhelm him. One such little sketch might be taken as a rudimentary version of a motif which recurs in ever more subtle and polished form throughout Čexov's work. It is one of four very short sketches which were written in 1881 and are grouped together under the title "This and That" (*I to, i se*).

A cold, beautiful midday. The sunlight plays in every snowflake. There are neither clouds nor wind. On a bench along the boulevard a little couple sits.
  "I love you," he whispers.
  On her cheeks play rosy little hints.
  "I love you!" he continues ... "Seeing you for the first time, I understood what I live for, I recognized the purpose of my life! My life must be with you, or else I absolutely will not exist! My darling! Marja Ivanovna! Yes or no? Manja! Marja Ivanovna ... I love you ... Manečka ... Answer or I shall die! Yes or no?"
  She raises her large eyes towards him. She wants to say "yes" to him. She opens her little mouth.
  "Oh," she cries out.
  On *his* snow-white collar, chasing after each other, run two very large bedbugs. ... O horrors!! ... (I, 129).

In its crudest form this is the young Čexov debunking romantic love. With various types of disguises, with all kinds of technical embellishments, and with great subtlety these bedbugs somehow make their way into every tender scene in Čexov. One later treatment of this same motif is the 1896 story "The House with a Mezzanine" (*Dom s mezo-*

ninom). To see these bedbugs as analogues for Lidija Bolčaninova in the later story may seem farfetched, but the fact is that as a motif this tendency to destroy the course of true love never leaves Čexov's work.

Another similar interrupted romance occurs in "A Confession, or Olja, Ženja, Zoja" (*Ispoved, ili Olja, Ženja, Zoja,* 1882). The narrator is writing to a friend to explain why he is thirty-nine and still unmarried. He relates three incidents in which the course of true love was diverted by various practical considerations. The first incident occurs on 'a wonderful June morning'. The narrator is walking in the country with Olja. He is in the midst of proposing to her when she starts coyly playing with some nearby geese. Apparently annoyed, the geese begin chasing her, snapping at her dress with their beaks. In her fright Olja loses her composure, and by the time the narrator has freed her from the attacking geese, his romantic image of young Olja has been destroyed forever so that he is unable to finish his marriage proposal.

A more typical pattern for these early stories, however, is the one in which the tenderest, most sincere, and most self-sacrificing of feelings is in one way or another negated by the sudden appearance of more practical concerns. One such story is "An Affair That Fell Through" (*Propaščee delo,* 1882). In this instance a young writer is proposing to a girl who comes from a rather well-to-do family. The girl accepts the young man's proposal; however, he feels it is his duty to make her aware of the sacrifices she must endure if she is to give up the easy life with her parents to live with him. She maintains that she is willing to follow him anywhere, no matter how difficult their life may be. The young writer persists, pointing out the luxuries which she must give up, until at last he actually convinces her that it is not worth the sacrifice of material welfare merely to marry a headstrong young writer. The story concludes with the man cursing himself for his honesty.

In another such piece, "A Bad Story" (*Skvernaja istorija,* 1882), a young woman seeks to force a marriage proposal from a young painter. Her father arranges to invite him to their summer dacha, but time there passes slowly because of the artist's continued indifference to the young lady. Finally, on a typically romantic night the artist makes what seems to be a proposal of marriage to the girl. Actually, he only wants her to model for him. In still another piece, "In Our Practical Age, When, and So Forth" (*V naš praktičeskij vek, kogda, i t. d.,* 1883), one of Čexov's most typical attacks on romance occurs. Once again it is a concern for money which suddenly diverts the course of true love. The scene takes place on a railroad platform, where a young man is seeing off the girl he loves. She will be gone two weeks, and they are overcome by the sorrow of parting. The man gives the girl twenty-five rubles to repay a debt to a friend, and amidst many tears they at last say goodbye. Just as the train is pulling away from the station the young man frantically runs after the train shouting to his beloved, but he is unable to catch her. He walks home slowly, terribly vexed because he has forgotten to obtain from the girl a receipt for the twenty-five rubles.

Čexov's use of romantic scenes as the butt of his jokes marks him as belonging to an age in Russian literature which was in open revolt against the romanticism of the early nineteenth century. Tolstoj in his Sevastopol stories and in *War and Peace*, for example, had debunked the romantic canons of war, and in such stories as "Family Happiness" had indicated the same distaste for romantic love as the young Čexov exhibits in these early contributions to the Moscow weeklies. Of course, the differences in treatment between the young Tolstoj and the young Čexov loom far larger than the similarities. Even as early as the fifties Tolstoj had a consciously formulated program, a concept of reality, which he wished to represent, and the debunking of romantic canons was only a part of his intention. The early Čexov, on the other hand, was perfectly content merely to take a stock situation – romantic young lovers overwhelmed by the most trivial practical problems – as the source of humor in the vast majority of his first sketches.

In the light of Čexov's later extremely delicate use of atmosphere in his stories it is somewhat curious to find the beginning artist not only indifferent to such effects, but downright contemptuous of them. One of his sketches in "This and That" begins, "The air was full of odors inclining one towards the tenderest feeling: it smelled of lilacs and of roses; a nightingale was singing, the sun was shining... and so forth" (I, 130). Such parodies of romantic settings are standard procedure in this early period, though even the young Čexov rarely exhibits such obvious distaste for atmosphere as this example indicates. In "A Confession, or Olja, Ženja, Zoja" the technique is a bit more subtle. The first episode begins, "It was a wonderful June morning. The sky was clear, like the most clear Prussian blue. The sunlight played in the river and its rays glided along the dewy grass. The river and the verdure, it seemed, had been strewn with expensive diamonds. The birds sang in perfect tune. ... We walked along the path, covered with yellow sand, and with happy breasts inhaled the aromas of the June morning. The trees looked on us so sweetly, whispered to us something which had to be very good, very tender..." (I, 188-189). Here Čexov has tried to do something more complicated than simply borrow the tritest and most typical elements from romantic descriptions of nature: he has attempted to create a convincing scene of spring romance, only to destroy it with the appearance of the geese, who chase Olja. In another story he comes close to writing a parody of the kind of atmospheric description which he himself was to use seriously sixteen years later. "The Meeting, Though It Took Place, Nevertheless..." (*Svidanie xotja i sostojalos', no...*, 1882) concerns a young man who has arranged a rendezvous with his sweetheart for the evening. During the afternoon, however, he inadvertently drinks too much, and is barely able to walk when the hour of the meeting comes. Nevertheless, "In the courtyard it was already growing dark. It was ten o'clock. Stars glimmered in the sky. There was no moon, and the night promised to be dark. Gvozdikov could smell the May freshness of the forest. All the attributes of a lover's rendezvous had gathered to meet him: the rustle of the leaves, the nightingale's song, and... even 'she', pensive and pale in the mist" (I, 216-217). This setting bears some resemblance to the graveyard scene in "Ionyč". In the present story the source of the satire is not so much the choice of atmospheric elements as their gross incompatibility with Gvozdikov's drunken stupor, though Čexov tends to overplay his hand in the self-conscious phrase, "All the attributes of a lover's rendezvous...".

The pieces cited here are but random samples of the most typical sketches and stories Čexov wrote during the first four years of his literary activity. The number of works which use the same thematic material – the debunking of romantic concepts of love – runs into the hundreds. None of these pieces can be singled out for individual excellence; they hold to a rather mediocre level of accomplishment. Their interest is engendered not so much by their literary qualities as by the indications they offer of Čexov's early tendencies and emphases. These pieces also give the reader an insight into some of the characteristics which are to persist in his writing: his basically critical attitude toward subject matter, theme, and literary style. The opportunity to observe his sceptical attitude toward love is particularly revealing. It suggests the possibility of a certain amount of ambiguity in his later treatment of such themes; it may even suggest an ambivalent attitude in Čexov himself toward such affairs as those depicted in "The House with a Mezzanine" (*Dom s mezoninom*), "Ionyč", and "The Lady with the Dog" (*Dama s sobačkoj*), as we shall see in chapter nine.

In analyzing these attacks on romantic love one faces a further problem. It is possible to look upon them primarily from the point of view of subject matter, as has been done here, but beyond that there is also the question of how Čexov manipulates reality. In all the examples discussed thus far the debunking process results in a shift of the hero's attitude toward his experience; invariably there is a sudden reversal of all the material in the story. In "A Confession, or Olja, Ženja, Zoja", for example, the narrator's consciousness of Olja is completely transformed at the end of the story. This process of transformation in the external world is, of course, a basic device for comedy, especially when it occurs suddenly and unexpectedly, but for Čexov this process is also important later in the more serious stories. I think we may say that in the 'love stories' one of Čexov's basic motifs makes its first appearance, for these transformations set up a tension between actuality and man's perception of it which ultimately denigrates the actual; since all action is based on perception one gets an ever more complex series of interpenetrations between perception and actuality.

In the earliest period this motif is probably most prominent in the political and socio-political satires written between 1883 and 1885 – "A Certificate" (Spravka), "The Chameleon" (Xameleon), "Fat and Thin" (Tolstyj i tonkij), "Two in One" (Dvoe v odnom), "Vint", "Abolished!" (Uprazdnili!), and "The Album" (Al'bom). In these stories the comic base is the exploitation of absurdities indigenous to the hierarchical system in Tsarist Russia. But within this framework what is revealed is the implication that man's consciousness of existence is extremely tenuous, and that his concept of the external world is almost always mistaken because the nature of reality itself is constantly being transformed. This vision, implicit in nearly all of Čexov's work, forms one focus for this study. The chameleon with his capacity for complete transformation of his identity is a symbol of this vision.

What might be called 'the chameleon act' is performed in nearly all these stories. Its most notable use occurs of course in the story of that name, but the same device occupies a central position in almost all these pieces. In essence, it consists of a sudden about-face on the part of one of the characters. An apparently trivial detail suddenly causes the character to change his behavior in such a complete and unexpected manner that it is difficult to recognize him as the same person. The chameleon act is performed not just once but several times in the story of that name. It concerns police inspector Očumelov and his assistant, who encounter a very ordinary dog and a man who claims the dog has attacked him. Očumelov's first reaction is to castigate the dog's owner. He delivers a little diatribe aimed at owners of dogs which are allowed to run about freely, attacking people. When he asks who owns the dog, someone suggests that it belongs to a general. At this point Očumelov goes into his first chameleon act. Not only does his manner change, but it is as if the climate, the very world in which he finds himself, has suddenly altered. Upon discovering this news, Očumelov observes, " 'Hm! . . . Help me get my coat off, Eldyrin. . . . It's terrible how hot it is! It must be going to rain . . .' " (III, 49). All at once Očumelov's chief concern is how such a small dog could possibly be capable of attacking such a very large man. He accuses the fellow of simply making the story up after having cut himself on a nail. Now the assistant recollects that it could not possibly be the general's dog, for his are all pointers. Očumelov goes through his chameleon act for the second time, now attacking the dog itself. The assistant has second thoughts about the dog's owner, however, and decides it must be the general's. For the third time Očumelov's whole world is transformed " 'Hm! . . . Help me into my coat, brother Eldyrin . . . Something in the way of a wind has blown up . . .' " (III, 50). When Očumelov demands that someone establish the dog's ownership once and for all, the general's cook maintains that the dog does not belong to his employer. Očumelov goes into his chameleon act for the fourth time, and is about to kick the animal when the cook adds that the general's brother owns it. For the fifth and final time he reverses himself; he begins to fondle the dog, offers a parting shot at the man who was bitten by the animal, and, "wrapping himself up tighter in his greatcoat, continues his march along Bazaar Square" (III, 51). "Chameleon" is the only story in which Čexov uses a whole series of such devices. But the sudden, complete, and unexpected reversal occurs many times in this group of satires.

Another aspect of the chameleon act is emphasized in "Two in One" (*Dvoe v odnom*), where the personal transformation is so complete that it actually seems as though two different characters have been depicted. The story concerns a meek clerk who, when away from his supervisors, becomes a boisterous, overbearing loudmouth. As in "Chameleon" Čexov explicitly draws the parallel between his character and the lizard. The story opens, "Don't believe these Judases, these chameleons! Nowadays it is easier to lose one's faith than an old glove – and I have lost it!" (II, 103). The supervisor encounters on a streetcar a person who bears a marked resemblance to one of the clerks in his office, but he is unable to believe that this rambunctious loudmouth is his own meek and mild Ivan Kapitonyč. Unaware of his supervisor's presence, Ivan sits up straight, discusses politics with his companion, dresses down the conductor for dimming the lights, commands the passengers to make room for a lady to sit down, and flies into a rage when the conductor tells him that smoking is not allowed on the streetcar. He aggressively protests this invasion of his liberty until he recognizes his supervisor. "Instantaneously his back curved, his face momentarily fell, his voice died away, his arms stiffened along the seams of his trousers, he sagged at the knees. Momentarily he changed completely. I no longer doubted: it was Ivan Kapitonyč, my clerk" (II, 105).

Without explicit reference to the device, the chameleon act appears again in "A Certificate", "The Album", and in probably the finest story of the whole lot, "Fat and Thin". In "A Certificate" the minor detail which sets off the device is the necessity of giving a clerk a few kopecks in order to obtain a badly needed certificate. The narrator, who is the central character, approaches the clerk's window, but is completely unsuccessful in his efforts to catch the clerk's attention, even when he resorts to shouting at him. As he leaves the window, someone advises him to slip the fellow a few kopecks. When he tries this ploy, the clerk is instantly transformed into the most zealous, helpful, and cheerful of men. In the story "The Album" the transformation is somewhat less sudden but nonetheless occurs. Upon the occasion of his anniversary an official is presented with a commemorative album by his clerks. He appears to be sincerely touched by this sign of affection in his workers, and takes the album home to display it before his guests that evening. The transformation occurs when his children get hold of the album. His daughter removes the photographs of many of the clerks and substitutes those of her schoolmates, while the official's son adds mustaches to the faces of the remaining clerks. When the children show the album to their father, he is vastly amused and even more impressed than he was when he originally received it.

But the most distinctive of all these stories is "Fat and Thin". Here the satire penetrates considerably more deeply than in any of the other stories Čexov wrote in this period. The story concerns two old friends who encounter one another in a railroad station. One is fat, the other is thin. They had been classmates in school and are delighted to see each other. The fat one is alone and smells of sherry and cologne. The thin one is surrounded by his wife and son, and smells of ham and coffee grounds. In previous examples of the chameleon act Čexov has tried to hide from the reader the nature of the transformation, but here in the opening lines he makes it evident. While the bond of friendship which ties them together is real enough, their different smells imply the conflict which will alter their responses to one another. The friends relate their adventures since the last time they had met, and it develops that the fat one has advanced several ranks over the thin one. At this point the thin man is transformed. His familiar forms of address are dropped and his speech becomes extremely formal. His friendly and relaxed manner is replaced by an uneasy stiffness and confusion. In this instance, however, Čexov does not rely purely on reversals for his effects. Here many of the same traits and mannerisms affected by the thin man at the beginning of the story are repeated after the transformation, but in a new and ominous key. Thus, the thin man is all smiles at the beginning when he recognizes his old friend. At the moment the fat one announces that he has attained the rank of privy councillor, "The thin one suddenly grew pale, became petrified, stood stock-still, but quickly his face became wreathed in smiles..." (II, 11). The thin man's original identity must come to a halt, must, as it were, cease to exist, before the chameleon can perform its act. The new man smiles broadly as did the old one, but there is a world of difference in these two smiles. Similarly, near the beginning of the story, after the friends have recognized each other and exchanged kisses, Čexov observes of their meeting: "Both were pleasantly surprised" (II, 10). At the very end of the story he makes the same observation, but now of the thin man and his family, rather than of the two friends: "All three were pleasantly surprised" (II, 12). The first observation refers to the mutual surprise and pleasure of the two old friends, the second to the formal and false respect which underlings are expected to show toward their superiors. Thus, Čexov makes a considerably more subtle and expert use of the chameleon act in "Fat and Thin" than in the other stories discussed in this group.

In his parodies of romantic scenes and in several stories which simply depict prosaic moments from daily life he employs the chameleon device for purely comic effects. In "Surgery" (*Xirurgija*, 1884) a minor church official, troubled by a toothache, visits the local doctor's assistant, where a polite exchange of pleasantries between the two ensues. The assistant decides the tooth must be pulled, but he bungles the job badly and by the end of the story the pleasantries are transformed bit by bit into the crudest of insults, as the hysterical church official flees from the doctor's office. Another piece of this period, "In Hotel Rooms"

(*V nomerax*, 1885), concerns a mother and daughter who are extremely upset by a young man in the neighboring room. He holds raucous parties, uses the wall for a shooting gallery, and in general seems to delight in shocking conduct. The outraged mother complains to the manager about the situation, viciously deprecates the young man, and demands that he be ordered to leave. In the course of the conversation it develops that he is unmarried. All at once the mother is transformed, and begins making excuses for the boisterous behavior of young men. The story ends with the mother asking the manager to transmit to the young man an invitation to tea.

In the more serious satirical stories the chameleon device almost always carries with it far-reaching implications about the nature of a society in which bribes and rank play so important a role, subjugating and transforming all other human values. Ultimately, the implication of most of these stories is that one has no real existence independent of his official position in the social framework. In "Chameleon" the absurdity of these implications is exploited for its humor: the plain and rather ordinary fact that a dog has bitten a man is somehow lost in the heavy shifts of sympathy on the part of Očumelov. A seemingly irrelevant point – the official rank of the dog's master – is the only significant reality in the topsy-turvy atmosphere of "Chameleon". As noted above, the whole world in which Očumelov operates is transformed through the various suppositions as to the dog's ownership: the weather is alternately humid and stuffy, and troubled by a cold wind; and this too becomes dependent on the rank of the dog's owner.

"Fat and Thin" explores these implications more intensively. Here real human values are at stake: the bond of friendship between two men. This value is negated and transformed once again by official rank. The very title of the piece, "Fat and Thin", may suggest either that the difference in rank is just as basic as their physical shapes, or that one difference is as essentially immaterial as the other. As Viktor Šklovskij has noted, the thin man's family acts as "his whole world, his social commentary, and chorus for his tragedy".[1] This world too is transformed when it is discovered that the fat one is a privy councillor. Thus, the transformation takes place not simply in the thin man but in his entire entourage. At the news, "His suitcases, bundles, and hatboxes shriveled, and made a wry face. The long chin of his wife became even longer; Nathaniel [his son] snapped to attention and did up

---

[1] Viktor Šklovskij, *Xudožestvennaja proza: Razmyšlenija i razbory* (Moskva, 1959), p. 485.

the buttons on his frock coat..." (II, 11). It is as though the previous
scene and all the years of their acquaintance had suddenly been denied
their existence by this new order of reality, which must take precedence
over all else. Early in the story the thin one introduced his family to
the fat man. After the transformation he goes through the same introduction in the same words. On one level this repetition may be read as
merely the result of his confusion. On another level, and taking into
consideration the explicit references to the transformation in the thin
man's whole world, not excluding his luggage, this repetition might well
be read as the denial of all previous existence; he introduces his family
again because the world which had hitherto existed has been nullified.
In this sense the thin one is not repeating the introductions but making
them for the first time in a wholly new order of reality. Almost all the
stories which employ the chameleon device, then, carry with them implications which deny, nullify, and dehumanize the world of ordinary
human relationships. In its place a wholly new set of values dependent
on official rank is established.

In two of his most grotesque social satires, "Abolished!" and "Vint",
hypothetical transformations produce a totally dehumanized vision of
the world. "Abolished!" starts from the fanciful premise that titles no
longer exist. A retired ensign wanders about from one former official to
another trying to discover just what he is now, but no one knows. The
implication is that if titles are abolished, people who bear titles are also
abolished. In a world where title and official rank count for everything,
their absence implies the absence of any meaningful existence. "Vint"
develops a similar denial of man's humanity. Andrej Stepanovič Peresolin, the chief of a department, finds his subordinates late one evening
engaged in a weird new card game. The clerks have assigned card
values to everyone in the office. Even the officials' wives have been
assigned compensatory values. Thus, state assessors rank as kings, and
so on down through the deck. Four different districts have been substituted for the four suits. Peresolin is tempted to try his hand at the
game. In the early hours of the morning the janitor overhears him
loudly proclaiming, " 'Oh, my boy, you can't think that way! That's not
a game! Only shoemakers play that way. Think about it: when Kula-
kevič led with a Court Councillor you should have discarded Ivan
Ivanovič Grenlandskij, because you knew that he had Natalja Dmitrevna
and two more in that suit, and Egor Egoryč besides. You upset everything! I'll prove it to you right now. Sit down, gentlemen, we'll play
one more rubber!' " (III, 65). In the previous stories it has only been

one or two characters whose world has been transformed, as they displayed their chameleon-like features. In "Vint" the transformation seems to take on universal proportions. Here it is not only the supervisors and more important officials who are reduced to the status of playing cards; even the lowliest clerk has his value in the game. With one of Čexov's most inspired touches a clerk points out that he himself is a three. Thus, it is not simply the reduction of the higher ranks to their official existences; everyone in the world of the story is reduced to his titular actuality. The final irony, of course, is Peresolin's easy acceptance of this parody of the world of officialdom. It is as though the parody itself were being accepted as the real thing. To put the implications of the story another way, the nature of the old reality is so close to absurdity in itself, that parody can no longer be distinguished from that which it ridicules.

In all these stories Čexov employs the chameleon act for essentially comic purposes, but despite the predominantly humorous note here, they carry a whole series of terrifying implications: if the stories are in any sense plausible, both reader and writer must make the assumption that man lacks a sense of personal identity. This is an extremely distasteful premise the consequences of which Čexov pursues later in his career, particularly in "A Dreary Story" (*Skučnaja istorija*), and more generally in those stories treated in Chapter VI. A lack of personal identity implies a correlate absence of any clear-cut notion about the nature of reality. Finally, a world whose nature is indefinable because it is constantly changing must forsake any sense of moral value. I believe that Čexov was aware of these implications and that many of the stories written during the years when his own world view was crystallizing reflect his struggle to deny the implications of "Fat and Thin", for example. This effort at denial dominates the stories of 1886 and 1887.

IV

PATHOS AND THE FAILURE OF FEELING

Pathos takes on a moral flavor when we see the protagonist who invokes our pity at the mercy of a villainous tormentor. Čexov depicted such situations from the very beginning of his career, and by 1886 had refined the basic elements to a point where their crudities, best exemplified in a work like *Uncle Tom's Cabin*, had completely vanished. Insofar as this kind of pathos involves a moral sense, a number of early stories implicitly contradict the vision of a chameleon-like world, although through the later refinement of the pathetic element, in "Veročka" and "On the Road" (*Na puti*), Čexov's own artistic vision abrogated the sense of moral stability which his earliest sallies into pathos had suggested. A classic instance of fairly crude pathos appears in "Because of Little Apples" (*Za jabločki*, 1880), in which a landowner torments a pair of lovers whom he discovers eating apples in his orchard. After a fairly extended episode of verbal taunts, he forces them to beat one another; the lovers finally part, never to see each other again. The outer frame of the story involves a narrator who is describing the moral depths to which human nature can sink: the landowner is his *prima-facie* evidence, and thus, it is made explicitly clear who the villain is. The situation exhibits none of that ambiguity of villainy which characterizes another story from the same period, "A Daughter of Albion" (*Doč' Al'biona*), where the picture of "a well-fed squire's mockery of a person lonely and strange to her surroundings'" is modified by a sense that the English governess may very well be receiving the treatment she deserves.[1] What distinguishes "Because of Little Apples" is the unrelieved description of the ways the landowner baits his victims. This focus on the process of torment is a continually recurring motif throughout Čexov's early work.

Another such piece is "The Head of the Family" (*Otec semejstva*,

[1] W. H. Bruford, *Anton Chekhov* (New Haven, Connecticut, 1957), p. 12. Bruford is quoting Gor'kij at this point, but apparently approves his reading of the story.

1885). A father who has had bad luck at cards proceeds to take out his irritation on his family at dinner. Once again at the core of the story is a close study of the tormenting process, as the man infuriates his wife and brings his children to tears. But neither "Because of Little Apples" nor "The Head of the Family" is intended to be amusing, and thus they stand out from a large group of similar stories where the tormenting process is turned into a source of humor. Perhaps the most successful instance of this is the story "A Name Like a Horse's" (*Lošadinaja familija*, 1885). When Major General Buldeev gets a toothache, one of the servants recalls knowing a man capable of charming away the pain. The servant is able to recall the first name and patronymic of the tooth charmer, but the surname escapes him. He has the impression that it was derived from the name of a type of horse. The household is turned into a frenzy as its members feverishly conjure up a barrage of family names derived from types of horses. The source of humor here is not the pain suffered by Buldeev, to which it is indirectly related. Instead, the general's real agony is transformed into a comic one in the servant who tries desperately to recall the forgotten name. And this comic agony spreads through the entire household, even to Buldeev himself, in its efforts to provoke the servant's recollection.

Quite early, however, Čexov begins experimenting with the kind of pathos represented particularly by "Because of Little Apples", where the separate roles of villain and victim are clearly distinguished. In the 1884 story, "The Tutor" (*Repetitor*), a single character enacts both parts, thereby creating a situation of greater moral complexity. In a number of early pieces the role of tutor is exploited as a source for a situation in which one person can tyrannize over another. "The Tutor" appears to be simply another such story at the outset, when the pupil must humbly listen to his instructor's berating of him. The situation is abruptly reversed, however, when the young boy's father comes to observe the tutor at work. By the end of the story he must ask the father for six months back wages and humbly agree to a postponement of payment. The reader's sympathies inevitably go out to the figure who appeared at the beginning as the villain of the piece. Much the same kind of implicit reversal occurs in "Sergeant Prišibeev" (*Unter Prišibeev*, 1885). Here a retired sergeant has taken upon himself the enforcement of absurdly repressive laws. The sergeant operates on the principle that whatever the law does not explicitly permit it necessarily prohibits. With this sort of reasoning he breaks up groups of young people singing songs at night, because there is nothing in the law which says that people should sit about and sing. Just a year or so earlier Čexov might have depicted such a character at the height of his powers, but now Prišibeev himself is on trial for disturbing the peace; the tyrannizer is represented as a pathetic figure when the reader sees him at his most vulnerable in the act of defending himself.[2]

Čexov brings a further refinement to this type of pathos in "Oysters" (*Ustricy*), written just ten months after "The Tutor", near the end of 1884. The narrator recounts an episode from his childhood when bad times had forced him and his father onto the streets to beg. The story is written entirely from the point of view of the young boy, who sees a sign on a hotel which reads "Oysters". He has no idea what they are, but in a kind of delirium begins shouting the word. Some young gentlemen are amused by the shouting and take the boy into a restaurant. A plate of oysters is set before him and his exquisite hunger compels him to eat wolfishly. To the vast amusement of the onlookers he bites into a shell. Had Čexov written such a story a year or two earlier the incident might well have been the core of a comic piece, but here the situation is pathetic. Even in the chameleon stories Čexov viewed the protagonists from outside, producing an attitude of contempt toward the victims of the social order, but in "Oysters" the point of view has shifted to that of the victim. The nature of villainy, as well, has shifted from the simple view of it in "Because of Little Apples". Here the spectators' laughter implies indifference to the boy's misery. This introduces Čexov's most important variation on the pathetic story – the transformation of villainy into indifference. Speaking of realistic fiction, which he places in the low mimetic mode and considers particularly inclined toward the pathetic, Northrup Frye notes that: "The exploiting of fear in the low mimetic is also sensational, and is a kind of pathos in reverse. The terrible figure in this tradition, exemplified by Heathcliff, Simon Legree, and the villains of Dickens, is normally a ruthless figure strongly contrasted with some kind of delicate virtue, generally a helpless victim in his power."[3] What Čexov has started to do in "Oysters" is to reduce the figure of the villain to his most essential nature: ruthlessness is

---

[2] However pathetic Prišibeev becomes, the story enjoys another significance in the body of Čexov's work: in his mature period the prime object of villainy is *futljarnost'* – encasing oneself physically, psychologically, morally, and spiritually in order to reduce the points of contact between oneself and the rest of the world. Prišibeev tries unsuccessfully to use the law in this spirit and in doing so establishes himself as an early forerunner of a type most explicitly delineated in "The Man in a Case" (*Čelovek v futljare*, 1898).

[3] Northrup Frye, *Anatomy of Criticism* (Princeton, New Jersey, 1957), p. 39.

most clearly exhibited not in acts which do positive harm, but rather in total indifference, where there is a complete absence of feeling. Laughter here does not intensify the boy's unhappiness, which is the product of hunger, but reveals a ruthless attitude toward his suffering.

Although he was certainly not consistent in employing this refinement, the reducing of ruthlessness to its essential indifference is a characteristic of those stories involving pathos which Čexov produced in 1886.[4] "The Chorus Girl" (*Xoristka*) is a fairly well-known story from this period, though a routine instance of the exploiting of pity and fear as Northrup Frye has described it in the passage cited above. A prostitute, Paša, is entertaining a gentleman friend whose wife unexpectedly calls on the girl. The man hides in the next room while the wife demands that Paša give her the husband's presents, apparently purchased with embezzled funds. Actually, the man has given her almost nothing, but goaded and threatened by the wife, she finally turns over the jewelry which other men had given her in the past. Having reproached Paša with her contempt, the wife leaves, and the husband emerges to heap further abuse on the girl for causing his wife the embarrassment of visiting the room of a prostitute. Whatever irony there is in the story resides in the figure of Paša, the noble but misunderstood girl of the streets. But by 1886 the good prostitute had become a stock figure in nineteenth-century literature, and the pathos is unrelieved by any hint at a more complex arrangement of the story's moral elements. Renato Poggioli, who feels that this is a 'marvelous story', has aptly pointed out the moral: "The sad moral of this fable is of course that the Pashas will never change, and will be ever dressed and treated by men and women alike as 'chorus girls'. Yet the tale carries another lesson, perhaps a wiser one, teaching that it is not dress that makes the man, or even the woman, at that."[5] The 'wisdom' which Poggioli finds here is precisely the kind of banality which places "The Chorus Girl" among the most unsuccessful of all Čexov's stories.[6]

In another 1886 piece, "Requiem" (*Panixida*) he begins with a stock

---

[4] Once he had established the importance of indifference in pathos he could continue with variations on the motif. One of the most unusual in this respect is "Enemies" (*Vragi*, 1887), where two men, each with his own grief, become aggressively ruthless toward one another, each out of resentment at the other's unhappiness.

[5] Renato Poggioli, *The Phoenix and the Spider* (Cambridge, Massachusetts, 1957), p. 114.

[6] It is curious that this story appeared only two years prior to "A Nervous Breakdown" (*Pripadok*), in which Čexov deliberately contradicts the image of the noble prostitute, who is here treated sympathetically.

situation for pathos – a father who has lost his daughter – but quickly shifts the direction of the emotional impetus. Andrej Andreevič, a shopkeeper, has gone to church to request a requiem service for his daughter, but when he slips a note containing his request to the priest, we discover that his response to bereavement has been sidetracked by a queer sense of decorum. In the note he refers to his daughter as the 'harlot Marija'. The morally squeamish priest is shocked by the use of the term 'harlot' in reference to the dead, whose sins must be forgotten. Andrej Andreevič exhibits a similarly narrow moral outlook: on the one hand, he wants to do the proper thing by his daughter – to have services held; on the other, his sense of decorum compels him to judge his daughter's profession, that of an actress, in the harshest of terms.

During the service Andrej Andreevič recollects a walk that he and his daughter had taken during their last meeting. She had reflected on the beauty of the landscape, while Andrej condemned the land as bad for farming. It now becomes clear that the father had been simply unable to understand his daughter. Renato Poggioli has observed that Čexov has here taken one of the commonest tricks of the hack writer – a vulgar word uttered in all innocence – and transformed it into a highly meaningful incident: "This flashback reveals immediately how and why those two hearts and two minds, with their opposite concerns for beauty and utility, were destined never to meet. Now the problem whether the father did or did not know the real meaning of 'harlot' does not matter any longer: the point is that he misunderstood his daughter, to be misunderstood in return. The semantic confusion thus becomes merely a sign of man's inability to know himself, as well as others, including his next of kin." [7] The father's lack of understanding further reveals a suggestion of that indifference towards others which had begun to appear in "Oysters".

By an unusual twist, here it is the dead who are virtually ignored, rather than the mourners, in contradistinction to a number of stories from 1886 where the pathos hinges on the indifference of those surrounding the bereaved person. "Easter Eve" (*Svjatoju noč'ju*) is a classic instance of this. The ferryman-monk, Ieronim, is compelled by circumstances to work overtime through the night, while lamenting the loss of a fellow monk who has died on Easter eve. By way of contrast with Ieronim's unhappiness we see the generalized feeling of joy in all those who have come to church on this night and their indifference to the

[7]   Renato Poggioli, *The Phoenix and the Spider*, p. 121.

beauty of the dead monk's lauds to the saints. Ieronim's misery is somewhat palliated by the presence of the narrator to whom Ieronim describes the death and unusual talents of his friend. At the service the narrator becomes a sympathetic mourner opposed to all those unaware of the delicate and sensitive monk who has died. Thus, the pathetic element is subdued through the narrator's own sensitivity to the beauty of both the deceased monk's lauds and the beauty of the night.

But the most intriguing story in this group is "Misery" (*Toska*). At first glance it appears to be a tale of pathos, employing the countermotif of universal indifference to a man's sorrow. The cabman, Iona Potapov, whose son has died, further seems to exemplify the ideal object of pathos in that he is entirely incapable of expressing his grief. He apparently fits perfectly into the description Northrup Frye offers when he writes: "Again, in contrast to high mimetic tragedy, pathos is increased by the inarticulateness of the victim. The death of an animal is usually pathetic . . .".[8] Although no animal dies here, still the victim, Iona, is implicitly identified with his horse – ultimately the only object in which he can confide his grief. But in this instance Iona's very inarticulateness becomes a source of his misery, as we shall see shortly. Going about his evening's work, he attempts to find a sympathetic person to whom he can express his sorrow. Here Čexov successfully avoided what might have become a trap in which pathos turned into bathos: he might have tried to write about the unhappiness of a man who has lost his son, a subject which would almost inevitably have become sentimental. But the subject matter of the story is not this sadness, but another one, which lends itself considerably more readily to literary narrative: Iona's misery is that he can find no one to whom he can talk about his son's death. Thus, Čexov managed to transform a really incommunicable emotion – sadness at a son's death – into another kind of sadness. Iona is pathetic because no one will listen to him, not because his son died.

His first passenger is a military man who departs just as he begins describing his son's death. This incident is by way of introduction, and the later repetitions of this basic incident become more complex. In the second episode a party of drunken men enter Iona's cab. In this incident he becomes particularly pathetic through his poignant confusion of feeling. It is perfectly obvious that his passengers are drunk, quarrelsome,

---

[8] Northrup Frye, *Anatomy of Criticism*, pp. 38-39.

and boastful; sensing that their mood is the antithesis of his own, he makes a pathetic attempt to bridge the distance between himself and his passengers. Iona begins chuckling, and as the others argue about how much they have had to drink and about a certain Nadežda Petrovna, Iona periodically repeats a single epithet, "Jo-olly gentlemen", as though through this utterance he can bring his own feelings in harmony with theirs. "He hears oaths directed at himself, sees people, and the feeling of loneliness begins little by little to lift away from his breast. ... Iona looks at them. ... Having waited for a pause, he turns around once more and mutters, 'But this week my ... or rather ... son died'" (IV, 137-138). Thus, through the confusion of feeling Čexov further intensifies the pathos as Iona seeks in the jollity of his passengers an answer to his search for understanding. But something more is intimated here as well: not only is Iona inarticulate, this episode casts some doubt on his very capacity for feeling. We begin to wonder whether his inarticulateness may not be due to a confused understanding of his own feeling. Is he capable of evoking a response in others if he can so misinterpret their mood? Later, back at the stable he conjures up an image of the sort of sympathy he seeks: "The listener must moan, sigh, lament ... But to speak with women is still better. They, even though they be fools, bellow at two words" (IV, 139). Once again we see in Iona himself an admission that what he seeks is rather the form than the substance of sympathy.

The final incident in "Misery" is a highly ambiguous one, and has produced a variety of reactions in readers. Iona goes to the stable and begins talking to his horse. By degrees he brings the subject of discourse around to his son's death. "The horse chews, listens, and breathes on the hands of her master ... Iona is carried away and describes to her everything ..." (IV, 140). By emphasizing different aspects of this concluding scene it is possible to interpret and evaluate the event in several different ways. If we view Iona as victim in a tale of pathos, this scene apparently casts the final aspersion on a humanity that takes no interest in one man's sorrow. In a different reading of the story Renato Poggioli believes that this last scene redeems "Misery" from the pathetic element: "The story thus ends almost good-humoredly, relieving the almost unbearable tension, and relaxing the strings of pathos, which were about to snap." [9] I am not entirely certain what is meant by the word 'good-humoredly', but it might convey this – that Iona has found a solution

---

[9]   Renato Poggioli, *The Phoenix and the Spider*, p. 119.

not only to the indifference of mankind, but also to his own imprecision of feeling and consequent inarticulateness: he has found the form of lament which is perhaps the only one in which he is capable of relieving his distress. In such an interpretation the pathetic element tends to vanish entirely, the greater the degree of responsibility the victim bears for his own grief.

One of the finest stories from this period, "Veročka" (1887), unites this sense of the victim's responsibility with the idea of the villain as his own victim, an aberration which we have already noted in "The Tutor" and "Sergeant Prišibeev". While collecting data in the local district, Ognëv, a statistician, has spent a very pleasant summer as the Kuznecovs' guest. He says goodbye to his host and prepares to walk back to the hotel. Leaving the estate, he encounters Veročka, Kuznecov's daughter. Unexpectedly, she tells a bewildered Ognëv that she loves him, but he is unable to respond to her feelings; when they part, he realizes that he has allowed his only opportunity for married happiness to slip past.

As is usual in Čexov's more mature work, the basic sequence of events reveals almost nothing of the content of the story. Čexov is not a narrator, but rather an analyst. His real field of investigation lies in the revelations he achieves through the collective impact of details of appearance and feeling. "Veročka" is constructed through a series of recollections of former recollections which double back on themselves with ironic bitterness. The story opens, "Ivan Alekseevič Ognëv remembers how on that August evening with a sharp noise he opened the glass door and went out on the terrace" (VI, 60). The reader is given two pieces of information here which become significant only later: first, the narrative form of the story is to be a recollection in the present of an event which occurred in the past; secondly, Ognëv's present recollections are extremely vivid and concrete. There is no veil of haziness cast by his memory of the past; he recalls distinctly that the glass door made a noise when he opened it. His next recollection is of the cloak and straw hat which he had been wearing on that evening. They now lie in the dust beneath his bed. There is the suggestion here that some change had taken place in Ognëv himself since that evening: the cloak and hat which were satisfactory enough at that time have now been rejected. Significantly, he has not thrown them out or discarded them, but simply consigned them to the dust.

As he parts with Kuznecov, his remarks are the kind which may or may not express real feeling. The point is that he says what one is expected to say when he takes his leave of those who have shown him hospitality. " 'Goodbye, and once again thank you, my dear fellow ... for your cordiality, for your kindnesses, for your love. ... Never throughout all my life will I forget your hospitality' " (VI, 60). Actually, the insincerity of his words is shortly revealed. As he leaves the estate he falls into reflection:

> He walked and thought about how often in life we must meet good people and how unfortunate that from these meetings nothing remains except memories. It often happens that on the horizons cranes may appear, the weak wind carries their plaintive cries, but in a moment, with what eagerness we search the blue distance, there are no points to be seen, no sounds to be heard. So it is that people with their faces and words appear in our life and disappear in our past, leaving nothing more than insignificant traces of memory. Living since the beginning of spring in the N district and being almost daily at the home of the cordial Kuznecovs, Ivan Alekseevič had become one of the family to the old man, the daughter, the servants. He had studied every detail in the whole house, the sheltering terrace, the turns in the garden paths, the silhouettes of trees over the kitchen and bathhouse; but in a moment he will leave through the garden gate, and all this will turn into memories and will lose for him forever its real significance. A year or two will pass, and all these dear forms will become hazy in his consciousness, on a level with fancies and the fruits of fantasy (VI, 62).

From this passage we learn much about Ognëv's attitude toward experience. For him its substantial reality disappears almost immediately. He is not even out of the gate before he is turning his acquaintance with the Kuznecovs into the very flimsiest kind of fancy. It must be kept in mind, however, that this *was* his viewpoint at some time in the past, but not at the present. Since the whole story is narrated as a recollection, he is here recollecting in the present a prognostication of a future recollection. If we recall the first line of the story, we realize that his reflections do not jibe with actual memory: in his revery Ognëv believes that the reality of experience will "become hazy, on a level with fancies and the fruits of fantasy"; and yet we have already seen from the first line that this is not the case at all; on the contrary, his recollection in the present is extremely concrete and detailed. By this point it is plain that something has occurred in the past to upset Ognëv's neat theory of experience. This revery concludes the first section of the story.

He now meets Veročka in the garden. As he first sees her, she appears as 'a dark shadow', which apparently is about as close to real experience as Ognëv wishes to come. He moves about in a world inhabited not by people who love and suffer, but by dark shadows. Sitting down for a moment with Veročka, he begins to recollect aloud his arrival in the town. Keeping in mind the framework of the story, we realize that he is recollecting a recollection. The significance of Čexov's device lies in its great aptness for Ognëv. He is at least two removes from actual experience by this time, seeing the world through a very complex set of screens which ought to protect him from gross reality. The irony of the device is that they have not protected him in the least.

This part of the story reaches its climax as Ognëv remembers describing to Veročka how their meeting will soon become but a dim memory: "'And suddenly after ten years we will meet,' he said. 'What will we be like then? You will already be a respectable mother of a family, and I will be the author of some respectable statistical volume which no one needs and which is thick like forty thousand other volumes. We will meet and remember the old days. ... Now we feel the actuality of it; it fills and excites us, but later, when we meet, we won't remember either the date or the month, or even the year when we last saw each other on this little bridge'" (VI, 67). This is, as it were, Ognëv's swan song; it is his last effort to project the present moment into a future where actual experience will be but a dim memory. The futility of this effort is his tragedy.

Veročka, who is the exact opposite of Ognëv, now becomes the center of attention. She has been so involved in the feelings which she is experiencing that she has not even heard his reflections on the present moment from a vantage point of ten years hence. She tells him that she loves him, that she will follow him anywhere, but this only makes Ognëv uncomfortable. "The sadness, warmth, and sentimental atmosphere which goodbyes and liqueurs had inspired in him, suddenly disappeared, making room for a sharp, unpleasant feeling of awkwardness" (VI, 68). His neat arrangement of experience has been abruptly destroyed, and he is powerless to respond. After Veročka leaves him, he realizes that "he had lost something very dear, close to him, something which he would not find again. He felt that with Vera had slipped away part of his youth, and that those minutes through which he had fruitlessly lived would never be repeated" (VI, 71). Now Ognëv is aware that in his efforts to transform experience into a vague memory, he has lost life, and that he did not wish to lose it. In the final scene he returns later that night to the Kuznecovs' house. He wanders around it, looking powerlessly toward Vera's window. He is now suffering intensely from his lost opportunity. The final irony of the story, of course, lies in the framework of the narrative; Ognëv's vivid memory of the experience he had lost out on belies with a vengeance his former desire to transform it into a vague past.

In one sense the story falls into a familiar pattern: the indifferent and emotionally unresponsive Ognëv causes Vera's unhappiness. But Čexov views this process in a considerably more complex light here; Ognëv has failed to respond to Vera's feelings, but in so doing he has caused himself even greater suffering, for he is now aware that he must go on living a life which is like death; he lives but feels only the pain caused by his inability to respond, and thus, the villain suffers by his own hand.

Renato Poggioli, describing Čexov's central theme in this transitional period, speaks of a 'failure of communication': "Chekhov pays great attention to all those mistakes or equivocations that prevent the establishment of a communion of feeling between different human beings. ... What Chekhov is primarily interested in is what one might call, perhaps too technically, a failure of communication. Such failure, which takes place mainly on the moral plane, may operate on both sides, although the author attributes it preferably to the party at the receiving end. Thus the comedy of errors becomes pathetic and tragic, deriving from a defective condition which the message sender can hardly improve or correct: in brief from a fault in the reception." [10] Poggioli's statement implies, correctly, I think, that someone is to blame for the faulty communication, usually the receiver. However, for the term 'failure of communication' might be substituted 'failure of feeling'. Iona Potapov can find no response in other men to his suffering; Ieronim in "Easter Eve" finds no appreciation for the beauty of his friend's lauds to the saints; in "Requiem" Andrej fails to understand his daughter; and in "Veročka" Ognëv fails to respond to Vera's love. The failure of feeling is a theme which becomes central in Čexov's mature work, where it is frequently operative in a form designated by the Russian term *futljarnost'*.[11]

Another important new element in his work of this period is the role which natural setting plays. Apparently he began exploiting this element in 1885. Dmitri Grigorovič, one of the most prominent literary figures of the day, was the first to call attention to it in "The Huntsman" (*Eger'*) and "The Burbot" (*Nalim*). Much has of course been written on the poetic and lyrical mood of Čexov's stories. This quality is derived

10   Renato Poggioli, *The Phoenix and the Spider*, p. 118.
11   For a definition of *futljarnost'*, see note 2 above.

principally from his descriptions of natural setting. However, "Burbot" and "The Huntsman" exhibit very little indeed of that careful correlation of scene and emotional atmosphere which marks the later work. The only such moment in either of these stories occurs in "The Huntsman". Egor, the huntsman, looks up to see a flock of mallards flying over. He watches them as they disappear in the distance. The birds' flight has its parallel in Egor's own sudden appearance before his wife, and at the end of the story, just as he had watched the mallards vanish, so his wife sees Egor vanish. The event in nature acts as a metaphor for one type of human relationship.

The stories of 1886 exhibit something more of a solid correlation between scene and the predominating emotional tone of the story. In "Misery" the snow falling in the streets of St. Petersburg has its figurative correspondence in the 'coldness' of those who are indifferent to Iona's suffering. Here one detects a basic characteristic of setting in Čexov's stories – the dependent existence of the elements of nature within the story. The reader has the feeling that snow is falling precisely because Iona lives in a world which is cold and hostile. If one compares this piece with "Burbot", for example, he finds that in the earlier story the setting is an independent element, not directly related to the theme. The dependence of setting on character and emotional atmosphere is even more apparent in "Veročka", where the quality of the night at the beginning of the story attests perfectly to Ognëv's view of the world. Its typical features are darkness and warmth, and the evening mist duplicates the vagueness of experience in Ognëv's world. One wonders in fact if this setting really exists or is merely a reflection of his personality; after his moment with Vera, when he realizes there is something more than vague memory, the fog suddenly lifts, and there is a clarity in the night which once again corresponds to the changed state of Ognëv's feeling.

Towards the end of 1886 Čexov produced probably his finest story of that year, "On the Road" (*Na puti*), in which the setting assumes a major role for the first time. Here virtually every detail becomes a dramatic aspect of the theme, a minor protagonist in the story's central paradox. "On the Road" takes as its motto the opening lines of Lermontov's "The Rock". Because of the exact correspondence of theme in poem and story, I offer here a prose translation: "A golden cloudlet spent the night on the breast of a giant rock; she whirled away on her journey early in the morning, gayly playing on the horizon. But a moist track remained in the wrinkles of the old rock. It stands alone in deep meditation, and softly weeps in the wasteland." [12] The central paradox in the poem is the need which the protector experiences for that which he protects. A soft substance seeks the shelter of the hard, but when the cloudlet leaves, it is the rock which feels the loss, not the cloudlet. This is the central idea too in Čexov's story. It is acted out principally in the figures of two travelers, Lixarëv and a young lady, Ilovajskaja, who meet at an inn on a stormy night. But the paradox is embodied not only in the relationship between the protagonists; it appears in their physical features, in the room where they sit, and in the storm itself. Lixarëv is described in these terms: "... all the features each taken separately, were rough and heavy, like the furniture and the stove in the 'traveler's room', but taken as a whole they gave the effect of something harmonious and even beautiful. Such is, as they say, the lucky star of the Russian face: the coarser and harsher its features, the more it appears tender and good-natured" (V, 263). The room itself contains a paradox: on the walls holy pictures and cheap popular prints hang side by side, as though the owner of the inn wished to offer something for everybody. Even the intentions of the stove seem paradoxical: at one moment the whistling sound in the chimney seems to be trying to get in tune with the howling wind outside, but at the next the wind, which is trying to come into the room through the chimney, is violently repulsed by the flames shooting up.

It is one of the signs of the middle period in Čexov's writing that he attributes human characteristics to inanimate objects. "Outside a storm was raging. Something frantic and wrathful, but profoundly unhappy, seemed to be flinging itself about the tavern with the ferocity of a wild beast and trying to break in" (V, 264). The pathetic fallacy apparently came naturally to him, for he does not see nature as an independent existence, but either as a reflection of human moods or as a state in the mind of man. Čexov's critics point out that later he eschewed the pathetic fallacy, and, in a letter, criticized Gor'kij's writing for this fault. [13] Actually Čexov never really dropped this device; he merely transferred his observations from omniscient narrator to appearances and reflections in the minds of his characters. This is notably apparent in "The Lady with the Dog" (*Dama s sobačkoj*) and "On Official Business" (*Po delam služby*).

The storm itself is a complex symbol of the central paradox. In one sense, the travelers come to the inn because they are trying to escape

[12] Mixail Lermontov, *Polnoe sobranie sočinenij* (Moskva, 1936), II, 122.
[13] See his letter to Gor'kij of 3 January 1899 (XVIII, 11-12).

from the storm; and yet at the same time, it is the communion achieved because of the storm which gives meaning to their meeting. In addition, it functions as a literal reflection of the figurative storm which is taking place within the central characters. This is to become another characteristic device in Čexov's work. Frequently, a major upheaval in a character's attitude toward his life occurs upon the occasion of a storm. In "A Dreary Story" (*Skučnaja istorija*) he employs an elaborate metaphor of the storm at a crucial moment, and still another storm plays an important role in "Betrothed" (*Nevesta*).[14] On a minor scale this point is illustrated in the behavior of Lixarëv's young daughter. Disturbed and frightened by the noise of the storm, she cries, " 'Lord, Lord, how unhappy I am! Unhappier than all the others!' " (V, 267). Here the storm is a reflection of her own unhappy state; she has been travelling for several days in a carriage and would much prefer to return to the relatives whom the father and child recently left. Upon hearing the child's cries, Lixarëv and Ilovajskaja, the newly acquainted travelers, are roused out of their silence. When they have calmed the unhappy girl, they fall silent again, as though without the presence of an emotional or literal storm there is nothing to talk about.

The central paradox of the story, however, lies in the relationship between man and woman, as exemplified by Lixarëv and Ilovajskaja. Čexov first presents the paradox through the relationship between Lixarëv and his daughter. We are early presented with the physical contrast between the large man and the very small girl. We later discover that Ilovajskaja is also extremely small. In the natural order of things power and authority should rest in the hands of the father. But on the contrary, these qualities reside in the child. She continually reproaches him for having brought her on this unpleasant journey, while he behaves towards her like a child who has been caught in a naughty act. At one point Lixarëv gets up to soothe his daughter and walks "with a guilty gait that doesn't go with his solid frame" (V, 267). In the principal action of the story Ilovajskaja is transported by Lixarëv's amazing ability to experience faith. It is implied that he could lead her where he chose, and yet when they part after the stormy night, it is he who feels the loss of something precious. Once again each detail contributes to the central paradox. As they are getting acquainted, he describes to her how he was once a landowner, "but in good time went

---

[14] Two other important stories featuring literal storms that parallel the heroes' emotional upheaval are "The Duel" (*Duel'*) and "On Official Business" (*Po delam služby*).

bankrupt" (V, 268). She is returning to the estate of her father and
brother in order to take over the management of it because of the
incompetence of her two male relatives. Finally, as Lixarëv finishes
describing his enthusiasms and faiths, Ilovajskaja is transported: "All
that she had just heard rang in her ears, and human life seemed to her a
marvelous, poetical fairy tale in which there is no end" (V, 276). But
her sense of joy finds no counterpart in Lixarëv, who has inspired her
with a faith in himself – the one faith he cannot share. During the night
she hears the child crying, and along with and like the child the father
cries. It is the man who is the weaker sex. The image at the end of the
story brings us full circle and returns us to Lermontov's poem: "Soon
the tracks of the carriage disappeared, and covered with snow he became like a white rock, but his eyes still sought something in the clouds
of snow" (V, 279).

In a commentary on this story Caroline Gordon and Allen Tate have
said: "But the storm (symbolic of mortal life) which has been howling
about them all night now overwhelms them both; snowflakes are
'greedily' settling on his hair, beard and shoulders and he only stands,
gazing at the tracks left by her sledge runners. The Symbolism . . . is
plain: any man and any woman may be so blinded by our human
condition that they are incapable of seeing each other clearly." And
earlier they noted: "In "On the Road" Chekhov shows us . . . how Gri-
gory Petrovich Liharev did not marry Mlle. Ilovaisky." [15] Regardless
of their apparent ignorance of Lermontov's poem, I think this is an
invalid interpretation of Čexov's story. It is definitely not about how
Grigorij Petrovič Lixarëv did not marry Mlle. Ilovajskaja. He shows us
rather a paradox, or a series of paradoxes, in human experience, which
ultimately demonstrate why these two cannot come together; a man and
woman create their own unhappiness through the inability of each to
respond to the other in the customary way. We cannot be what we
would like to be because of the way we are. Pathos has been transformed to the point where the moral element inherent in the early
stories has simply vanished. The attempt to depict a world in which
blame can be fixed at all has crumbled. To put it another way, Čexov's
artistic vision belies the notion of a stable reality in which moral ab-
solutes can be found. This struggle between artistic vision and emotional
stability continues until roughly 1894.

Francis Fergusson, writing not about the stories, but about *The*

---

[15] Caroline Gordon and Allen Tate, eds., *The House of Fiction* (New York,
1960), pp. 97-99.

Cherry Orchard, has described the world of Čexov's stories more accurately than Gordon and Tate: "It is an imitation of an action in the strictest sense. ... the incidents are selected and arranged to define an action in a certain mode; a complete action, with a beginning, middle, and end in time. Its freedom from the mechanical order of the thesis or the intrigue is the sign of the perfection of Chekhov's realistic art. And its apparently casual incidents are actually composed with most elaborate and conscious skill to reveal the underlying life, and the natural, objective form of the play as a whole." [16] If we substitute 'story' for 'play' in the last sentence, I think we have a far more adequate definition of the kind of work which Čexov could produce at his best in this transitional period.

[16] Francis Fergusson, *The Idea of a Theater* (New York, 1953), pp. 174-175.

V

DREAMS

By 1886 the stories dominated by pathos had settled their attention on a figure whose chief shortcoming is an insensitivity to the feelings of those around him. In the same year Čexov begins to depict a complementary type who is distinguished by his unusual sensitivity to life. While the stories of pathos approached the moral issue in a negative way – attention was focused on the villainous figure – this new group of stories approaches the moral issue from a positive standpoint. Its hero constantly asserts the existence of beauty, mystery, and freedom in the world, even though he regularly comes into contact with people who deny the validity of these values. By 1887 Čexov's own faith in his hero seems to wither and the moral issue is once again undercut: even these sensitive figures lose their sense of conviction.

Their most distinguishing trait is that they are dreamers though there is irony in this epithet. As by some magical power, the dreamer is able to discern in ordinary life values and ideals utterly meaningless to a person caught up in the midst of the ordinary and the normal. That which the prosaic man sees as the workaday process may be a revelatory moment for the dreamer. Thus, while one person crosses the steppe to sell his wool at a profit, another makes the same journey to find a vision of life not limited by the necessity of getting along. Dreamer is an ironic designation because it envisions two opposing concepts of the one who finds the extraordinary in the ordinary; from the prosaic man's point of view his opposite number is a dreamer in the sense that he is out of touch with the workaday world. But from his own point of view the dreamer does not sever his connection with reality; on the contrary, there is an intensification of contact – an attempt to find another system of values within the daily sphere, a more meaningful reality within that of the ordinary and the normal.

What Čexov offers the reader in his new character type is a valuable distortion of the workaday world – valuable because it gives meaning to the ordinary. Of course, every artist strives to illuminate for us the tangled muddle of actual living. What distinguishes Čexov's effort is the double perspective – an ironic one, if you will – whereby ordinary reality and the distorted vision of it are seen in conflict. Such valuable distortions of the world were apparent in his early satirical pieces, in the presentation of the chameleon type, for example, where a typical aspect of the normal world – the importance of official rank – was distorted to reveal its real absurdity. However, the parallel can be carried no further. This period is, in fact, primarily important insofar as Čexov was engaged in an assiduous effort to deny, or at least counter, his vision of a shaky existence. The stories concerning dreams attempt to assert the presence in life of values rather more permanent, values which are not significantly altered by the process of living. Ultimately, the effort fails; neither the writer nor his characters can retain their faith in the validity of the dream.

In 1886 Čexov's preoccupation with the distorted point of view is most evident in his stories about children, whose appeal for him was apparently the very fact that they offered an easy vehicle for the distorted vision of reality. "Griša" is an instance of this fascination with the child's ability to see the world in wholly new terms, though here he exploits this faculty purely for its charm. A nurse is taking a small boy out for his first walk, and the appeal of the story rests on the child's sense of wonder at the world he beholds. "Griša" is only a minor effort; it is delightful but offers no real illumination through its distortion of the ordinary. In this same connection, Čexov was willing to exploit any point of view, it seems, to attain a new perspective, even if it limits rather than broadens one's comprehension. Thus, "Kaštanka", written late in 1887, offers a dog's perception of human motivation.

These two stories might serve as evidence for Viktor Šklovskij's theory that literary art perceives the ordinary as something strange (ostranenie).[1] But the distortion which the child's point of view offers is used with considerably more telling force in some of the other stories from this period. The child may reveal a reality outside the ordinary. In "At Home" (Doma, 1887) Serëža, a boy of seven, has drawn a soldier who is taller than the house he is standing next to. His father objects to this illogicality, but the boy insists that if the man were smaller his eyes would not be visible. What follows is not only an interesting observation on children, it is an extremely revealing account

[1] Viktor Šklovskij, "Iskusstvo kak priëm", O teorii prozy (Moskva, 1925), pp. 7-21. See also Victor Erlich, Russian Formalism (The Hague, 1955), pp. 149-154.

of the value which Čexov finds in the child's distortions of the normal world: "Was it really necessary to dispute him? From daily observations of his son the lawyer was convinced that like wild animals, children have their own artistic visions and original demands not accessible to the understanding of adults. Under intensive observation Serëža might appear abnormal to an adult. He found it possible and reasonable to draw people taller than houses, to render with his pencil not only objects but also his own feelings" (VI, 95). The last sentence could be taken as the author's own programmatic statement of the way he will render experience in many of these stories, as he becomes increasingly absorbed in portraying his characters' feelings about reality rather than reality itself.

The child's point of view may even reveal a system of moral and ethical values which are not usually perceptible to the man caught up in the normal and the ordinary. In "At Home", for example, Serëža is able to disrupt his father's rather conventional moral views. When he reprimands the boy for smoking his tobacco, the father tells his son that he has committed three crimes, one of which is taking an-other's possessions without asking permission. The father argues that he would not try to take Serëža's toys because they belong to Serëža. The boy innocently offers to let his father take any toys he likes at any time, and thereby introduces a set of values more basically Christian than those with which the father would inculcate his son.

In "A Common Trifle" (*Žitejskaja meloč*, 1886) a child's idealism receives its first shock of disillusionment. Nikolaj Beljaev has come to see his mistress, Ol'ga Ivanovna, who is estranged from her husband. In her absence her son Alëša greets Beljaev, and as they talk the boy describes how he and his sister visit their father once a week – a fact which Beljaev promises not to reveal to the mother. Incidentally, Alëša mentions his father's suffering at the thought that another man is living with Ol'ga Ivanova. Beljaev takes offense at this image of himself as the destroyer of a happy home. When Ol'ga returns he indignantly complains about the injustice of regarding him in this way. The mother is thrown into a turmoil when she finds that the children still see their father, but the most deeply hurt is of course Alëša, who has discovered that the values and ideals he had been taught to respect are frequently ignored by the adult world.

Children may imagine a different kind of existence in which the practical details of ordinary living simply disappear. In "The Boys" (*Mal'čiki*, 1887) Volodja, a student returning home for the Christmas holidays, has brought with him a young friend, Čečevicyn. The two boys plan a fanciful journey to America where they will become Indians. They have already projected themselves into their new world: Čečevicyn calls himself Montigomo, the hawk's claw. Their dream is suddenly quashed by Volodja's father, who intercepts them at the railroad station. They are scolded and the next day Čečevicyn's mother comes to take her son home. "The Boys" illustrates an important feature of Čexov's stories about dreamers: whether the stories are amusing, like this one, or deadly serious, the crass, normal world invariably resents the dream and attempts to destroy it. A kind of victory for the normal world is inevitable, because the dreamer is not trying to transform it; he merely seeks other values within it. However, he can be totally defeated only when his own faith in the dream is shaken, and this ultimate defeat recurs with ever greater regularity whenever there is a confrontation between the practical and the imaginative, though in this story the final victory goes to Čečevicyn. When he is carried off by his mother, he does not utter a word: "He simply took Katja's notebook and wrote as a memento: 'Montigomo, the hawk's claw' " (VI, 362). Volodja's father may be able to destroy the actual journey to a new land, but he cannot touch the reality of the dream.

It is significant that Čexov draws a sharp distinction between dreams and daydreams. Throughout his career he remained sympathetic toward the dreamer, but the daydreamer is a subject of contempt and ridicule. There are a number of stories from this same period in which the latter figure is the butt of contemptuous comedy. The daydream presents not another world, but merely a projection of oneself as hero or victor in the ordinary one. Unlike the dream, it attempts to defeat daily existence on its own terms, and the range of its vision is necessarily limited to the normal and the familiar.

An example of the pure daydream used for comic effect is the story "Intrigues" (*Intrigi*, 1887). Doctor Šelestov dreams of becoming president of his local medical society after he has made an impassioned speech to its members, eloquently exposing the intrigues which dominate it. Having attained this eminent position he proceeds to demonstrate his own skill at intriguing by arranging the removal of his rival from the society, and ends by purging the organization generally of all members who displease him. What he dreams of is nothing more than his own victory in the banal terms of the ordinary world. Čexov makes Šelestov an object of foolishness by contrasting the eloquence of his imaginary oration with the clumsiness of his actual speech at the meeting.

"Talent" (*Talant*, 1886) is particularly interesting in this regard because it presents in one story both the daydream and the dream. A
penniless artist, Egor Savvič, dreams of becoming rich and famous.
Čexov lends a sense of poetic justice to Egor's material poverty by
pointing up his complete lack of talent: "It is an afternoon in early
autumn. If one looks upon it with a painter's eye, this sadness of nature
is beautiful and poetic in its own way, but for Egor Savvič there is no
beauty. Boredom eats away at him ..." (V, 135). A similar stroke occurs
at the end of Egor's dream of fame and fortune: he picks up the works
of Gogol' and tries to read but falls asleep after two pages. The dreamer
is Katja, the landlady's daughter. She is in love with Egor, but he assures
her that he cannot marry, because an artist must devote his life to his
work. In the evening two of his fellow artists come to visit him. They
are apparently as barren of talent as Egor himself, for their conversation
is all of fame and fortune in the future. When they leave, Egor finds
Katja on the floor outside his room, where she has been listening to
every word: " 'I am thinking of how you will be a celebrity,' she says
in a half whisper, 'I see it all before me, what a great person you will
become ... Just now I heard your whole conversation ... I am dreaming ... dreaming' " (V, 139). While the artist's dream is a selfish one,
projecting a banally triumphant Egor in the ordinary world, Katja's
represents a faith in the possibility of happiness – a faith based on a kind
of simplicity incomprehensible to the artist. In Čexov's terms Katja's
dream is a real one, while Egor's is no more than a piece of comic
self-deception.

The first serious presentation of the dreamer occurs in the second
half of 1886 in a story entitled, significantly, "Dreams" (*Mečty*). The
central figure here is the first of Čexov's mature characters who seek
a more meaningful reality, who seek the extraordinary in the ordinary.
The dreamer is a vagrant whom two policemen are escorting to the
local magistrate's office. As a character type the vagrant is sharply
distinguished from the constables: "... perhaps, judging by that dull
patience with which he struggles against the clinging, autumn mud, this
is a fanatic, being trained as a monk, wandering among the Russian
monasteries doggedly seeking 'an existence peaceful and sinless' and
not finding it ..." (V, 225). The suggestion of fanaticism is typical of
Čexov's searchers. The world they seek, and sometimes momentarily
find, is always a distortion of everyday existence. If not mystical, their
experiences are at least mysterious. This vagrant has a number of rather
mysterious traits. He has forgotten his name. One of the policemen is

downright angry at this: for him it is incredible that a person could forget his own name. His origins also have an aura of mystery about them. He remembers that his mother was a nurse in a gentleman's household, but he has no idea who his father was. There is a suggestion that the mother had rejected men of her own class and had set her sights higher. The vagrant is a kind of classless person wandering about in a no-man's land, perhaps a peasant, perhaps the son of a nobleman. At any rate, Čexov clearly establishes his dreamer as a person completely out of touch with the normal order of existence.

His dream is of a free life in Siberia, to which he hopes they will exile him: " 'They will give me land to plow and for a garden and for a house, lad ... I will start to plow and sow like other people, raise cattle and all kinds of business, bees, sheep, dogs ... a Siberian tomcat so that mice and rats won't eat my goods ... I will build a house, brothers, icons I'll buy ... God willing, I will marry, have children.' ... The vagrant's small mouth was twisted by a smile, and his whole face and eyes and little nose hardened and became torpid from the sweet foretaste of a distant happiness" (V, 229). When the vagrant describes the fishing in Siberia in loving detail, we recognize another characteristic of Čexov's dreamers: they are often able to describe their wonderful visions with great eloquence.

For a while the guards seem to be caught up in the marvel of the dream, but then the grimness of everyday reality reasserts itself. "In the autumn silence when a cold, harsh fog from the earth lies on the soul, when it stands like a prison wall before one's eyes and informs man of his will, it is sweet to think of broad, rapid rivers with free, steep banks, of impenetrable forests, of limitless steppe" (V, 230). The constables suddenly recover their sense of equilibrium, and assure the vagrant that he could not possibly reach his dreamland. They point out that he is tired after a mere four versts and could not endure the journey to Siberia. When they hand him over to the authorities, he will almost certainly be consigned to a hospital. It is as though the guards resent the dream, or at least resent the vagrant's ability to experience it. They seem to fear that he might attain his goal, and ordinary existence must destroy such hope as best it can, for the dream implies the inadequacy of practical reality. Unlike the stories about children, "Dreams" depicts a conflict in which total victory is assigned to the workaday world: the vagrant's faith is shaken under the onslaught of the constables' objections. As they continue their march, "The tramp was still more bent over and he thrust his hands deeper into his sleeves. Ptaxa is silent"

(V, 232). However, the final sentence suggests that the constables'
triumph may conceal their own more fundamental defeat. Ptaxa, the
less experienced of the two guards, has been upset by the tramp's inability to recall his own name, and it is he who has drawn the vagrant
out into a more detailed account of his past and his vision of freedom.
He joins his comrade in deriding the tramp's hope for realizing his
dream, but the last two words of the story (*Ptaxa molčit*) imply that he
shares the depression of defeat.

The process of disenchantment is central in "The Kiss" (*Poceluj*,
1887). What really marks the excellence of the story is Čexov's newly
found ability to enter the individual consciousness, to penetrate the
inner world of his central character. The private life is a kind of dreamland, separated from external reality, and yet capable of illuminating
life as a whole. Although "The Kiss" describes a highly romantic adventure which takes place in the mind and feeling of the central character, Rjabovič, it opens on a far different note: "On the twentieth of
May, at eight o'clock in the evening, the entire six batteries of the N-
reserve artillery brigade, while on the way to their camp, stopped for the
night at the village of Mestečki" (VI, 338). The tone of the narration
clearly belongs to that public sphere which has no interest in the individual's dreams. This tone is maintained in the early pages of the
story, as the officers are invited to the home of a member of the local
gentry, von Rabbek. Remembering such occasions in the past, the
officers anticipate a tedious evening, listening to the war stories of an
old man. Von Rabbek turns out to be a different sort, though the party
is equally dull for another reason: he does not really wish to entertain
the officers, but feels that his position in the community has obligated
him to perform this social task. Thus, in the first few pages the reader
is introduced to a prosaic world indeed, dominated by boredom, indifference, and artificiality.

However, it is at the home of von Rabbek that Rjabovič, a shy young
officer, has a very different kind of experience. Losing his way in the
intricate corridors of the house, he wanders into a dark room and the
embraces of a woman he cannot see: ". . . two soft, sweet-smelling, undoubtedly feminine arms enveloped his neck; a warm cheek was pressed
against his and at the same time was heard the sound of a kiss. But
immediately the one who had kissed him uttered a soft cry and, as it
seemed to Rjabovič, jumped away from him in disgust. He too barely
uttered a cry and rushed toward the bright beam in the door chink" (VI,
344). The meeting is mysterious in two senses: he has no idea who the

woman is or why she was there; and it is a secret, private event, known only to the two of them. Rjabovič has an adventure denied to all the others in the house, and he is intoxicated by it.

The obvious explanation of this episode, mistaken identity, is powerless before his enchantment. However accidental it may have been, the experience was still his alone. Standing on the edge of the dance floor, he surveys the girls and tries to decide which of them it was he had met in the dark room. Characteristically enough, he rejects each girl in turn as being somehow not as lovely or not as charming as the lady of his mysterious meeting. Thus, in the real world there are no girls who can rival the one created by his imagination.

On the way back to the barracks the whole world becomes enveloped for him in this mysterious sense of delight. Here Čexov uses atmosphere to isolate the man with his dream. Out of boredom the officers stop to look at a fire shining from across the water. "Rjabovič too looked at the fire, and it seemed to him that this fire smiled and flickered at him as if it knew about the kiss" (VI, 346). In Rjabovič's private world he has established a special kind of relationship with the real one – a relationship which is denied to all the others. The romantic adventure is his alone in a world dominated by prosaic facts, boredom, and indifference. As he falls asleep that night he feels that "... someone had been tender and had filled him with a sense of joy, that in his life had occurred something out of the ordinary, stupid, but extraordinarily good and wonderful. This thought did not leave him even in his sleep" (VI, 348).

The following day, as the battery marches along the road, the struggle between dream and reality begins. Čexov offers an extended and detailed description of the battery marching. His purpose is obviously to communicate the sense of routine and business-as-usual which envelops Rjabovič, who is trying to escape this and preserve the world of his strange adventure. "At first, when the brigade had just moved out, he wanted to convince himself the incident of the kiss could be interesting only as a small, mysterious adventure, that in essence, it was insignificant and to think about it seriously was in extreme measure stupid; but swiftly he waved aside logic and gave himself up to dreams ..." (VI, 350). The struggle now becomes highly dramatic. The command is given, "To the brakes!" "He too shouted 'to the brakes!' and feared that this shout might destroy his dream and call him back to actuality ..." (VI, 350).

Rjabovič's foil is a fellow officer, Lobytko, who is a ladies' man. He

has the kind of success with women in actual life which Rjabovič has
only imagined. The brigade commander jokes with Lobytko about
being in love with a tall, fat woman past forty. The struggle becomes
clear now: the real world tries to reduce Rjabovič's strange adventure to common terms, to equate it with the kind of affair which
Lobytko experiences. The commander leaves in a cloud of dust which
settles over the brigade. The symbolism is apparent: it is the very texture
of the real world which is enveloping the dreamer. At this point, Rjabovič thinks, " 'I am the same as the others, and sooner or later I shall
endure what all the others have endured...' " (VI, 352). His final
defeat occurs that evening when he describes to Lobytko and some of
the other officers what had happened to him the evening before. He
finds to his surprise that what he has to tell is remarkably short and flat.
Obviously, as soon as he tries to put his dream into words before the
others, it has been transformed into precisely the kind of sordid experience which his comrades have known. Lobytko is reminded of an
adventure of his own, and what comes from his lips is really a parody
of Rjabovič's dream:

"Last year I was going to Kovno ... I take a second-class ticket ... The
coach is stuffed full of people and it's impossible to sleep. I give the conductor some money ... He takes my baggage and leads me to a sleeper ...
I lie down and cover myself with a blanket ... It's dark, you see. Suddenly
I hear somebody touching me behind the shoulder and breathing in my face.
I make a movement with my hand and feel somebody's elbow ... I open
my eyes, and, can you imagine, a woman is there! Black eyes, lips red like
a fine salmon, her nostrils breathe with passion, breasts like buffers ...!"
(VI, 352-353).

By this time the dream has been destroyed for Rjabovič. When some
time later he returns to the scene of the original adventure, he is an
utterly different person. Stopping at the spot where the officers had
watched the fire shining from the opposite bank, he realizes that the
concrete details of setting are the same, but, having lost his dream, he
finds no meaning in them: "The water flowed no one knows where or
why. It flowed just as it had in May; from the stream in May it had
flowed into a large river, from the river into the sea, then turned into
vapor, returned as rain, and, perhaps, the very same water flows again
now before Rjabovič's eyes... To what purpose? Why?" (VI, 355).
    The officers have again been invited to the home of a member of
the gentry, but it is too late for Rjabovič; it is literally already late in
the evening, and in a deeper sense it is also too late − he is no longer

the same person who attended the party at von Rabbek's; he is in-capable of such an experience again. The world of prosaic detail, bore-dom, and indifference has won a full victory. The complete destruction of the dreamer, his metamorphosis into a person who has lost his sense of beauty, mystery, freedom, marks a new attitude in Čexov's work – one characterized by a deeper gloominess.

In the spring of 1887 Čexov made a journey to his native town, Taganrog, and returned to Moscow through the steppe country of south-west Russia. This journey had an important effect on his career, for it inspired his first contribution to a thick journal, "The Steppe" (*Step'*). Both this story and another product of the trip, "Happiness" (*Sčast'e*) are particularly relevant to the problem of the dreamer. "Happiness" was the first piece he wrote after his renewed acquaintance with the steppe, and, in setting and theme, clearly belongs with his later more important piece. Like "The Steppe", "Happiness" is a search for a quality which hides itself mysteriously in the landscape. A sense of mystery pervades the narrative: the appearance of a horseman a few feet away from the two herdsmen who are the central characters is left strangely unexplained. One of the shepherds, an old man, speaks of his friend, Efim, who possessed mysterious powers: his melons whistled, and he once caught a fish that laughed. The old man goes on to tell of treasure buried in the steppe. The aura of mystery is reinforced as he describes how one needs talismans and charms to find it.

The conflict now develops between the younger shepherd and the old man. The younger fellow has little patience with talk of melons that whistle and of talismans, but at the mention of buried treasure his ears prick up. However, there is an ironic double meaning involved in the concept of buried treasure. In terms of the tangible world there may be gold coins buried in the earth, but in the story it is not really clear whether the old man is talking about this kind of treasure or whether he is thinking of a different type, happiness. " 'And really there is much happiness, so much, lad, that it would satisfy all those around, but not a single soul sees it' " (VI, 166). All the talk of talismans has its counter-part in the mystery of the night: "In the quiet air, scuttling through the steppe, passed a sound. Something in the distance gasped menacingly, struck against a stone, and ran through the steppe issuing 'Tah, tah, tah, tah!' When the sound died away, the old man looked inquiringly at the indifferent Pantelej, standing motionless" (VI, 166). In "Happiness" the conflict between the two kinds of buried treasure never really comes to a resolution, as the conflict between dream and sordid reality did in "The Kiss". In this sense "Happiness" is considerably more anecdotal than the previous story.

However, the most important fruit of Čexov's trip and the most revolutionary work of 1887 was "The Steppe", which at least begins with an implicit conflict between Ivan Ivanyč Kuz'mičov, a merchant crossing the steppe to sell his wool, and his nephew, Egoruška, a boy of nine. The uncle's journey is a practical one and the man himself is the chief representative of the workaday world. Egoruška's trip has a different purpose: he is crossing the steppe in order to attend a school, but for the purposes of the story, his studies are confined to the school which the steppe itself offers, and what his journey ultimately involves is a search for a kind of world not envisioned in Ivan Ivanyč's concept of the normal and the ordinary. At various points in the story Čexov reminds us of Egoruška's purpose: each time the travellers encounter a new person, the boy is asked why he is making the journey, and his reply is always, "To study." We have seen in previous stories how the practical world strives to destroy the dream, and here, typically, Ivan Ivanyč resents the fact that his nephew is going to school; he is certain that it would be better if the boy came into business with him. It is appropriate, too, that Egoruška parts with his uncle midway through the journey to continue travelling with a group of peasants: their paths diverge just as their motives do.

However, the conflict thus introduced continues to appear sporadically through references to Varlamov, a rich merchant whom Ivan Ivanyč sought to overtake. Egoruška associates a sense of mystery with the elusive Varlamov – a mystery which is dissipated when the boy eventually meets him: "In the small man dressed in grey, wearing high boots, sitting on a homely little horse and talking with the peasants at a time when decent people are sleeping, it was difficult to recognize the mysterious, elusive Varlamov, whom everyone seeks, who is always 'circling' . . ." (VII, 88).

There is no mystery about those who belong to Ivan Ivanyč's world, but in contrast to this there is the world of the steppe. It has been remarked that the central character in the story is not a human figure at all, but the steppe itself.[2] Certainly it is true that Čexov personifies it continually in passages like this one: "Scarcely has the sun set and the mist covered the earth when the daytime sadness is forgotten, all is forgiven, and the steppe lightly sighs with its vast bosom" (VII, 51). In

[2]   See David Magarshack, *Chekhov: A Life* (New York, 1955), p. 143.

addition, Egoruška's consciousness strangely distorts what he sees and hears, and thus the steppe itself and its distortion through Egoruška's perception creates a kind of mysterious, sometimes meaningful, but always very different, world from that of ordinary existence. At one point Čexov observes: "Everything presents itself as something other than what it is" (VII, 51). Such illusions include a bush which at night becomes a robber crouching by the roadside, imaginary chariots drawn by frenzied horses, and three peasants with pitchforks who appear to be giants carrying pikes. Some of the peasants with whom Egoruška travels also have this ability to see a different world: "Everybody started looking into the distance and seeking with his eyes the fox, but they found nothing. Only Vasja saw something with his dull, grey eyes and was excited. ... Thanks to such sharpness of vision, besides the world which others saw, Vasja had also another world, his personal one, denied to others and probably a very good one, because when he saw it and became excited it was difficult not to envy him" (VII, 62). The conflict between these two worlds recurs in the scene around the campfire, where Pantelej, who holds everyone with his tales of robbers, prefers to relate imaginary variations on the actual.

This conflict is largely acted out in terms of visual and auditory impressions. What can be seen on the steppe is peculiarly unrevealing. It seems to partake for the most part of the prosaic and ordinary world. Monotony dominates the scene: "The hot rays burned his back, his neck, and the back of his head. The plaintive song now died away, now again reached him in the stagnant, humid air, rooks monotonously screeched, the horses chewed, and time dragged on endlessly, as if it had congealed and stopped. It seemed that since morning a hundred years had passed already... Did not God want Egoruška, the carriage and the horses to perish in this air, and, like the hills turn to stone and remain forever in one place?" (VII, 31). Visual images seem unable to transport man beyond the conventional world. "The stars, peering from the sky for a thousand years already... indifferent to the short life of man, oppress the soul with their silence when one remains with them eye to eye and tries to comprehend their thought. That loneliness which awaits each of us in the grave comes to mind and the essence of life appears desperate and horrible ..." (VII, 72).

It would seem to be the inability of such visual images literally to 'say' anything which holds them to the ordinary; primarily auditory impressions appear at those moments when Egoruška comes into contact with the beauty of the steppe. The sounds of nature, particularly those of birds, play an important role in the story; when a storm occurs at the end of the journey, it is the sounds of the storm, rather than its visual aspects, which receive the greater attention;[3] Čexov seems to be most in his element when he is describing the sounds of the steppe at night, rather than the sights of the day, but even during the day the finest moments are auditory ones:

At that time, as Egoruška looked at the sleeping faces, a quiet singing was unexpectedly heard. Somewhere far off a woman was humming, but precisely where and on what side was difficult to determine. The soft, leisurely and plaintive song, which resembled weeping, scarcely caught by the hearing, was heard now from the right, now from the left, now from above, now from beneath the earth, as if an invisible spirit was floating over the steppe and singing. Egoruška looked and did not understand where this strange song came from; then, as he listened, it began to seem to him that the grass sang it; in its song, half dead, already perishing, without words, it sadly and sincerely assured someone that it was in no way guilty, that the sun had burned it up in vain; it affirmed that it wanted terribly to live, that it was still young and would be beautiful, if there were no heat and no drought; there was no guilt, but it nevertheless asked somebody's forgiveness and averred that it felt unendurably sick, unhappy and sorry for itself . . . (VII, 29-30).

In this passage one can also see how Egoruška's own distortions help to create this different world; we perceive all this through the oblique lens of his consciousness.

Even in the human realm the image for the dreamer's world is always a vocal one. One of Čexov's finest descriptions of the steppe concludes with a plea for verbal expression: "And in the solemnity of its beauty, in its excess of happiness you feel the strain and sadness, as if the steppe realizes that it is alone, that its richness and inspiration are perishing in vain for the world, unsung by everyone, unnecessary to everyone and through the joyful accents you hear its sad, hopeless call: 'A bard! a bard!' [*pevca! pevca!*]" (VII, 52). Zinovij Papernyj has pointed out the

---

[3]   Dmitrij Merežkovskij was the first to call attention to the distinctive aspects of similes describing the storm: the enormous effects of nature are compared to the most commonplace events. Of thunder, for example, Čexov writes: "There was the sound of someone somewhere far away walking across an iron roof" (VII, 91). The net effect, Merežkovskij argues, is not to reduce the magnitude of the natural forces, but rather to increase it through the contrast. See Merežkovskij's essay, "Čexov i Gor'kij" in *Grjaduščij xam* (St. Peterburg, 1906), pp. 43-105. For a discussion of such stylistic devices in Čexov's work generally, see George Ivask, "Čechov and the Russian Clergy" in *Anton Čechov, 1860-1960: Some Essays*, ed. Thomas Eekman (Leiden, 1960), pp. 83-93.

irony of the next line: " 'Tprr! Hello, Pantelej! Is everything all right?' "
The voice is that of Ivan Ivanyč, the last person who would be capable
of furnishing that expression for which the steppe calls.[4]

In another of the most important scenes of the story – the evening
spent around the campfire – the importance of verbal expression is
paramount. Pantelej beguiles the others with his tales, and toward the
end of this scene there arrives a stranger, who briefly joins the peasants
around the campfire to tell of how he won his wife. Having pursued her
through various intermediaries for three years, he finally visited her
town to speak with her: " 'I look, she is by a stream with her washing,'
he continued. 'Evil seized me ... I called her to one side and, can you
imagine, for a whole hour I plied her with various words ... She fell
in love! For three years she hadn't loved me, but for my words she fell
in love' " (VII, 84). One of the peasants, Emeljan, was at a former time
a wonderful singer, but he has now lost his voice. Inspired by the
stranger's story, he wants everyone to sing. But when he opens his
mouth, he is unable to produce anything but a croaking noise. This
desire to express the beauty and mystery of the steppe world lies at the
center of the whole story. The story itself is such an effort, and Egoruška's primary role is that of a recording intelligence upon which the
beauty and mystery are registered and thus expressed.

The fact that the central character performs such a function raises
fundamental questions about the structure of "The Steppe", the first of
Čexov's longer pieces actually to be realized. He had attempted to write
a novel before he began work on it in late 1887, but apparently destroyed the manuscript.[5] He was also under pressure from Grigorovič
to undertake the composition of a novel and was seriously engaged on
such a project throughout 1888 and well into 1889.[6] In Russia in the
eighties, after the examples of Gogol', Gončarov, Turgenev, Dostoevskij,
and Tolstoj, how could one lay serious claim to being a writer of prose
if he had not produced a novel? And yet for all its length "The Steppe"
is not even a short novel. In dealing with a longer prose form Čexov

---

[4]   Zinovij Papernyj, *A. P. Čexov: Očerk tvorčestva* (Moskva, 1960), p. 75. Papernyj
calls his chapter on "The Steppe" "Dreams Vast as the Steppe" (*Mečty širokie kak
step'*). He tends to view the story as a patriotic hymn to the land and its people,
which is a bit too specialized an interpretation to say the least, but still more
suggestive than most accounts of the story.
[5]   See the letters to his brother Aleksandr for 10 October 1887 (XIII, 373) and
21 October 1887 (XIII, 378).
[6]   See particularly the letters to Grigorovič of 12 January (XIV, 15) and 9 October
1888 (XIV, 183), as well as the letter to Suvorin of 11 March 1889 (XIV, 330).

somehow missed the point. He realized that a novel involves movement, and therefore his story abounds in it: to begin with, "The Steppe" is a narrative of a journey; what situation could be more ideal? There is a complementary movement on a smaller scale in Egoruška's transfer from the care of one person to another. He leaves his mother to follow his uncle; at Mojsej Mojseič's inn he is temporarily turned over to the innkeeper's wife; in the middle of the journey he passes from the protection of his uncle to that of an old peasant, Pantelej; at the journey's end he returns to his uncle, only to be given over in the last pages to the care of Nastasja Petrovna, an old friend of his mother. All this movement takes place on the first level of the story, and yet in the novel movement is seldom only a physical one. There must be an inner movement – a development which takes place within the character. Tom Jones is not the same person at the end of the novel as he was at the beginning; the experience of the journey has in some way changed him. Huck Finn began his journey on the river as a boy, but by the end of the novel he is no longer a boy. Egoruška, however, never really changes; he is the same small child at the end as he was on the first page, although there are occasional hints in his treatment of the death theme that Čexov may have been working towards the kind of movement which gives meaning and point to the journey.[7] At the beginning of the story the carriage passes the local graveyard, where Egoruška's grandmother lies buried. The child's inability to understand death is underlined in the passage describing his impressions of her funeral, which concludes: "and now she is sleeping, sleeping..." (VII, 20). The journey introduces the boy to a world in which death surrounds and awaits him. He meets it in a more violent form in his rival, the peasant Dymov, and in Pantelej's tales. But the theme of initiation into life is never consummated: Egoruška's attitude toward death becomes more serious during the journey, but he still cannot conceive of its ever coming to him. Hence, this theme touches the central character, but does not really involve him.

Actually, as suggested above, Egoruška fulfills another function, which seems to take precedence over the traditional role of the young hero embarked on a journey. After an extremely brief exposition, from the fourth paragraph to the very end of the story he becomes the point of view. "The Steppe" is, in fact, an extended experiment in the use of a recording intelligence. The memorable descriptions of the landscape

[7]   For a discussion of this theme in "The Steppe" see Thomas Winner, *Chekhov and His Prose* (New York, 1966), pp. 47-51.

owe much of their originality to the fact that we see it as it filters through the consciousness of a boy. It has been argued that the steppe itself is the hero of the tale; however, this is not quite accurate. We are not presented with the steppe itself; rather, we see the impression it makes on the boy's mind. The central interest of the story rests on the interaction of steppe and recording consciousness. Čexov had been experimenting with this method of rendering reality throughout this period. It is apparent in "Griša" and in nearly all the stories mentioned in this chapter, though without the presence of a recording intelligence other than the author. "Dreams", for example, begins: "Two rural policemen – one a black-bearded stocky man with unusually short legs so that if one sees him from behind, it seems that his legs begin much lower down than most people's . . ." (V, 224). Clearly, this is an impression of the policeman rather than an objective description of him, but in this case it is attributed to a hypothetical passerby rather than to a character in the story. "Typhus" (*Tif*, 1887) is built on a contrast between the way reality appears to a delirious person and the actual state of affairs. (Čexov achieves a similar effect in "The Steppe" when Egoruška contracts a fever after the storm.) The story which immediately precedes "The Steppe" chronologically, "Sleepy" (*Spat' xočetsja*) – so different in external features – obviously shares with its successor this interest in exploiting a character's impression of reality. Actually, "Sleepy" does this more dramatically within its narrower framework: the series of impressions in the mind of the thirteen-year-old Var'ka ultimately elucidates her murder of a baby: in her state of hallucination she associates the death of her father and his inarticulate murmurs (*"Bu-bu-bu-bu . . ."*) with the wailing baby and her own semiconscious lullaby, *baju-bajuški-baju* ('rockabye, baby'). The logic of her delirious state suggests that the present situation should conclude, as the episode involving her father did, in death.[8] In "The Steppe" the process of relating a character's impressions of the landscape creates that expression of its beauty which the steppe longs for; the story fulfills the yearning of its setting. In this lies the great originality of the story, and this is what gives point and meaning to the sustained attempt at employing the device of a recording intelligence.

But finally this narrative device rebounds on itself, for if it is not

[8] For extended analyses of the impressionistic technique in "Sleepy" see Gleb Struve, "On Chekhov's Craftsmanship: The Anatomy of a Story", *Slavic Review*, XX (October 1961), 467-477 and Constance Curtin, "Čexov's *Sleepy*: An Interpretation", *Slavic and East European Journal*, IX (Winter 1965), 390-400.

quite accurate to conclude that there is no beauty, mystery, or freedom
in the external world, it is no more accurate to conclude that these
values do exist in it. The implication, ultimately, is that the external
world has no objective reality; it is for us at any given moment whatever
we perceive it to be. Hence Čexov's artistic rendering of experience again
has belied his own assertion of values.

VI

THE QUESTION OF IDENTITY

With the publication of "The Steppe" in *The Northern Messenger* (*Severnyj vestnik*) Čexov had established himself as an important writer of the younger generation. Vsevolod Garšin and Saltykov-Ščedrin were extremely enthusiastic about the story;[1] its publication in one of the major 'thick' journals meant that his work would be taken seriously by those concerned with contemporary Russian literature. He might have been highly pleased with this new recognition, but, on the contrary, he seemed to be entering a period of deep depression. He begins to doubt his own powers: in a letter to Aleksej Pleščeev, editor of *The Northern Messenger*, he confesses: "I am a coward and nervous; I am afraid to hurry and in general am afraid to publish. It always seems to me that I shall become a bore and turn into a supplier of worthless stuff. As Jasinskij, Mamin, Bažin and others have done, so shall I too, 'having given great hopes'. This fear has its foundation: I have been publishing for a long time now; I have published a hundred and eighty pounds of stories, but up till now still do not know where my strength and where my weakness lie" (XIV, 78). Again in 1889 he writes to Suvorin: "I need to study, to learn everything from the beginning, for as a writer I am an utter ignoramus" (XIV, 454).

Plagued by doubts about the problem of thematic development, he feels that his pieces end at just that point where he should begin to expand them. Essentially, this is the same uneasiness he had exhibited only shortly before over the question of the novel. Try as he will, he cannot seem to produce an extended narrative work. Writing to Suvorin in October 1888, he admits possible weaknesses in "Name Day" (*Imeniny*):

You write that the hero of my "Name Day" is a figure who should be studied. Lord, really I am not a callous brute, I realize this. I realize that

---

[1] See the notes to "The Steppe", VII, 524.

I cut off my heroes and spoil them, that good material in my hands is wasted. . . . Frankly, I would readily sit over "Name Day" half a year. I love to take a rest and I don't see any charm in hasty publication. With pleasure, with feeling, and with care I would readily describe everything about my hero, would describe his soul while his wife gives birth, his trial, his mean feeling after the verdict of "not guilty," I would describe the rain. . . . This would give me only pleasure because I love to dig in and spend a lot of time (XIV, 208).

Čexov goes on to defend himself by pleading poverty – the necessity to publish quickly and often – and the limited financial resources of such journals as *The Northern Messenger*. In other letters from this same period he relates plans for novels he wants to write and at least occasionally refers to partially finished work. In March 1889 he tells Suvorin: "And what do you think? I am writing a novel!! I write and write, and there is no end to my writing" (XIV, 330). But like his earlier attempts at a novel, this one was never published, and presumably Čexov himself destroyed whatever part of it had actually been written. During this period of change and development the essential problem which perplexes Čexov is his own identity as a writer. He does not find any answer to it in his work, and the result, finally, is the only major retreat from literature during his entire career: the trip to Saxalin Island, undertaken in April 1890.

The stories and one play written in 1888 and 1889 take as their point of departure elements that had already been developed in the years immediately preceding, but now Čexov converts these elements into a formulation and articulation of his own crisis. He exhibits a new approach to the problem of the dreamer, a figure who is made happy by the vision of a world in which ideals seem attainable. Now the dreamer reverses his field of vision; if he could be sensitive to the beauty of his private world, he could be equally sensitive to the inadequacies, distortions, and horrors of everyday life. Most men can accept the empirical world uncritically, without, even, any awareness of its inadequacies. The dreamer cannot do this.

Unlike his earlier counterpart the new dreamer is not necessarily a sympathetic figure. In the previous chapter I referred to an ironic distortion of reality, ironic because it was the vehicle by means of which new values could be perceived. But now the dreamer's distortions become ambiguous; his criticism of the life he finds around him may be valid at one moment, but simply a manifestation of his own irritability at another, as in "Name Day" and "A Nervous Breakdown" (*Pripadok*).

The most obvious example of the unsympathetic dreamer is Ivanov in
Čexov's play of that name. The fact is that these characters are either
morally or physically sick. Although their sickness may be the source of
their insights, they nevertheless have warped visions, and there is both
objectivity and subjectivity in visions which can cut two ways. Čexov's
handling of point of view is not wholly successful in these stories, and the
variety of possible solutions with which he experiments may attest to his
awareness of this problem. In "Name Day", for example, he is interested
in observing the increasingly hysterical manifestations of physical and
spiritual distress in Ol'ga Mixajlovna; on the other hand, he is equally
interested in allowing her to be the vehicle for certain insights regarding
the dishonesty of social relationships. Shortly before he began working
on "Name Day" he had written to his fellow writer Ivan Leontev this
criticism of his friend's work: "You are a good writer, but you do not at
all know how to or do not want to generalize and look at things objec-
tively" (XIV, 30). The fact is that at this period Čexov already considered the objectivity of the writer a prime virtue, and yet he was not
always able to maintain that cool sense of control which his instinct
told him must be preserved. In "Name Day" he becomes at times the
victim of his own characters and creates effects not necessarily intended:
his problem is to represent a set of essentially good people and to show
how within a social context false values and lies can destroy the relationships between them. He selects as his principal character a pregnant
woman and uses her as a sympathetic point of view throughout most of
the story, though he occasionally finds it expedient to play the omniscient narrator when he needs to set us straight on Pëtr Dmitrič's motives.
At the same time he also wishes to show that Ol'ga Mixajlovna herself
is far from immune to this process of corruption, but the two functions
which she performs come into conflict in the course of the story. She
is simultaneously inside and outside the dramatic action. We see her
primarily outside with an implied capacity for judging accurately those
around her when she tries to confront her husband in his study. Ol'ga
enters to find him morose, apparently struggling with his own conscience after the scene at the dinner table. She feels sorry for him; she
wishes to tell him that he has become entangled in his own lies and that
he can free himself only by rejecting them. But when he turns to her, it
is Pëtr Dmitrič the official who speaks, rather than the man who loves
her. He then returns to his guests. "He could be heard with his solid gait
passing through the hall, then through the living room, laughing heartily
at something and saying to the young man who was playing: 'bra-o!

bra-o!' Quickly his steps grew faint: probably he had gone into the garden" (VII, 147). The intent of this passage is to indicate a physical parallel to the spiritual drifting apart of two people. But at the same time the point of view inevitably suggests that Ol'ga Mixajlovna is in a position of moral superiority, at this moment the process of corruption is taking place almost exclusively in Pëtr Dmitrič.[2] But if we can trust her in this scene, what are we to make of another, somewhat earlier passage? "There was also nothing out of the way in her husband's words and in the fact that before guests he would sit lolling and with his hat on the back of his head. He was spoiled by women, he knew that they found him attractive, and in his treatment of them adopted a special tone which everyone said was becoming to him. He behaved with Ljuboèka the same way he did with all women. But, nevertheless, Ol'ga was jealous" (VII, 142). Purportedly, this is Ol'ga's own analysis of her husband's behavior and her own rational, though unsuccessful, attempt to conquer an irrational jealousy. But another motif has slipped into the passage: Pëtr Dmitrič's behavior with women is clearly one aspect of his tendency to adopt a false role. In this sense, Ol'ga's irritation, if not specifically her jealousy, is justified. And yet I believe that this scene is primarily intended to dramatize Ol'ga's unhealthy sensitivity. It certainly provokes an ambiguous response in the reader, and the result is a blurred vision where no blur was intended. The writer's own objectivity and sympathy alternately come into play.[3] In a different genre one sees a similar confusion in *Ivanov*. The fact that the public misinterpreted the play cannot be blamed entirely on the public's dull perception. The fault lay at least partially with Čexov himself, who could not apparently present a clear image of his character. The numerous revisions of the play are clear testimony to Čexov's repeated failure to clarify the image.

---

[2] The irony that she herself had assumed an identical social mask shortly before, exclaiming, " 'Bravo, bravo' " on her way to the study, does not seriously alter either our sympathy for Ol'ga at this moment or our sense of the justice of her own attitude toward Pëtr Dmitrič.

[3] For a discussion of the unintended ambiguities which can result from the absence of a trustworthy authorial voice see Wayne C. Booth, *The Rhetoric of Fiction* (Chicago, 1961), pp. 311-339. He makes an especially telling point when he writes: "Confusions of distance did not begin with modern fiction. In all periods and in many different genres we find speakers who win credence when they should be doubted, or who lead critics to dispute the precise degree of their untrustworthiness" (p. 316). The confusion of functions in "Name Day" is analogous to, though less complex than, the situation which Booth describes in his analysis of James' "The Aspern Papers" (pp. 354-364).

This conflict between objectivity and sympathy on Čexov's part goes considerably deeper, however. It is imbedded in the very nature of the theme which occupies him during these years. While the dreamer gives expression to the corruption and falsity which can engulf human relationships, Čexov is necessarily sympathetic towards him, because he is sympathetic to the revelation itself. Therefore, there is to a degree at least a feeling of identity between artist and dreamer. But apparently Čexov's sense of the artist's objectivity forces him to see this very corruption in the dreamer himself: no one can be free from it. It is only in his long story of 1889, "A Dreary Story" (*Skučnaja istorija*), that he is able to come to terms with this conflict and to evolve a dramatic and narrative form which can encompass both the strengths and weaknesses of the dreamer in reverse. In "A Dreary Story" Čexov finds a framework in which his own double vision of the dreamer can exist without one element tending to drive the other out. One of the major distinctions of the work is the fact that he resolves this ambiguity in a first-person narrative where, seemingly, he would run the danger of invalidating the professor's judgments by allowing an admittedly neurotic character to control the reader's perception. Rather ironically, the professor frees himself of this limitation by implying that no one has been more seriously crippled by a public identity than he has; the fact that he is in many ways an empty shell permits us to sustain our faith in his disinterested evaluation of others.

In at least one way these stories are related to some of Čexov's very earliest satirical pieces from the eighties. It will be recalled that in such stories as "Chameleon", "Fat and Thin", and "Two in One" he had exploited for comic effects the sudden transformation of a character from one pose to another. The impetus for transformation came from the character's sudden realization that he was dealing with a person whose civil service rank was either distinctly higher or lower than he had supposed. The comedy is derived from the completeness of the transformation, as well as from its suddenness. In relation to the present period the importance of this device lies in the implication that a person may put on a variety of mutually contradictory masks, and when these transformations now occur, they are explicitly related to the question of the individual's identity. His characters persistently inquire: "Who am I? In what sphere of human relationships do I have a meaningful existence?" These transformations seem to imply that one's identity is open to question; the fact that a person can perform different roles at different moments suggests that he does not himself know who he is or in what kind of activity he can be himself. A variety of identities means that there may be no real identity at all. This problem is treated particularly in "An Unpleasantness" (*Neprijatnost'*), "Name Day", "A Nervous Breakdown", "The Princess" (*Knjaginja*), and "A Dreary Story". What is essential in these works is that the dreamer's vision of a world whose potentialities have gone to seed should constantly come up against this problem: what is the real identity of the individual, who is constantly at the mercy of public pressures to become something other than what he thinks he is or can be at his best?

A corollary trait in Čexov during this period is an almost peevish tendency to turn his artistic attention inward – to refuse to see his characters' problems in a social context. His attitude in this respect seems somewhat belligerent in view of the pressures around him to write socially meaningful stories, in which the issues of the day occupy a central position. In a famous letter to Pleščeev, written in October 1888, there is a passage which is particularly relevant to his attitude at this period: he complains that he fears those who seek a tendency in his writing, who insist on classifying him as a liberal or a conservative. The real issue for Čexov, however, is not simply the question of a political tag; he emphatically refuses to accept any kind of public role whatsoever: "... I feel no special predilection for either gendarmes, or butchers, or writers, or young people. I consider trademark and label a prejudice" (XIV, 177). In view of this refusal to be identified by his public with any special tendency, one must necessarily see Čexov's political indifference as only an isolated instance of a more generalized attitude.[4] His writing itself supports this view: in this period he is concerned with the representation of the human personality in the private domain; any time the public sphere impinges on it, it is a destructive force. He steadfastly refuses to see his characters in the public realm. Even in a work like *Ivanov*, where the protagonist obviously represents a social type,[5] Čexov studiously avoids public questions. Ivanov's prob-

---

[4] Čexov's famous refutation of all labels and trademarks might also be read as a relatively early modern declaration of independence from the 'reliable narrator', as Wayne C. Booth defines him in *The Rhetoric of Fiction* (Chicago, 1961), pp. 169-271. Actually, Booth himself quotes the repudiation of labels manifesto as an instance of the way a writer is hopelessly incapable of avoiding commitment, for, as Booth points out, only a few words later Čexov affirms his stand as a 'free artist'. See Booth, pp. 68-69.

[5] See particularly Čexov's own discussion of his central character in a letter to Suvorin of 30 December 1888 (XIV, 268-271).

lems may have social repercussions, but he is represented only in his private, personal relations.

In connection with "Name Day" Čexov comes close to teasing his editor, Pleščeev. He writes to him: "I just finished a story for *The Northern Messenger*. ... The story turned out a little long... a little dull, but life-like and, just imagine, with a 'tendency'..." (XIV, 172). When Pleščeev replies that he finds no tendency at all in "Name Day", Čexov taunts him further: "Is there really no tendency apparent in my last story? You once told me that the element of protest is absent in my stories, that there are no sympathies and antipathies. ... But isn't it true that from the beginning to the end of the story I protest against the lie? Isn't that really a tendency?" (XIV, 181). It is obviously not the kind of tendency which Pleščeev had in mind, as Čexov very well knew. This was simply another of his ways of telling the editor that he would not concern himself with the public realm.

"An Unpleasantness" is the first story to reflect a conflict between external and internal identities. The central character, Doctor Ovčinnikov, is a 'nervous' man, as we are informed on the first page. The characteristic seems trivial enough in itself, and yet when one sees Ovčinnikov against the background of other characters in this period – Ol'ga Mixajlovna in "Name Day", Vasilev in "A Nervous Breakdown", the title character in *Ivanov*, and Nikolaj Stepanovič in "A Dreary Story" – such traits can be seen to isolate and identify the dreamer type: he becomes both more sensitive and at the same time more prone to confusion than those with whom he comes into contact. At any rate, these characters as a group exhibit ailments of a nervous order, and Čexov associates this nervousness with a sensitivity toward their environments which is not shared by their fellows.

Thematically, the story centers on Ovčinnikov's confused response to his own action – striking his drunken assistant while on duty. Among other alternatives he considers a duel or an apology. This is part of the unhealthy element in the dreamer's make-up; he has a tendency to over-respond to stimuli. At the same time Ovčinnikov quite correctly sees the difficulty of the situation: all the avenues of response open to him would prove ineffective because they involve the official identities of the two men, and yet the issue between them is essentially a private matter. There is, in fact, no course of action through which they can settle their differences on a personal basis. The situation is finally resolved by a public hearing, which actually resolves nothing. When the doctor later reflects on the hearing, "He was ashamed that in his personal

matter he had involved outsiders. .... Having returned to the hospital he
immediately set about his inspection of the wards. His assistant walked
beside him, stepping softly like a cat, and softly answering questions. ...
And the assistant ... and the nurses acted as though nothing had happened and that everything was fine. And the doctor himself tried with all
his strength to appear indifferent. He gave orders, grew angry, joked with
patients, but in his brain words kept swirling: stupid, stupid, stupid . . ."
(VII, 190). In the realm of public actions there can be no solution to
private questions. Ovčinnikov seems to be the only character capable of
realizing this. The conflict is between the apparently normal world in
which all such problems are really ignored and the private sphere of the
'nervous' Ovčinnikov. He is aware of the absurdity of such solutions;
he knows that the way in which the official world disposes of personal
problems is utterly irrelevant to the problem itself. The fact that everyone acts as though nothing had happened cannot undo the incident between the doctor and his assistant. It is this kind of revelation – that
there is something essentially absurd about the relationships between
people in the world of officialdom – which characterizes the dreamer.

The next story in this group goes a step further than "An Unpleasantness"; in "Name Day" Čexov denies the sphere of public
relationships any validity whatsoever. Only the private world can be
meaningful. The story is more complex than "An Unpleasantness", but
once again its central character is in a state of nervous imbalance. The
setting is a name-day party being given for Ol'ga's husband, Pëtr
Dmitrič. As the story opens, Ol'ga, who is pregnant, has escaped the
company of her guests and tries now to focus her consciousness on the
infant she will soon bear. As a symbol for the rejection of the social
sphere and the private direction towards which Ol'ga turns, Čexov could
scarcely have invented a more perfect situation. She is caught between
the public world of the party and a private one of personal relationships. In a letter Čexov himself specifies that his central characters are
caught between their own lies, which he associates with their public
roles, and the truth about them – i.e., their essentially good natures
when they are being themselves: "But I counterbalance not conservatism
and liberalism, which do not appear to me to be the chief essence, but
the heroes' lies with their truth. Pëtr Dmitrič lies and plays the buffoon
in court, he is heavy and hopeless, but I cannot cover the fact that by
nature he is a fine and gentle person. Ol'ga Mixajlovna lies at every
step, but it's unnecessary to hide the fact that these lies cause her pain"
(XIV, 184).

The essential assertion of the story is that the social relationships of the public world are invalid because they are made up of lies. The burden of the narrative is an attempt to show how public values and images may corrupt private relationships as well. At one moment in the story there is a comic incident which illustrates this point. A student and two young boys arrive at the party rather late. Ol'ga asks them if they want something to eat: "The student begged her not to disturb herself, the children were silent; evidently, all three wanted to eat" (VII, 150). This might be called the logic of the lie in the public world: if one seeks the truth, he must assume that the opposite of what is said represents the real feeling.

The private relationship between Ol'ga and her husband is the dramatic center of the story and the field in which Čexov observes the process of corruption. When Pëtr assumes his public role with his wife, he is allowing the lie to destroy his private relationship with her: "She understood that Pëtr Dmitrič was tired, dissatisfied with himself and ashamed, but when one is ashamed he hides it first of all from those close to him and is open with mere acquaintances" (VII, 145). She contrasts his relationship with others and with her, and comes to the conclusion that he "hides his soul and conscience from his wife" (VII, 145). What is beginning to appear here is that transformation which we spoke of earlier. At one point in the story she goes to her room and finds Pëtr: "It was not the same Pëtr Dmitrič who quarreled at dinner and whom the guests knew, but another man – tired, guilty, dissatisfied with himself whom his wife alone knows" (VII, 161). In other words, will the real Pëtr Dmitrič please stand? Clearly, the author would expect that other man – 'tired, guilty' – to rise. When Pëtr becomes the public figure, he is false, and it is the public image which corrupts the world of private relationships when a public identity is assumed in private relationships too. In one scene Čexov develops Pëtr's public image at some length. Ol'ga recalls seeing her husband at court in his official capacities: "In the president's chair, in uniform, with the chain of office on his breast, he was utterly transformed. Stately gestures, thunderous voice, 'what?' 'yes of course', a careless tone. . . . Everything ordinary and human, his own self that Ol'ga Mixajlovna was accustomed to seeing at home, disappeared in grandeur, and in the chair sat not Pëtr Dmitrič, but some other man who everyone addressed as Mr. President" (VII, 148). Throughout the greater part of the story it is this public self which Ol'ga finds confronting her, and it is because of this that the narrative erupts into a violent quarrel near the end.

In short, the public image necessarily perverts the private identity in its relations with others. Their quarrel is caused by the projection of the public image each of them holds and it is finally dissipated when Ol'ga's labor pains begin. She is utterly indifferent to the fact that the baby is still-born, while Pëtr comes to himself through the shock: " 'Olja,' he said, wringing his hands, big tears suddenly dropping from his eyes. 'Olja, I don't care about your property qualification, nor the Circuit Courts,' he gave a sob, 'nor dissenting opinions, nor those visitors, nor your dowry. . . . I don't care about anything! Why didn't we take thought for our child? Oh, it's no good talking!' " (VII, 171-172). From the list of attainments which Pëtr rejects here it is clear that he is speaking of his final awareness and rejection of the public self. The story has been brought full circle from Ol'ga's contemplation of the infant inside her on the first page to Pëtr's awareness of the dead baby. If one follows this line of development, there is also the implication that the attention they have devoted to the public world has somehow killed the baby. Pëtr's despair at the end is the shock of recognition – an awareness of the destruction which the public self has wrought.[6]

The temperamental affinities between the central character in "A Nervous Breakdown" and the type of personality presented in the two previous stories is unmistakable. The student Vasilev's state of anxiety resembles that of Ovčinnikov and Ol'ga but it is now greatly intensified. He over-responds to the point of psychic disturbance, but at the same time the stimulus is such that his reaction is perhaps healthier than that of the ordinary man. His repugnance at viewing prostitution leads to his nervous collapse, but when the doctor to whom his friends take him turns out to be a psychiatrist, Vasilev delivers an important speech: " '. . . it all seems amazing to me! That I should have taken my degree in two faculties you look upon as a great achievement; because I have written a thesis which in three years will be thrown aside and forgotten, I am praised up to the skies; but because I cannot speak of fallen women as unconcernedly as of these chairs, I am being examined by a doctor, I am called mad . . .' " (VII, 194-195). The sickness of the dreamer produces once more a revelation of the absurdity inherent in the relations of the public world.

---

[6] For a similar interpretation of the story see Rufus Mathewson, "Afterword" in Anton Chekhov, *Ward Six and Other Stories*, trans. Ann Dunnigan (New York, 1965), p. 382: "The real connections between birth and death, between the flesh and the spirit, between the social occasion and the biological tragedy, are caught in the magnified power of the symbol: death is the only possible issue of lives that are eaten away by lies and hatred."

The narrative technique in "A Nervous Breakdown" relies considerably more on symbolic representations than earlier stories in this group. Čexov complained on one occasion that everyone was praising the content of his latest story, but only Grigorovič had been aware of the devices which conveyed it.[7] Vasilev's state of innocence at the beginning of the evening is conveyed by the image of fresh snow. Its purity seems to confirm his vision of a world full of beauty. However, the ironic juxtaposition of this pure snow with the atmosphere of a brothel is surely not accidental. In contrast to the beauty of nature is the 'taste' and 'style' characteristic of the furnishings in these houses; it is something utterly unnatural and false. The image of the snow occurs once again at the end of the evening after Vasilev has been thoroughly exposed to this new world. " 'And how can the snow fall in this street!' thought Vasilev. ... 'These houses be damned!' " (VII, 185). What he cannot reconcile is the fact that this utterly foreign world of the prostitute can be enveloped in the same pure snow which falls in his. It is too cruel that the virgin snow can fall meaninglessly, or perhaps with a vengeance even, in the prostitute's world as well. In this way Čexov uses his setting to dramatize Vasilev's turmoil.

Once more a transformation occurs, at least in Vasilev's mind, when he is trying to discover the identity of the prostitute. His conversations with these women have convinced him that their moral world is one entirely foreign to him. "He thought that he saw not fallen women but some other, utterly special world which was foreign and incomprehensible to him; if he had seen this world before on the stage in the theater or had read about it in a book, he wouldn't have believed it . . ." (VII, 181). One of the minor triumphs of the story, in fact, is the way in which Čexov reveals Vasilev's horror when he finds that in outer respects these women resemble any woman, but live in a moral world utterly foreign to his own.

The original impetus for writing "A Nervous Breakdown" was apparently Pleščeev's proposal that Čexov should contribute a story to the memorial volume honoring Vsevolod Garšin, a man of extreme nervous sensitivity who committed suicide at the age of thirty-three. It is quite apparent that Garšin's own character closely resembles that of Vasilev. The similarities between the two are easily recognizable in this

[7]   In a letter to Suvorin written on 23 December 1888 he said: "The literary society, students, Evrejnova, Pleščeev, young girls, and so forth have praised my 'A Nervous Breakdown' to the extreme, but only Grigorovič has noticed the description of the first snow" (XIV, 257).

description of Garšin written by a school friend: "It often happened that this student, gay in appearance and carefree, would grow quiet, stop talking, as if dissatisfied with himself and those around him, as if he were bitter that those around him were not sufficiently intelligent and good. Sometimes at these moments observations on the need to struggle with evil would escape from his lips, and at times he would utter very strange views on how to establish the happiness of all mankind." [8] What has perhaps not been so obvious is the fact that a temperament like Garšin's fitted in perfectly with the kind of character which absorbed Čexov's creative interest at this period. Another reflection of Garšin's personality, particularly relevant to a study of "A Nervous Break-down", is Garšin's own short story "An Occurrence" (Proisšestvie, 1878), which also deals with the identity of the prostitute.[9] Interestingly enough Garšin's interpretation of the moral world of the prostitute is negated by Vasilev's experience in the houses, and it would be difficult to reject the notion that Čexov had "An Occurrence" in the back of his mind when he describes the uninitiated Vasilev, who "... would recall a story he had read somewhere at some time: a young man, pure and self-sacrificing, loved a fallen woman and asked her to marry him; considering herself unworthy of such happiness, she took poison" (VII, 174). The first half of the story follows a Tolstoyan pattern in which Vasilev's expectations are completely negated.[10] Specifically, he discovers that the prostitute is incapable of any 'consciousness of guilt' (VII, 185).

Garšin's prostitute, Nadežda Nikolaevna, on the other hand, exhibits just that sense of guilt which Vasilev had expected to find. Nadežda Nikolaevna is pursued by a young man who wishes to marry her and

[8]   Quoted by G. Bjalyj in his introduction to V. M. Garšin, Sočinenija (Moskva, 1960), p. vii.
[9]   In dealing with the question of literary influence on Čexov, P. Bicilli notes the parallel between "An Occurrence" and "A Nervous Breakdown", but then goes on to point out some of the complexities involved in questions of influence: "An Occurrence", he says, is derived from Gogol's story "Nevskij Prospekt", and it is impossible at third remove to say precisely what combination of influences may have been at work on Čexov. Perhaps his model was Garšin, perhaps he returned to the original source, Gogol', or perhaps it was a combination of the two which had some role in the creation of "A Nervous Breakdown". For an exceptionally full discussion of the question of influences on Čexov's work see Bicilli, Tvorčestvo Čexova: Opyt stilističeskago analiza, Godišnik na universiteta sv. Kliment Oxridski; istoriko-filologičeski fakultet, XXXVIII, 6 (Sofia, Bulgaria, 1942), pp. 1-138.
[10]   The pattern I have in mind is that which Tolstoj uses in the Sevastopol stories, where he first sets up his hero's romantic preconceptions about battle and then proceeds to enlighten both hero and reader on the real nature of war.

provide a better life, but a sense of guilt pursues her throughout the story and causes her to refuse Ivan Ivanyč's marriage proposal. She knows too that this guilt will eventually force her to commit suicide. In short, Garšin's view of Nadežda Nikolaevna closely approximates Vasilev's own preconceptions of the prostitute. It would seem, however, that Čexov could no longer be satisfied with the image of 'the good prostitute', as he had been only a few years earlier in his own story, "The Chorus Girl".

Čexov produced only two stories in 1889, but both are relevant to the problem of lost identity. The first of them, "The Princess", concerns a woman so thoroughly enmeshed in her public role that she has completely lost her private identity. We see her at a moment when a doctor, once employed on her estate reveals to her the way she has corrupted any sense of decency her employees may once have had. He tells her: " 'A young man cannot be in your service three years without becoming a hypocrite, a slanderer, a flatterer...' " (VII, 216). The scene between Vera Gavrilovna, the princess, and the doctor is the first instance in Čexov's work of a dramatic device which occurs in several later stories at key points, notably in "The House with a Mezzanine" (*Dom s mezoninom*), "An Anonymous Story" (*Rasskaz neizvestnogo čeloveka*), and "My Life" (*Moja žizn'*). This device might be called the telling-off complex; it is a scene in which one person ruthlessly exposes the emptiness and meanness of another's life. The motivation of the device is somewhat curious. On one level, it obviously provides a fine dramatic scene, but on another level it is always completely ineffective; when the doctor exposes Vera Gavrilovna, it may alleviate his pent-up disgust at her hypocrisy, but purportedly its real aim is to reveal Vera Gavrilovna to herself. However, the telling-off complex never achieves its ostensible purpose. The truth revealed in these scenes never changes anybody or even brings about a realization of personal failure. In this sense, the device is meaningless. Actually, Čexov uses it ironically; the whole point of the telling-off complex may very well be just this: that no matter how clearly the truth is laid before one, it is utterly ineffective. In "The Princess" there is a double irony about the scene: not only does it fail to bring about any change in Vera Gavrilovna, but the doctor bears testimony to the truth of his assertions by becoming himself a hypocrite when he apologizes later for his outburst. These ironies are neatly contained in the nature of the doctor's profession: he is compelled to retract his own diagnosis and to reverse his role by confessing that it is he who is ailing.

"A Dreary Story" is probably the finest achievement of this period. Here Čexov was able to bring together his own contradictory attitudes toward the dreamer in a form which could accommodate opposing views. He achieves this by attributing all views to his central character, who is the narrator; he transfers the conflict to his hero, and thereby attains that degree of objectivity which he sought in his writing.[11] "A Dreary Story" is one of the most discussed and quoted of all Čexov's works. The apparently pointless lives of its characters seem somehow highly typical of the Čexovian situation. Critics usually fix their attention on that moment when Nikolaj Stepanovič decides he has no 'general idea', no sense of purpose in his life. It is customarily taken for granted that herein lies the story's 'message'. There have been many explanations of just what sort of 'general idea' Nikolaj Stepanovič lacks, depending on the bias of the critic. For a Marxist like Vladimir Ermilov he lacks a plan for the advancement of society;[12] for Boris Zajcev a Christian, he lacks religious faith.[13] Such speculations, however, are really beside the point; "A Dreary Story" is not about the kind of 'general idea' that the central character lacks. As a result, these analyses cannot illuminate the story in any way. Indeed, one critic, no doubt weary of such speculations, has suggested that some of Čexov's lesser known stories might offer more profitable lines of investigation.[14]

However, there is still a great deal in the story which has never been discussed. By concentrating on a few catch phrases, such as 'general idea', critics have failed to take into account many elements in the work which deserve attention. The central problem which the story poses is this: what happens when the dreamer – the man of exceptional sensitivity – turns his critical insight on himself and his own life? Based on the series of actions narrated and emotional states described, the answer would seem to be a terrifying disorganization of self. I shall elaborate on this aspect of the story shortly, but first it will be useful to look at some of the literary problems which were vexing Čexov at the time he was working on "A Dreary Story".

He had been writing for the theater off and on for some time. In this particular period his play *Ivanov* was enjoying a great deal of

---

[11] For an interesting discussion of objectivity in Čexov's writing see John Hagan, "Chekhov's Fiction and the Ideal of 'Objectivity' ", *PMLA*, LXXXI (October 1966), 409-418.

[12] See *Čexov* (Moskva, 1949), pp. 216-222.

[13] See *Čexov: Literaturnaja biografija* (New York, 1954), pp. 87-89.

[14] See Gleb Struve, "On Chekhov's Craftsmanship: The Anatomy of a Story", *Slavic Review*, XX (October 1961), 467-477.

attention in both Petersburg and Moscow, but his experience with it had been far from satisfying. In his view the public badly misunderstood two of the central characters, Ivanov himself and Doctor Lvov. He could not seem to get his meaning across even to his closest literary associates.[15] As a result, he had spent an enormous amount of time and labor in revising and adding speeches to his play, but *Ivanov* was a work which never seemed wholly satisfying to him. There is no doubt that the frustrations engendered by the play were fresh in Čexov's mind when he began writing "A Dreary Story".[16] What I would like to suggest is that some of the basic elements in the play found their way into the story and that Čexov was perhaps subconsciously trying to work out once more those elements in *Ivanov* which the public had seriously misinterpreted. I would further suggest that the narrative form, rather than the dramatic, permitted him to express at least one aspect of his character more successfully. The external resemblances between Ivanov and Nikolaj Stepanovič are not at all striking; the professor is an old man, while Ivanov has just reached middle age. However, the closer one looks, the more striking their similarities appear. The professor is on the point of physical death, but his spiritual death has taken place even before the story opens; Ivanov, too, has gone through a spiritual death. Nikolaj Stepanovič worries constantly about what has gone wrong with him; in the play everyone talks about what has gone wrong with Ivanov. Some of the details of situation in the play and story are also alike. Both men have fallen out of love, and both have turned away from their families. There is an identical understanding of the past in the two works: it is a period when all was right with the world. Ivanov is constantly reflecting on that period just two years prior to the present when he had been full of love, good intentions, fine schemes, vitality, and ambition. Nikolaj Stepanovič looks back similarly on his early years. "A Dreary Story" is narrated almost entirely in the present tense, which gives to every event a sense of stifling boredom and repetition. Whenever the past tense is used, it evokes a period of bustling activity when

15   See his letter to Suvorin of 30 December 1888 (XIV, 268-275).
16   In the letter to Suvorin cited above he concludes: "If the audience leaves the theater with the consciousness that Ivanovs are villains, while the Doctor Lvovs are great people, I will be forced to resign from the theater and throw my pen to the devil. And you can't accomplish anything with revisions and interpolations. . . . I simply cannot add any more to Ivanov and Lvov. I wouldn't know how. If I add anything I merely feel that I will spoil it even more" (XIV, 273). However, in February 1889 he was once more engaged in reworking the fourth act. (See the notes to the play, XI, 510 and 531.) By March he had begun work on "A Dreary Story". (See the notes to the story, VII, 559.)

everything one did seemed eminently worth doing. In this connection
it is interesting to observe the process of transformation which Nikolaj
Stepanovič sees in his own wife and family: "I have the feeling that
at one time I lived at home with a real family, but now I dine with
guests at the table of an unreal wife and see an unreal Liza [his daugh-
ter]" (VII, 250). Frequently, Nikolaj Stepanovič is so overwhelmed by
the present image of his wife that the contrast between past and present
confounds him:

In bewilderment I ask myself: really is this old, very stout, awkward woman,
with a dull expression of trivial anxiety and fright before a piece of bread,
with a look obscured by constant thoughts of debts and needs, who knows
how to speak only of expenses and to smile when she has found a bargain
– really was this woman at one time that very slim Varja whom I loved
passionately for her fine, clear mind, for her pure soul, beauty and, as
Othello loved Desdemona, for her "compassion" towards my knowledge?
Is this really that very wife, my Varja, who once bore me a son? (VII, 227).

The allusion to *Othello* indicates not only the extent of change in the
wife, but also serves as an ironic verdict on the professor himself; the
reference is to Othello's words: "She lov'd me for the dangers I had
pass'd,/And I lov'd her that she did pity them" (I, iii, 168-169). But
here the dangers which the general has endured have been transformed
into the professor's scholarly pursuits. The environment in which Nikolaj Stepanovič moves seems also to have changed for the worse; the
shop which he passes each day on his way to the university was once
run by a fat woman who loved all students because " 'each of them
has a mother;' now a redheaded merchant sits there, a very indifferent
man" (VII, 230). At these moments one is never really sure, of course,
whether the signs of change in the external world are valid, or only reflections of the changes which have taken place in Nikolaj Stepanovič
himself. In any case, Ivanov and the old professor share similar ideas
about both the past and present.

One of the major contemporary misconceptions about the play was
the image of Ivanov himself. The public took him for a villain, while
Čexov had wanted to portray, if not a positive character, at least a
sympathetic one. Part of Čexov's difficulty, I think, was the medium in
which he was working – the drama. The public could easily understand
Doctor Lvov's criticisms of Ivanov and accept them at face value. Therefore, one might say that the alleged objectivity of the drama itself
hindered Čexov. When he came to write "A Dreary Story", he was able
to enlist sympathy for his central character simply through the medium

of the first-person narrative: critics invariably accept Nikolaj Stepanovič's evaluation of his own family and sympathize with his preference for
the company of Katja, even though the neighbors gossip about their
close relationship. Did the story not have the advantage of the single
point of view – if the same story were put on the stage where each
character's point of view carries equal weight – one could easily imagine
a public reaction similar to that which *Ivanov* received. Hence, in regard
to the presentation of his central character Čexov succeeded in the short
story form where he had failed on the stage.[17]

The theater is relevant to an understanding of what Čexov is doing
in this story in another way as well: throughout "A Dreary Story"
Nikolaj Stepanovič is absorbed by the omnipresence of the 'role' he is
playing. At every step he has the sense that he is acting out a part
rather than actually living. This question of a role is, of course, closely
connected with the sense of disorganization in his life and with the
question of identity, which has recurred throughout this period. Indeed,
the metaphor of the theater is perfect in this story if we accept Eric
Bentley's conception of the theatrical occasion: "To say that the theatrical occasion points up the problem of illusion and reality, confusing
us as to which is which and where we stand in it all, would be a gross
understatement. The theatrical occasion is a supreme instance of such
confusion . . .".[18] The story opens upon a very strange note indeed:
"There is in Russia an honored professor, a certain Nikolaj Stepanovič,
a privy councillor and cavalier... And so forth, and so forth. All this
and much else that one might add comes to this, that it is personified
by my name" (VII, 224). There is an extraordinary disassociation between name and person. He goes on to speak of his name as if it had an
existence all its own, entirely separate from his identity: "In Russia it
is known by every educated person. ... It is happy" (VII, 224-225).
There is, indeed, a feeling that the person who goes by the name of
Nikolaj Stepanovič is someone entirely different from the old professor's
own conception of himself.[19] Towards the end of the story this extraordinary sense of disassociation between reputation and actual identity
is made explicit: "Apparently, great names are created to live independ-

---

[17]   However, even in the case of "A Dreary Story" the single point of view did not
dispel all traces of ambiguity: some readers apparently read into the story hints
at a sexual attraction on Katja's part for the half-dead professor. See Čexov's letter
to Pleščeev of 21 October 1889 (XIV, 419-420).
[18]   *The Life of the Drama* (New York, 1965), p. 181.
[19]   The original title for this story was "My Name and I" (*Moe imja i ja*). See
N. Gitovič, *Letopis' žizni i tvorčestva A. P. Čexova* (Moskva, 1955), p. 235.

ently, apart from those who bear them. Now my name serenely walks through Xar'kov; in about three months, carved in gold letters on my grave stone, it will shine like the sun itself – and this will be at a time when I am already covered with moss" (VII, 280). The 'I' does not even look like the name. He describes himself as sixty-two years old, growing bald, with false teeth, and with a tic. "As bright and fine as my name is, I am dim and featureless" (VII, 225). Nikolaj Stepanovič can speak of his voice also as something almost separate from himself – something, like his name, that presents to the world an image of a man, though not the man himself. The actor has the facility to present an image other than that of the actual man; he can embody an imaginary character, even though it may be far different from his real identity. It is in this sense that Nikolaj Stepanovič sees himself playing a role; in this sense he is an actor. The problem of a role lies at the basis of the professor's dilemma – the loss of any real identity. He has in fact several parts; one is that of the well-known professor, the privy councillor. We can say that in some sense this is not his real self. But neither is that private life which he describes particularly real. He can always predict what his wife is about to say to him, just as though she too were reading a part in a play. Perhaps it is because he has had to perform a public role that even in his private life he has become an actor; he can no longer look upon living as something real, but only as a series of parts which it is apparently necessary to act out. Čexov has come a long way from the tentative gropings toward this idea in "Name Day".

One sustained instance of Nikolaj Stepanovič's sense of a role is his description of a typical lecture delivered before his students. He is extremely nervous just before the class meets and can never think of how he will begin. The similarity of feeling between the actor about to go on stage and the professor about to go before his class is unmistakable. A thorough examination of this scene would reveal any number of detailed parallels between the lecture platform and the stage. One such parallel might be Nikolaj Stepanovič's ability to manipulate his audience: he is extremely sensitive to that moment when his students' attention begins to wander, and like the good showman, he can produce a joke precisely when it is needed to relieve the weariness of his audience.

I have already mentioned the fact that the story is related entirely in the present tense, except for an occasional flashback to the bright past when there at least seemed to be an organized self that could be identified. This use of the present tense serves several purposes: it is an effective means of conveying the sense of boredom and purposelessness in the professor's daily routine. But the present tense also suggests an allusion to the stage: the even tenor of his life is like a play – a series of actions performed repeatedly without any significant change. Each night he cannot sleep; each morning his wife comes in, asks about his health, and discusses their son.

There is still another way in which "A Dreary Story" is concerned with the theater: Nikolaj Stepanovič's one close friend, Katja, is literally an actress. Their reactions to the theater are, on the surface at any rate, diametrically opposed. Katja loves the theater and sees in it a summation of all the arts; she considers it the highest expression of man's potential. The professor, on the other hand, dislikes the theater. He believes it is essentially false, and continually emphasizes its artificiality. At one point he says: ". . . under present conditions the theater can serve only as a diversion. But diversion is too expensive to continue using it. It takes from the government thousands of young, healthy and talented men and women, who, if they had not dedicated themselves to the theater, could be good doctors . . ." (XII, 242). There is, of course, an irony in this statement, for, if not caught up in the theater literally, nevertheless Nikolaj Stepanovič's own 'role' has terribly restricted his life. Katja says to him: " 'You are a very fine fellow, Nikolaj Stepanyč. . . . You are a rare specimen and there is no actor who would know how to play you. Me, for example, or Mixail Fedorovič even a poor actor could play, but you no one. And I envy you, I envy you terribly!' " (VII, 270). The fact is, no actor would know how to play Nikolaj Stepanovič because there is nothing there to play. There is no real identity, only the several roles which he performs.

Katja's own character is extremely complicated, and it is difficult to decide whether she has a real existence for Nikolaj Stepanovič. At times she seems to be simply his *alter ego*. The similarities between them are striking in spite of the obvious differences of age, sex, and attitude toward the theater. Katja is going through the same kind of personal crisis which the professor is enduring. Whenever she comes to him for advice, he is unable to help her, precisely because he does not know how to handle the same problems in his own life. Even their attitudes toward the theater are not as dissimilar as they may at first appear: ultimately, both are actors, whether they want to be or not. At the very end of the story there is, however, a kind of resolution of the question of Katja's identity. She finally realizes that she must escape from the trap of non-identity into which Nikolaj Stepanovič has fallen. When she goes to his room in Xar'kov to ask him what she is to do with herself, he is unable to advise her. She knows that she must divorce herself from his influence, that he can only lead her down a blind alley. They shake hands and she leaves his room. Nikolaj Stepanovič is familiar with the role which each of those around him plays, and he thinks that at this moment he can predict Katja's actions. "... she is walking down the long corridor, not looking back. She knows that I am following her with my eyes, and, probably, at the turn she will look back." But for once he is not in a play world. The final paragraph of the story reads: "No, she didn't look back. Her black dress disappeared for the last time, her steps grew faint. ... Goodbye, my treasure!" (VII, 282). The sudden shift to the past tense is significant here. It implies that Nikolaj Stepanovič has come up against a human being with an identity of her own, who ultimately is not simply playing a part, and whose actions cannot be easily predicted. While this could certainly not be described as an optimistic ending – Nikolaj Stepanovič's own dilemma remains – it does offer a kind of resolution; it testifies to a world in which personal identity has not been completely lost. And yet Čexov himself was left at this point with nowhere to turn. What is central in the story ultimately is not the vague possibility of someone somehow finding himself, but the overwhelming representation of a personality almost totally annihilated. If these five stories represent a series in which Čexov comes to grips ever more surely with the problem of identity, there was nothing more for him to write. A trip to Saxalin was as reasonable an answer as any.

VII

THE DIALOGUE WITH MELODRAMA

The Saxalin expedition came as an alternative to further creative work for Čexov. After "A Dreary Story" the three-year span 1890 to 1893 was the least productive period of his entire career, with the exception of the final years when physical exhaustion prevented his usual prolific industry. But if Saxalin was an alternative, it still raises questions, specifically, why this particular alternative? Why make a trip of nearly five thousand miles to visit an island inhabited by convicts? None of Čexov's biographers has ever found a wholly satisfactory answer to this question, and it seems likely that there will always remain a certain mystery about the motives for the trip. It is extremely doubtful that Čexov himself could have given a complete account of them. Undoubtedly, there were many factors which entered into the decision, probably no single one of which was decisive; strangely enough, because on different occasions Čexov mentioned different motives, many of his biographers have been led to assume that one of them was decisive, while the others were either lies, rationalizations or deliberate efforts to confuse his friends.

The very distance of the trip and the remoteness of its goal naturally suggest that he was either trying to forget something in his Moscow life or that in an environment which was the extreme opposite of that in Moscow he was searching for something that had eluded him at home. A variety of decisive motives has been suggested: David Magarshack argues that the principal one was an effort to forget and extinguish his love for Lidija Avilova.[1] This argument has been subjected to a hard look by Čexov's latest biographer, Ernest Simmons, who most convincingly rejects it.[2] There is no special reason for doubting any of the motives which Čexov himself mentions: "I want to write at least one or two hundred pages and with this to pay a little of my debt to medicine, before which, as you know, I am a swine" (XV, 28-29). And as

[1] David Magarshack, *Chekhov: A Life* (New York, 1955), pp. 173-188.
[2] Ernest Simmons, *Chekhov: A Biography* (Boston, 1962), especially pp. 207-209.

a matter of fact, the journey did produce a work of some social and medical benefit, *Saxalin Island* (*Ostrov Saxalin*), in 1893. In the same letter to Suvorin Čexov mentions another reason for the journey – a sense of social responsibility:

> ... you write that nobody needs Saxalin and that no one is interested in it. Can this be so? Saxalin can be unnecessary and uninteresting only for that society which does not exile thousands of people to it and does not spend millions on it. .... All Europe is interested in it, but for us it is unnecessary? ... From the books I have read and read, it is apparent that we have driven millions of people to prison, have driven them for no reason, without thinking, barbarously; we have driven people in chains through the cold thousands of miles, infected them with syphilis, corrupted them, multiplied the number of criminals, and shifted the blame on red-nosed prison officials. Now all educated Europe knows that not the prison officials but all of us are guilty, but we're not up to this, this isn't interesting. ... No, I assure you that Saxalin is necessary and interesting, and we need feel sorry only that it is I who am going there and not someone more knowledgeable in the matter and more capable of awakening an interest in society (XV, 29-30).

Not only the Saxalin trip, but also Čexov's efforts in the cholera epidemic of 1892, his interest in contributing to the construction of schools, medical centers, and libraries in his own village, Melixovo, and in Taganrog attest to a new interest in social projects.

In addition to the medical and social motives there were distinctly personal reasons for undertaking the trip, and in the light of Čexov's literary work these are certainly the more relevant. In a letter to Leontev-Ščeglov he clearly denies any literary purpose in his trip and emphasizes the personal nature of his motives: "Please don't place any literary hopes on my Saxalin trip. I am going neither to observe nor to collect impressions; but simply to live for half a year differently from the way I have lived up until now" (XV, 43). In spite of such disclaimers it is surprising how little direct reflection of the Saxalin experience there is in Čexov's writing. He was always a writer who relied for his raw material on personal experience: examples can be chosen from almost any story, but suffice it to mention the reflections of his love for fishing, episodes based on medical experiences, and the apparent necessity for reviving at first hand his impressions of the southern steppe before he could set about writing "The Steppe". Yet the Saxalin trip engendered very little – "Gusev", "In Exile" (*V ssylke*), and perhaps the finale of "The Murder" (*Ubijstvo*). While on the island he had spent enormous time and effort preparing a census, visiting and talking with very nearly every inhabitant. One might expect that such an experience would supply raw material for any number of stories; if nothing else, the creative barrenness of this expedition testifies to an amazing capacity to separate one's artistic interest from more personal ones. The fact is that among Čexov's reasons for the trip clearly a major consideration was the need to forget his creative work for a time; he had reached an impasse with "A Dreary Story" and was uncertain of the direction his work was now to take.

Did the journey to Saxalin answer adequately to the various impulses which had prompted it? One's reply to this varies according to his formulation of the decisive motive. Ernest Simmons feels that "Chekhov's long and difficult journey and his experiences on Saxalin had quite clearly brought about a catharsis of the incessant and agitating inner promptings that had sent him off on this implausible adventure."[3] But Simmons never really makes clear what the nature of this catharsis is. If part of the complex of 'inner promptings' was the effort to break with literature for a time in order to put his emotional house in order, as Simmons suggests, then one must conclude that the journey was a failure. In spite of financial necessity Čexov found himself absolutely incapable of settling down to protracted work. Scarcely three months after he had returned from the arduous Saxalin expedition, in March 1891, he was off once again, this time with Suvorin, bound for Europe.

This whole period is in fact studded with all kinds of projects other than literary ones and with numerous confessions of the difficulty he found in writing. In 1891 a large part of his time was taken up by the Saxalin book, into which he poured an enormous amount of energy that might otherwise have been directed along more creative lines. Early in 1892 he purchased an estate in Melixovo, and the needs of the estate, together with a newly awakened interest in gardening and farming, cut into his creative hours. The winter of 1891-92 was a period of widespread famine in Russia; with great gusto Čexov threw himself into efforts to relieve the sufferers. In the latter year he took an active role in medical work for the local *zemstvo* as well. All these activities – either pleasant or praiseworthy in themselves – obviously left him considerably less time for writing than he had been accustomed to. I would suggest that part of the reason for all these newly discovered interests is the continued effort to escape from literature, much as Tolstoj had done in his spiritual crisis. Unfortunately, Čexov did not have the financial

---

[3] Ernest Simmons, *Chekhov: A Biography*, p. 232.

independence which Tolstoj enjoyed; as a result, material necessity forced him to ply his trade at least some of the time when he would have preferred to turn his back on it entirely.

His letters of the period abound in references to the difficulties he experienced in trying to write. Concerning "The Wife" (*Žena*) and "The Grasshopper" (*Poprygunja*) he tells Suvorin:

From morning to night I am unpleasantly irritated; I feel as if someone were dragging a blunt knife across my soul, while in external form this irritation is expressed by the fact that I rush early to bed and avoid conversation. Nothing works out well for me; I am stupidly clumsy. I began a story . . . wrote half of it and threw it away, then I began another. I have already struggled with this story for over a week, and the time when I shall finish it and write and finish the other one . . . seems to me remote (XV, 252).

Of "The Duel" he says: "Thanks to working too fast, I wasted a pound of nerves on it. Its composition is a little complicated. I got confused and often tore up what I had written, was dissatisfied with my work for whole days – that's why I still haven't finished" (XV, 228). By way of contrast, one might recall a remark made to Korolenko in 1886 when Čexov was still filled with a youthful bravado in regard to his work: " 'Do you know how I write my little stories? Here,' he glanced at the table, took in his hands the first object his eyes fell on – it happened to be an ashtray – placed it before me, and said, 'Do you want it, tomorrow there will be a story . . . the title, "The Ashtray".' " [4] Finally, in April 1892 Čexov had this to say of his general disposition:

I have aged not merely in body, but in spirit. I have become somehow stupidly indifferent to everything in the world and for some reason the beginning of this indifference coincided with my trip abroad. I get out of bed and go to bed with a feeling as if I were running out of interest in life. This is either the illness called in newspapers strain from overwork, or else emotional activity not consciously observed and called in novels emotional upheaval . . . (XV, 366-367).

Obviously, the Saxalin experience had failed to settle his own inner conflicts. In fact Čexov never seems to have resolved his doubts about his writings and himself, but after 1892 they gradually subside.

It is generally agreed that the Saxalin expedition coincides with what Thomas Winner has called "a search for a more clearly defined world

---

[4] V. G. Korolenko, "Anton Pavlovič Čexov", *Čexov v vospominanijax sovremennikov*, ed. N. L. Brodskij (Moskva, 1952), p. 75.

view".[5] This search is reflected in the stories of 1890 through 1893 as the last major attempt to assert the existence of constant, recognizable values. In this sense it parallels the kind of largely unsuccessful search carried on between 1885 and 1888 in the stories of pathos and the stories about dreamers, and in its treatment of character it further represents a counter-offensive launched against Čexov's own portrayal of meaningless identity.

One manifestation of the attempt to represent clear-cut issues is the regular appearance in these stories of a new character type, the reformer, the man who sets out to correct the wrongs he sees on every side. Following a pattern already established in the stories about dreamers, Čexov regularly undermines the reformer's efforts to make a better world, but the type which emerges may be a distant relative of the traditional hero found in melodrama. Looking at these stories while keeping that particular type of writing in mind, one is struck by various features ordinarily associated with melodrama, but by and large absent from Čexov's work heretofore, with the exception of some very early parodies. For one thing, these stories involve unusually violent action for Čexov; e.g., adultery and murder with revenge as its motive in "Peasant Wives" (*Baby*), hysterical outbursts between Ol'ga Ivanovna and Rjabovskij in "The Grasshopper" (*Poprygunja*), political terrorism in "An Anonymous Story" (*Rasskaz neizvestnogo čeloveka*). For another, fairly unadulterated figures of villainy appear in these stories – Matvej Savvič in "Peasant Wives", von Koren in "The Duel", Semën Tolkovyj in "In Exile", Orlov in "An Anonymous Story". Eric Bentley has argued that in his plays Čexov regularly employs such traditional dramatic elements as 'violent action' and a "... Villain who serves the traditional purpose of villains in dramatic plots, namely, to drive the Action toward catastrophe. The Professor in *Uncle Vanya*, Natasha in *The Three Sisters*, and Madame Ranevsky in *The Cherry Orchard* do just that."[6] I do not want to imply that in this period Čexov produced anything like the first-class melodramas of Victorian fiction, say, but rather that he was engaged in a dialogue with melodramatic elements as he had never been before. I would further suggest that the relatively black and white drama of villain versus hero helped him define his own moral position in these stories. The most lasting result of this dialogue is the explicit representation of evil in the form of *futljarnost'*.[7]

---

[5] Thomas Winner, *Chekhov and His Prose* (New York, 1966), p. 81.
[6] Eric Bentley, *The Life of the Drama* (New York, 1965), pp. 11 and 55.
[7] For a definition of this term see above, Chapter IV, footnote 2.

Several aspects of this new orientation can be seen in "Thieves" (*Vory,* 1890), the last story completed before the Saxalin journey. The action is unusually violent for Čexov: a doctor's assistant, Ergunov, is forced to seek shelter from a snowstorm in a house occupied by two horse thieves and a Čexovian *femme fatale,* Ljubka. In the denouement Ergunov is held captive in the arms of Ljubka while one of the thieves steals his horse, and when the enraged Ergunov discovers the theft, his fury is transformed into an impassioned attack on the girl, who eventually beats him off. In this story the dialogue with melodrama takes the form of authorial refusal to cast the thieves in the obvious role of villains. Instead, we see them romanticized through the eyes of Ergunov, who associates all three of his companions with mystery, passion, and freedom. The older thief, Kalašnikov, comes from a village full of romantic associations for the medical assistant: "The village is large and lies in a deep ravine so that when you go there on a moonlit night along the broad road and look down below into the dark ravine and then up at the sky, you think that the moon is hanging over a bottomless wasteland and that the end of the world is here" (VII, 286). The second thief, Merik, has even a diabolic side, inasmuch as Ergunov had once mistaken him for a kind of devil in the night. He envies Merik as he watches him engaged in a torrid dance with Ljubka. But it is not only the couple's passion which excites him; in their wild dance he senses a freedom denied to him. He wishes that he might be a 'simple peasant', that he could exchange his official jacket for a blue shirt and rope belt. "Then he could boldly sing, dance, drink, grab Ljubka with both hands, as Merik did . . ." (VII, 292).

Ergunov constantly contrasts the thieves' freedom with his own life, bounded by official restrictions, and out of this contrast emerges the real villain of the piece, the implied *futljarnost'* of societal organization. At the end of the evening he reflects:

Why was he a doctor's assistant and not a simple peasant? He was confused in the head and he thought, why are there doctors, assistants, merchants, clerks, peasants in this world, and not simply free people? There are indeed free birds, free animals, the free Merik, and they fear nobody, and they need no one. And who thought this up, who said that one must get up in the morning, have dinner at noon, go to bed at night, that a doctor is senior to his assistant, that one must live in a room and can love only his own wife? Why shouldn't it be the opposite: to have dinner at night, to sleep during the day? Oh, to jump on a horse, not asking whose it is . . . (VIII, 297).

Structurally, the story has led Ergunov in an ironic circle. Seeking shelter from the violence of a storm, he has fallen into the hands of thieves whose life force is a freedom and violence unfamiliar to him. Ljubka's dance is like the free forces of nature itself, and significantly Čexov compares the girl to a bird with its wings spread during her dance. Thus, in his effort to escape violence Ergunov stumbles into its midst. Čexov adds an epilogue in which Ergunov, now unemployed, returns to the neighborhood a year and a half after his disastrous evening, and as if to drive his moral home, the author includes Ergunov's somewhat broader indictment of society, even though this passage nearly duplicates the earlier one, quoted above:

The quiet, starlit night looked down from the heavens on the earth. My Lord, how deep the sky and how immeasurably vast it spreads over the world. The world has been well-made, but why, the assistant thought, why should people categorize one another as sober and drunk, those who serve and those who have been dismissed, and so forth? Why do the sober and well-fed ones sleep peacefully in their homes, while those who are drunk and hungry must wander in the field without shelter? Why is it that those who don't serve and receive no wages must absolutely be hungry, naked, shoeless? Who thought up this plan? Why should birds and forest animals be free of service, without wages, but live to their own satisfaction? (VII, 298).

One could paraphrase the moral stance of "Thieves" by saying that guilt has been shifted from the traditionally wicked thief to the society which denies man that freedom which is only a secondary effect of the thief's break with society.

Because he refused to say that thieves are wicked, Čexov was taken to task by his contemporaries, among them Aleksej Suvorin, who had reproached him for his "objectivity, calling it indifference to good and evil, the absence of ideals, ideas, and so forth" (XV, 51). Čexov answered this criticism in one of his most frequently quoted pronouncements on the short story,[8] but a more definitive answer is implied in the story itself – a refusal to accept the easy division of men and their behavior into categories of good and bad. He would not play the game according to the simplified rules of a Suvorin. It is curious, though, that in a roundabout fashion the editor of New Times should put his finger on one of the central issues of this period for Čexov.

---

[8] See his letter to Suvorin of 1 April 1890 (XV, 50-51). One could make a case for the position that Suvorin's major service to literature was a by-product of his frequently unperceptive reading of Čexov's works; the result was Čexov's rebuttals, which include a number of his most important observations on his craft.

Like "Thieves", "Peasant Wives" (*Baby*, 1891) attempts to fix blame on society itself for arbitrarily establishing rules which ignore real human problems. Hence, Čexov again points the accusing finger at *futljarnost'*, whose principal representative here is Matvej Savvič, a man who hides behind the sacredness of the marriage vow in an attempt to dispel a conflict in which he is actually a major protagonist. He has entered into a liaison with the wife of a soldier who is away on duty. Because he insists that their affair must end when the husband returns, despite the woman's attachment to Matvej and loathing for her lawful mate, he bears a responsibility for the woman's violent resolution of the impasse – the murder of her husband.

This summary of the most sensational aspect of the story has, of course, some bearing on Čexov's continuing dialogue with melodrama. However, in this case the violence and intensity of feeling are muffled through the device of a frame story. The reader does not see these actions directly, but instead learns of them at second hand, as Matvej relates them to a family with whom he spends the night. The outer frame is a considerably more sedate, more typically Čexovian scene, in which a set of characters listens to Matvej's account of the woman's fate – a fate which in many respects parallels that of the female listeners. Like Mašenka, the woman who loved Matvej, they too have been forced into marriages which spell a vile life. Lying awake at night, they toy with the possibility of murdering their husbands. Such violence will never disturb the tedious misery of their existences, but all the same their sympathies lie with Mašenka. They hear people singing in the night: "From the sad song came a longing for a free life; Sof'ja started to laugh; she was ashamed and horrified but to listen was sweet, and she envied her [sister-in-law] and was sorry that she herself hadn't sinned when she was young and beautiful..." (VII, 323). The interaction of the frame story and of Matvej's story tends to suppress the emotional impact of the latter, as though Čexov could not quite consent to writing a story about murder out of passion. Making Matvej the narrator shifts the responsibility from the author's shoulders. This device also somewhat confuses the focus of the entire work. Are we to see Matvej as the central character and are we to read the story as a revelation of hypocrisy? [9] Are we to see the misery of peasant wives, which also embraces the two separate stories, as the central issue? The title would seem to support the latter reading. Another possibility is that

[9] Thomas Winner in *Chekhov and His Prose* does read the story in this way. See pp. 83-85.

Čexov here dramatizes the kind of conflict between villains which was more directly stated in "Thieves" through the rhetoric of Ergunov's reflections. In "Peasant Wives" the legal villain is Mašenka and the two women in the outer frame are her potential compatriots. But Čexov manipulates his story to show that Matvej, hiding behind his *futljarnost'*, bears the greater guilt. Society at large is implicitly indicted inasmuch as Matvej supports its own verdict. Hence, what finally emerges from the story is a moral conflict, and neither Matvej nor the peasant women, the respective agents of each side in the drama, can take precedence.

That the attempt to establish his moral bearings was a central problem for Čexov throughout this period is born out by what might be called his famous 'lemonade' letter to Suvorin, written in November 1892. It is important to realize that what he was struggling to articulate about the artist's mission at that late date is inherent in "Thieves" and "Peasant Wives", the first two stories of this period:

In our works [his own and those of his contemporaries] there is no alcohol whatsoever ... Aren't Korolenko, Nadson, and all the present-day play-wrights really lemonade? ... Remember that writers whom we term im-mortal or simply good and who make us drunk share one very important trait: they are going somewhere and they call you there, and you feel not with the mind but with your whole being that they have some purpose, as the ghost of Hamlet's father has, who didn't come and stir up the imagina-tion for nothing. Some of them, judging by their caliber, have immediate aims – abolition of serfdom, the liberation of their native land, politics, beauty, or simply vodka, as Denis Davydov did; others have more distant aims – God, life beyond the grave, human happiness and so forth. The best of them are realists and describe life as it is, but owing to the fact that every line is saturated, as though it were a juice, with the awareness of purpose, besides life as it is, you feel also life as it ought to be, and this captivates you. And we? We! We describe life as it is, but we can't budge beyond that even if you whip us. We have neither immediate nor remote aims, and in our souls there is a void. We have no politics, we don't believe in revolution, there is no God, we're not afraid of ghosts, and personally I'm not even afraid of death and blindness. He who wants nothing, hopes for nothing, is afraid of nothing cannot be an artist. ... You and Grigorovič find me intelligent. Yes, I'm intelligent, at least sufficiently so not to hide from myself my disease and not to lie to myself and not to cover up my emptiness with others' rags, such as the ideas of the sixties and so forth. I won't throw myself down a flight of stairs like Garšin; but neither will I kid myself with hopes for a better future (XV, 446-447).

With regard to the two stories we have just considered, Čexov has done himself an injustice in this letter, for if he has not given us a vision of 'life as it ought to be', he has accomplished nothing in them, and in nearly all the stories of this period his criticism of life persistently implies a vision of 'life as it ought to be'. If this letter gives us Čexov's definition of the writer's role, it also can be considered as a statement of his entire generation's dilemma – the existence of a society cut off from its moral and ethical foundations. He devotes the last ten years of his life to following out the implications of this moral and ethical collapse. He moves from rage at a society in which moral perception is so arbitrary that the society itself shows signs of insanity, in "Ward No. 6", towards an ever more comic vision of the absurdity to which such rootlessness – or rather a false pretense at roots – leads. *The Cherry Orchard* is perhaps the most finished example. In the present period, however, his representation of moral confusion is colored by the presence of the 'ought to be'.

"The Duel" is quite possibly the most confused work Čexov ever wrote.[10] The 'ought to be' appears at the end of the story in the chastened characters of Laevskij and von Koren, whose progress through the story certainly contributes to the confusion. In these two characters Čexov's tampering with traditional villain and hero is especially interesting. In any ordinary story Laevskij would be the hero and von Koren the villain. In fact, von Koren does fulfill the villain's role by driving the action to the brink of, if not actually into, catastrophe at the moment when he aims his pistol at Laevskij and all but shoots to kill. One of the ironies of the story is the fact that by this point the duel has become a superfluous part of the action. The Laevskij who had become involved in a duel had already begun his own reform the previous night; this is part of the reason why its participants feel they have been placed in an artificial situation. In other words, von Koren is in the awkward position of fulfilling his proper role at a point when a villain is already superfluous to the story.

While von Koren emerges most clearly at an inappropriate moment, earlier in the story both he and Laevskij constitute a motley gathering of qualities. Čexov deliberately blends traditional virtues and vices in each. Not only do they dislike one another, each is a perfect complement to the other. Laevskij is lazy; he talks a great deal but does nothing except lie to himself. On the other hand, he is sympathetic to the faults of others and capable of overlooking their shortcomings. By contrast, von Koren is a man of action rather than a talker, but he is merciless

---

[10]   I have discussed a number of the confusions in "The Duel" in Chapter II.

towards those of whom he disapproves. Take the virtues of each and you have a model hero; place their combined vices in one man and you have an arch villain. Actually, in the double reformation at the end of the story, Čexov tries to make heroes of both by purging each of his vices: Laevskij accepts his moral responsibilities by marrying his mistress and working to pay off his debts. Von Koren's regeneration is not quite so apparent, but he is forced to retract his zealous condemnation of others; he acknowledges that Laevskij, whom he would have shot as a danger to society, has become a useful social being. There is at least one other clear sign of von Koren's regeneration. Throughout the story he has been trying to convince the deacon that he should join him on his Far East expedition. Von Koren says: " 'I don't understand your hesitation. If you continue being an ordinary deacon, who is obliged to hold a service only on holidays, and on the other days can rest from work, you will be exactly the same as you are now in ten years, and will have gained nothing but a mustache and a beard; while on returning from this expedition after these same ten years you will be a different man, you will be enriched by the consciousness that you have done something' " (VII, 357). Given von Koren's character, one would expect him to have nothing but contempt for the deacon, who elects to remain behind, and to be incapable of appreciating the virtues the deacon may find in remaining at home. But at the end of the story, in his chastened character, von Koren can say only: " 'Goodbye, deacon. ... Thank you for your company and for our pleasant conversations. Think about the expedition' " (VII, 429). Finally, it is the deacon who announces von Koren's transformation: " 'Nikolaj Vasilič ... let me tell you that today you have conquered the greatest of man's enemies – pride' " (VII, 428).

But at this moment, as Ralph Matlaw has noted,[11] Čexov apparently begins to suspect that everybody's regeneration has cheated on life, and von Koren replies to the deacon: " 'Conquerors ought to look like eagles, but he's [Laevskij] pitiful, timid, crushed, bows like a Chinese idol, while I ... I am sad' " (VII, 428). Nevertheless, in spite of Čexov's temporizing with a desire to wipe the slate clean at the end, there is an element here which is not quite convincing. There is a certain honesty about the assertion that both von Koren and Laevskij have paid a price for their salvation, but what they have lost bears only a peripheral

---

[11] Ralph Matlaw, "Čechov and the Novel", *Anton Čechov, 1860-1960: Some Essays*, ed. Thomas Eekman (Leiden, 1960), p. 165.

relation to what they have gained. What we have here is an undigested fragment from the canon of melodrama. Eric Bentley has spoken of exaggeration as one of its major components: "The exaggerations will be foolish only if they are empty of feeling. Intensity of feeling justifies formal exaggeration in art, just as intensity of feeling creates the 'exaggerated' forms of childhood fantasies and adult dreams." [12] The trouble with the denouement of "The Duel" is that Čexov does employ exaggeration without any intensity of feeling. Certainly one of the basic exaggerations in melodrama is the assumption that there exists a clearly marked dichotomy between virtue and vice, personified in the separate roles of hero and villain. Now the regeneration of Laevskij particularly involves this kind of dichotomy. He is transformed from a worthless will o' the wisp into an industrious and useful member of society. The exaggeration is contained in the notion that such mutually exclusive categories exist and that a person can move from one extreme to the other. This kind of exaggeration is not justified by any intensity of feeling in "The Duel". Thus the failure of the ending may be attributed to the timidity of the story throughout.

Whatever else Čexov does or fails to do in "The Duel" he establishes a new character type in Laevskij – the reformer, in this particular case, a self-reformer. Laevskij is distinguished from his successors in that Čexov does try to convince us of his hero's moderate success in achieving his purpose. In this sense he is the most positive character in any of these stories.

The self-reformer reappears in Čexov's next work, "The Wife" (*Žena*, 1892). Asorin, the narrator, personifies the villainy of this period; and he goes through a process of regeneration at the end, but now the price of regeneration is the virtual destruction of the man. Asorin's fault lies in his coldness, an insensitivity to the feelings of others.[13] This failure of response is to be found in all the villains of this period, and it is one

---

[12]   Eric Bentley, *The Life of the Drama*, p. 204. In this chapter I am particularly indebted to Mr. Bentley's first-rate discussion of melodrama (pp. 195-219).

[13]   Avram Derman has developed the interesting theory that Čexov wrote the stories under discussion here in an attempt to purge himself through his art of a certain emotional coldness in his own nature, and that this literary purging followed an unsuccessful effort to resolve the problem during his trip to Saxalin by exposing himself to people for whom it was all but impossible not to feel compassion. The only difficulty with this theory is that none of the characters in these stories manages successfully to purge himself of his emotional coldness, as Professor Derman claims they do. See *Tvorčeskij portret Čexova* (Moskva, 1929), particularly pp. 172-219.

of the quintessential elements in *futljarnost'*. Von Koren also has this
coldness, as well as another mark of the disease, the urge to become
a despot, for only through absolute control over others can he hope to
fend off the touch of the outside world. Asorin is also something of a
despot. Unsuccessful at organizing assistance for the peasants during
famine, he resents his wife's facility for collecting funds throughout
the neighborhood. He decides he must take over her drive lest some
unscrupulous landowner accuse her of misappropriating funds. Here is
both the timidity of *futljarnost'* and its despotism, for as he interferes
with his wife's work he takes from her the only source of satisfaction
in her life.

But in "The Wife" the emphasis is not so much on despotism as on
Asorin's desperate need to hide himself away. He has retired from his
work as an engineer to bury himself in the country. His actions are
always carefully prepared and thought out; even if he wishes to speak
with his wife, Natalja, he plans in advance each word he will say.
Natalja characterizes him aptly when she says: " 'You are an educated,
cultured man, but in essence what a Scythian you still are! That's because you lead a secluded existence, you are hostile to life, you don't
see anybody and you don't read anything, except your engineering
books. But there really are good people, good books! Yes...' " (VIII,
36).

Their marriage, of course, has been a failure for many years. Apparently, what Asorin seeks in his marital relationship is not a wife,
but the security and protection offered by a mother or a nurse. He
reflects: "I miss her as once in childhood I missed my mother and
nurse, and I feel that now as I approach old age, I love her more purely
and more highly than I had loved her before, and therefore I felt like
going to her room..." (VIII, 21). And again, "In childhood when I
was sick, I would press close to my mother or the nurse, and when I
hid my face in the folds of the warm dress it seemed to me that I was
hiding from the illness. So now for some reason I felt that I could hide
from my uneasiness only in this small room near my wife. I sat down
and covered my eyes from the light with my arm. It was quiet" (VIII,
33).[14] It is this search for the security of a child in its mother's arms
which finally brings about his strange regeneration. In accordance with
Natalja's wishes he leaves her and his house, but at the railroad station

---

[14] Interestingly enough, this reflection by Asorin comes at the end of a moderately
violent scene in which Natalja has demanded that he leave her for good.

on a snowy night he is frightened at the thought of returning to Petersburg and to "the acquaintances whom I have already left, the loneliness, dinners in restaurants, the noise, electric lights, which make my eyes ache..." (VIII, 38). He prefers to return to his jeering wife, and when he reaches home, he tells her: " 'You can't bring back that time when we lived as husband and wife, and you don't need to, but you will make me your servant. Take my whole fortune and give it away to whomever you want. I am happy, Natalie, I am satisfied... I am happy' " (VIII, 49). Thus, Asorin foregoes his despotic role, but he does so in exchange for another kind of security, that of the slave who can rely on the protection of the master, or perhaps of the child obeying its mother. Ultimately, then, Asorin is rendered harmless, but at the expense of his manhood.

In "The Grasshopper" (*Poprygunja*) Čexov evokes one of his most striking effects in his continuing dialogue with melodrama. In this instance there is nothing in the story itself to suggest its exaggerated effects, except in the mind of the heroine, Ol'ga Ivanovna. Because she conceives of herself as a melodramatic persona, she brings its effects into an essentially undramatic narrative. Her personality is exactly opposite from that of her rather prosaic husband, Dymov, whose death, even, would pass quietly were it not for the intensity of her reaction to it. One example of her bombast is Ol'ga's relationship with her lover, Rjabovskij. This is in essence a pretty ordinary affair, but when the lover grows tired of his mistress, she creates a violent scene, shouting hysterically: " 'Well, kill, kill me!... Kill!' " (VIII, 63).

The superb irony of the finale is that she creates her own terrible loss when Dymov dies. She is at least temporarily crushed at the realization that she has actually been married to a man of enormous talent and has thus innocently let an attachment to a great man slip by. But her misery is a product of her own conception of life in extravagant terms. If she were the kind of person Dymov is, it would be impossible for her to become a victim of herself in this way. The suggestion that Ol'ga may belong to the self-reformer group by virtue of her apparent self-realization at the end is vitiated by the fact that she is miserable only because she does *not* respond to the real significance of her husband's death – the loss of a potentially great scientist.

But in order to bring off this ironic effect, Čexov had to pay a price in his portrayal of Dymov, the self-effacing man, who will permit Ol'ga and her artistic friends to use him virtually as their lackey. Dymov's ostensible merit – his complete dedication to his scientific studies –

is obfuscated by his naive faith in a set of vainglorious aesthetes.[15]

"In Exile", one of the few pieces to emerge from the Saxalin expedition, depicts a potential reformer who goes down to defeat at the hands of yet another spokesman for *futljarnost'*. "In Exile" may be said to mark a shift in Čexov's treatment of the reformer, for in this and the three longer stories which follow it the reformer turns his attack away from himself and consistently encounters frustration in his efforts to change those around him. The 'reformer' here is a tartar and the villain a ferryman, Semën, who asserts that to survive one must break off all bonds of affection. Semën recounts the experiences of an exiled Russian who suffered torments away from his family. The tartar finally delivers a crushing verdict on the ferryman: " 'God created man so that he should live, so that there would be joy and sadness and misery, but you want nothing, so you are dead, a stone, clay! A stone needs nothing and you need nothing... You are a stone – and God does not love you, but the Russian He loves' " (VIII, 87). Semën is of course the same villain who has appeared in "The Wife", the emotionally indifferent person, seeking by indifference to protect himself. But he has the last word: commenting on the tartar, who is now lying on the ground crying over the separation from his own family, he observes: " 'He'll get used to it!' " (VIII, 87). The only expectation is either that a future of unlimited sorrow awaits him, or that he will become like Semën; in either case his future is bleak.

The reformer reappears in Čexov's next story, "Neighbors" (*Sosedi*), only to find that no one really needs reforming. Čexov seems to be playing with a series of ironic reversals, as Pëtr Mixajlovič, another in the group of cold men, prepares to rescue his sister Zina from a patently immoral relationship with a neighbor, Vlasič. When Pëtr arrives at the neighbor's home, he finds, instead of the anticipated depravity, that Vlasič worships Zina as a divine being.

Henry James' *The Ambassadors* has for its basic scheme the reversal of Lambert Strether's expectations. What appears to be a depraved affair turns out to possess values of which Strether had been completely unaware. Up to a point "Neighbors" seems to follow this scheme, but

---

[15] Interestingly, Soviet critics are very fond of "The Grasshopper". Their sympathies lie wholly with the quiet little doctor, devoted to his work and capable of greatness in his chosen field. He is the proletarian hero, unrecognized prior to the Revolution, except by such perceptive writers as Čexov. In short, for Soviet critics Dymov is one of the literary prototypes for the hero of socialist realism. See particularly V. Ermilov, *Čexov* (Moskva, 1949), pp. 253-262, and V. V. Golubkov, *Masterstvo A. P. Čexova* (Moskva, 1958), pp. 127-136.

as Pëtr Mixajlič looks more closely at his sister's affair he finds it is not all that Vlasič had claimed. Vlasič himself, in contrast to Pëtr, is a man of strong feelings and noble inclination. He is in fact quixotic; he had married his present wife out of compassion – at eighteen she was already the rejected mistress of an army officer. But Vlasič found his life with the girl miserable. Gradually, it becomes clear that Zina is performing the same kind of compassionate act for Vlasič as he had performed for his wife. There can never be any love between them, only reverence on one side and pity on the other. Pëtr's original moral indignation has been replaced not by a new awareness that there may be something of value in a seemingly depraved affair, but by a sense of the unhappiness which their devotion and selflessness will bring them.

In his only major work of 1893, "An Anonymous Story" (*Rasskaz neizvestnogo čeloveka*), Čexov presents what are by now the classic ingredients for a story of this period: he toys with the possibilities of violent, dramatic action;[16] his hero is a reformer *par excellence* who enjoys a total lack of success; and his villain, Orlov, is the typical cold man, whose protective coat is a sense of irony before any feeling outside himself. There is one extremely effective moment in the story when Orlov loses his sense of irony. During a quarrel his mistress, Zinaida, bursts into tears. This display of emotion is more than Orlov can cope with, and he surrenders to her completely. Why does he suddenly become defenseless? Apparently, because his protective coating of irony is worthless before direct emotional contact with another being.

But for Čexov's concerns of this period, obviously the primary character is the narrator himself. By making his central figure a revolutionary, Čexov manages very neatly to merge the various lines of the story, for the revolutionist disillusioned converges on the reformer of mankind, and by the end of the story he has devoted himself heart and soul to correcting the misguided, though ultimately he is a stupendous failure. It is interesting to note during this series of stories how the self-reformer gradually becomes the reformer of others and at the same time becomes ever less successful in his task. Here the narrator strives to reform both Orlov and Zinaida. In the latter half of the story it is the desire to save the girl – to show her that her life with Orlov has been sordid and nothing more – which is his driving force. The very fact that he carries her away is an implicit effort towards reform. After she has become disillusioned with her savior as well, there is a moment when

---

[16]   For a discussion of the way Čexov manipulates plot in "An Anonymous Story" see Chapter II.

his effort becomes explicit: " 'Listen to me,' I continued, catching at a thought which suddenly, dimly came into my head and which could still save us both" (VIII, 242).

The call to salvation by this point has become extremely familiar to the reader. When the narrator leaves Orlov's, he cannot resist the temptation to write a note telling his former master what he thinks of him, and in it he observes: "No powers can now warm your damnably cold blood, and you know this better than I. So why do I write? But my head and heart are burning, I go on writing, am somehow moved, as though this letter might still save you and me" (VIII, 224). The letter, of course, does not. When he returns from abroad with Zinaida's baby, he is still the reformer, however. He knows he will soon die and he hopes to convince Orlov that he must accept his moral responsibility for the child. In a scene of scathing irony they meet and discuss the narrator's letter. But while Orlov freely admits his faults, it is apparent that he does not at all understand what the narrator has been talking about. In a final gesture of gross misunderstanding, he agrees to take responsibilty for his child – i.e., to locate a boarding school for her.

As we have seen already, the anonymous man bears a certain resemblance to Insarov, the hero of *On the Eve*. In speaking of the way Turgenev handles the Insarov type, George Woodcock writes: "... he knew and observed well the more individualistic type of revolutionary intellectual who failed precisely because he could not or would not suppress all this human normality in favor of what Ibsen called 'the claim of the ideal'." [17] If this is true of Turgenev, what must we say of Čexov's revolutionary? Here the 'human normality' comes to dominate the character to a point where the 'claim of the ideal' is all but usurped, or where the revolutionary energy is diverted wholly to the sphere of the personal moral problem.

The masterpiece of this period, "Ward No. 6" (*Palata No. 6*, 1892), had appeared one year before "An Anonymous Story". Its position at the tail end of this series puts it in the same relation to its period as "A Dreary Story" bears to the works of the previous series, and, like "A Dreary Story", "Ward No. 6" owes at least part of its distinction to the fact that Čexov had in effect been working over the same thematic and formal problems for an extended period. Central to the story is the study of *futljarnost'*, although now the evil is embodied not in a single individual, but rather in the social fabric itself. Certainly, a large measure

---

[17] George Woodcock, "The Elusive Ideal: Notes on Turgenev", *The Sewanee Review*, LXIX (Winter 1961), 46.

of the story's power is derived from the all-pervading breath of evil. If we compare "Ward No. 6" with "Peasant Wives", we find that in his portrayal of Matvej Savvič Čexov is talking about the same kind of evil. But Matvej had served as the single embodiment of *futljarnost'*, and it is difficult, if not impossible, to respond in the same way to a disgusting individual as to an entire society which we identify with our own and yet whose values are repugnant. We may react to an individual case, such as Matvej's, with anger, but to an entire society our reaction is certainly one of fear, and perhaps also of awe. The most obvious candidate for villain in "Ward No. 6" is Nikita, the porter, but he is at best a pawn. While he does embody the evil of the society, the power stands well behind him and becomes all the more effective for doing so.

The ward has frequently been taken as a symbol of Russia and the cruel Nikita as a symbol of Alexander III's rule by force.[18] One of the great strengths of this story is certainly that the significance of this particular ward in this particular hospital in a Russian village seems to spread out in all directions and that the madness which it either shuts in, or, perhaps, shuts out is equally a part of our own world. In connection with the central theme, *futljarnost'*, the ward is an extraordinary symbol of the community at large trying to enclose and isolate, as it does with Gromov and ultimately with Ragin, any threat to the stability of its own absurdity. I referred above to the fact that Čexov sees a close connection between *futljarnost'* and despotism. The despotism in the *futljarnost'* of society at large is of course implicit in ward six, where it is only through force that the community can hope to silence the critical voice.

In addition to the ward itself, the story presents many other forms of *futljarnost'* and manages to reveal images of madness and absurdity only dimly concealed. The word 'order' (*porjadok*) – in the sense of a state in which everything is in its right place and functioning properly – occurs frequently and always with an ironic effect in this story. The various orders exhibited here all prove to be meaningless, illogical, and chaotic. The ultimate 'order' under attack is that society which tries to hide its own madness by isolating and barring any suggestion that it is itself finally absurd.

Nikita is the first keeper of this society whom we meet. He "belongs to the class of those simple-hearted, staid, careful, dull-witted people who more than anything else in the world love order and are therefore con-

---

[18] Reference to this symbolism – or more properly, allegory – can be found in virtually every Soviet commentary on the story. See particularly V. Ermilov, *Čexov*, pp. 245-253.

vinced that they must beat people. He beats you about the face, the chest, the back, whatever is handy, and he is sure that without this there would be no order here" (VIII, 108). Through his earlier description of the hospital Čexov has established the absurdity of Nikita's principles: the building over which he has charge is surrounded by an unkept yard; it has a chimney and front steps that are falling to pieces. Inside "along the walls and near the stove whole mountains of hospital rubbish are piled up" (VIII, 107). In short, the appearance of the ward makes a mockery of Nikita's love for order.

The first of the two central characters, Gromov, a victim of persecution mania, emphasizes the fact that the kind of 'order' upon which society is based may well send an innocent man to prison. "Under this same formal", – note the variation on the idea of order – "callous attitude toward the individual, to deprive an innocent man of all rights of ownership and to send him to prison, the court needs but one thing: time" (VIII, 113). When Gromov tries to reason sensibly, he becomes all the more convinced of his danger: "Facts and common sense persuaded him that all these fears were nonsense and morbidity, that if one looked at the matter more broadly actually there was nothing frightening in arrest and imprisonment – so long as the conscience is at rest; but the more sensibly and logically he reasoned, the more acute and agonizing his distress became" (VIII, 114). In short, to reason logically about this society is to become more convinced of the chaos hidden just beneath its apparent order.

Dr. Ragin, the only other major character, is like a microcosm of the community as a whole. His entire life is a series of minor orders which amount to nothing more than futljarnost'. Čexov emphasizes this point in describing Ragin's nightly routine, including the ritualistic visits of his friend Mixail Aver'janyč, who rather ridiculously affirms 'absolutely right' to all of Ragin's opinions, even though this friend has not the vaguest idea what Ragin is talking about. Indeed, the doctor's advice to Gromov to imitate Marcus Aurelius and seek peace in one's mind rather than in the external world is an attempt to make the mind itself into a kind of box where one can conceal himself. But there are gaps in Ragin's sense of order; for example, he is sometimes bothered by the incongruity between the advances of modern medicine and the savage conditions of ward six. The story as a whole is concerned with exposing the chaos barely hidden by an orderly society. Specifically, with Dr. Ragin it is the revelation of his own futljarnost' which moves the story forward. Given such a society, once Ragin has seen the truth, his death at society's hands is inevitable. That there is a basic absurdity – even madness – in the order of human society was a vision that never deserted Čexov, though he never again returned to a treatment of the stark horrors such a vision entails.

It has been said that "... the most developed and critical handling of Tolstoyan issues and the most direct attack on the crucial Tolstoyan doctrine of non-resistance may be inferred from... *Ward No. 6*".[19] I would like to suggest the very opposite, that there are overwhelming affinities between Tolstoyan doctrine and views expressed in "Ward No. 6"; indeed, they form the very basis of the story. The view that Čexov was here attacking Tolstoyan doctrine is usually based on the fact that Ragin advises Gromov not to resist the injustice of his confinement, but to seek internal peace and that ultimately, when forced to put his own advice to the test, Ragin finds his prescription useless. This view would make a Tolstoyan of Ragin. I do not deny that Čexov possibly intended some such interpretation. However, it seems to me that the whole tenor of the action tends rather to make Gromov the primary Tolstoyan, even though he is an extremely sympathetic character. Actually, he never resists by force; physically he remains passive in the ward. But verbally, he constantly protests, just as Tolstoj the writer protested every kind of injustice he found in his world.

Gromov's attack on the system of justice administered by the law courts expresses precisely the views to be found in *The Kingdom of God*. Further, his observations on the ease with which a judicial error could be committed, quoted above, read like a theoretical statement of the process by which Maslova is condemned in *Resurrection*. At one point in Gromov's reflections he virtually espouses the Tolstoyan doctrine of non-resistance: "And isn't it absurd even to think of justice when every kind of force is accepted by society as a reasonable and consistent necessity..." (VIII, 113).

But the basic harmony expressed here and in Tolstoj's writing lies in the incongruity between professed attitudes and actions. The more logically Gromov reasons, the more he fears a miscarriage of justice. Speaking of just such inconsistencies, Tolstoj writes: "A man with a sensitive conscience cannot but suffer if he lives this life. The only way to avoid this suffering is to stifle his conscience, but even if such men succeed in stifling their conscience, they cannot stifle fear."[20] Thus,

[19]   Thomas Winner, "Čexov's *Ward No. 6* and Tolstoyan Ethics", *The Slavic and East European Journal*, XVII (Winter 1959), 325.
[20]   Lev Tolstoj, *The Kingdom of God*, trans. Aylmer Maude (New York, 1951), p. 143.

"Ward No. 6" affirms a number of Tolstoj's views, without of course sharing their Christian basis.[21]

We have already noted that "A Dreary Story" and "Ward No. 6" occupy similar positions as penultimate moments in the process of Čexov's growth from 1888 to 1892. Certainly these two periods encompass his most difficult years, and it is tempting to suggest that these two stories represent a creative catharsis, at least, which goes far beyond the Saxalin expedition in its effect. "A Dreary Story" and "Ward No. 6" are the two most powerful and devastating stories in all of Čexov's work. The artist was fortunate for never again having been pressed to attempt the expression of such despair.

[21] The question of Tolstoj's influence on Čexov is a complicated one. Part of the complication stems from Čexov's own statement, in a letter to Suvorin of 27 March 1894, to the effect that he had at one period been receptive to Tolstoj's philosophy but that by 1894 his enthusiasm had cooled. His disillusionment is generally taken to coincide with the Saxalin trip; before it he had been in raptures over "The Kreuzer Sonata"; upon his return his attitude was distinctly critical. There is room to speculate that Čexov's own description of his attitude toward Tolstoj exaggerates the proportions of both his early enthusiasm and his later rejection. There are no stories which will demonstrate that Čexov ever accepted Tolstoj's major theoretical positions. There are, however, stories, including "Ward No. 6", which indicate Čexov's sympathy for a number of Tolstoj's specific indictments of his society and for the predicament of a man who stands up to his society as Tolstoj did. These stories appeared both during and after the period of purported enthusiasm for Tolstoj. In "A Nervous Breakdown", for example, the intensity of Vasilev's indignation at what he considers wrong suggests the personality of Tolstoj, as well as of Garšin. In a very late story, "My Life" (*Moja žizn'*, 1896), Čexov may have demonstrated a satirical attitude toward Tolstoj in making Misail a house painter, and yet there is no denying that this Tolstoyan is far and away the most sympathetic figure in the story. Another type of Tolstoyan influence is exhibited by "A Dreary Story", a work which upon first publication was hailed as a rather poor rewriting of "The Death of Ivan Il'ič" (see N. I. Gitovič, *Letopis' žizni i tvorčestva A. P. Čexova* [Moskva, 1955], p. 248). But perhaps the most apt discussion of the relationship between these two stories is that by Lev Šestov in his essay "Anton Tchekhov: Creation from the Void", *Chekhov and Other Essays* (Ann Arbor, Michigan, 1966), pp. 3-63: "Nietzsche once asked: 'Can an ass be tragical?' He left his question unanswered, but Tolstoi answered for him in *The Death of Ivan Ilyich*. Ivan Ilyich, it is evident from Tolstoi's description of his life, is a mediocre, average character, one of those men who pass through life avoiding anything that is difficult or problematical, caring exclusively for the calm and pleasantness of earthly existence. Hardly had the cold wind of tragedy blown upon him, than he was utterly transformed. The story of Ivan Ilyich in his last days is as deeply interesting as the life-story of Socrates or Pascal. ... In his work Tchekhov was influenced by Tolstoi, and particularly by Tolstoi's later writings. ... I think that had there been no *Death of Ivan Ilyich*, there would have been no *Ivanov*, and no *Tedious Story* ... Had Tolstoi not paved the way, had Tolstoi not shown by his example, that in literature it was permitted to tell the truth, to tell everything, then perhaps Tchekhov would have had to struggle long with himself before finding the courage of a public confession, even though it took the form of stories" (pp. 10-11).

VIII

STORIES OF TIME

Čexov had reached the apex of his creative development by roughly the beginning of 1894. It might be said that everything he wrote prior to this date was part of the development *toward* the stories which he produced during the last ten years of his life. Up to this time he was in the process of becoming, while the final years mark his ultimate fulfillment. Unfortunately, Čexov died when he was only forty-three. Although there is no way of knowing what direction his work might have taken had his life continued, still one does get a sense that the evolution of all his previous work culminates in the thirty-three stories written between the summer of 1893 and the summer of 1903, when he returned to his publisher the final proofs of "Betrothed" (*Nevesta*). Many of the earlier works could, of course, stand on their own, and had Čexov's literary career come to its end at some earlier date, it would no doubt be possible to see all the previous work pointing toward a different goal. Nevertheless, the final years represent a more sustained period in his work than any other group of years.

There are no basic thematic or stylistic shifts after mid-1893 when he wrote "The Black Monk" (*Černyj monax*). By this time he had apparently found himself in his creative work as he never had before. Perhaps the chief evidence for this statement lies in the absence of spiritual or creative crises during the ensuing years. As we have seen, the crisis which apparently ran its course between 1889 and 1892 rather abruptly disappeared, and there is no indication that it ever recurred. This may be a further indication that "A Dreary Story" and "Ward No. 6" performed a cathartic role in Čexov's creative life. Furthermore, with the possible exception of a late-discovered concern for peasant problems in several of the major works, notably "Peasants" (*Mužiki*) and "In the Ravine" (*V ovrage*), nearly all these stories continue the exploration of man's tenuous and precarious grasp on reality.

What is new in this period is the fact that the struggle which Čexov had carried on throughout his career against his own vision of the world has finally come to an end. There is a spirit of cheerful resignation – even an occasional flicker of hope – and willingness to accept in matured form the idea of man's constantly shifting relationship to himself and everything outside himself – to a world in which the only constant is the relativity of all values.

The world itself has not changed. The reality Čexov now depicts differs in no essential from that of "Ward No. 6", but instead of the 'savage indignation' with which he had so recently viewed his creation, his tendency is to accept such a world as essentially comic. In this sense, it is certainly no accident that he identified his last finished work, *The Cherry Orchard*, as a comedy. Logical absurdities in the social condition, the complete absence of rational connection in the emotional exchanges between people, human response based on a misconception of one's relationship to existence – Čexov now views all such irrationalities as manifestations of a ludicrous world. Perhaps this was the only possible defense against insanity.

A predilection for the ridiculous and the absurd had always been an omnipresent aspect of Čexov's personality. Certainly one of the major reasons why his letters continue to charm readers is that he had the capacity – almost a compulsion – to describe any and every event in whimsical terms. Descriptions of third persons or references to his correspondents almost invariably turn into capricious portraits. Least of all can he resist making himself appear grotesque at every turn. Granted that the whimsical is pure comedy in the letters, nevertheless, this undercurrent in Čexov's character can be documented for virtually every day of his adult life, thanks to his copious correspondence, and in itself attests to an inherent concept of reality which erupted only spasmodically in his creative work prior to 1894.

It would be possible to cite examples from the correspondence for almost any period; I would suggest particularly the letters to his family and to Suvorin while he was travelling – the journey to Taganrog in the spring of 1887 or to Saxalin from April to December 1890. There are enormously comic descriptions of the adventures of a mongoose which he brought back from India, particularly of the difficulties encountered by both mongoose and Čexov's neighbors in adjusting to life together in Moscow. However, at this point it seems most appropriate to select from the final period illustrations of Čexov's predilection for the grotesque, for one might say that the truth of the letters – the constant presence of the absurd in life – does not really come into its own in the artistic prose until the last ten years. Any incident, any topic is grist for the mill: on one occasion Čexov had asked Suvorin to lend financial support to a failing medical journal. Upon receipt of Suvorin's check he writes: "As regards the *Annals of Surgery*, the journal itself, all the surgical instruments, bandages and bottles of carbolic acid bow to the ground before you. Their joy is, of course, enormous" (XVI, 273-274). His relations with female friends invariably place both Čexov and the lady in the most grotesque circumstances: to Lidija Mizinova he writes: "Sweet Lika, when you become a famous singer and are paid a wonderful salary, be kind to me: marry me and support me, so that I can do nothing. If you are really going to die, then let Varja Eberle do this, for, as you know, I love her" (XVI, 135). He tells Marija Malkiel' that he has become an honorary Mohammedan in a Tatar society near Yalta: "I thank you for your letter and send cordial regards to you and your prophetic sister, and I hope you both land in the harem of a distinguished gentleman..." (XVIII, 256). Between Anton and his brother Aleksandr a completely imaginary epistolary relationship was established in which Anton plays the role of a wealthy snob, while Aleksandr is a thoroughly depraved pauper: "I haven't answered you for so long, in the first place, out of pride, inasmuch as I own property; you, on the other hand, are poor . . .". In a postscript he adds: "I have put twenty-three rubles in the savings bank. My wealth is accumulating. But when I die, you won't get a kopeck, as you are not mentioned in my will" (XVI, 149-150). Imaginary characters pop up regularly in his correspondence. Before his marriage to Ol'ga Knipper he had invented a wholly fictitious lady named Nadenka, who sometimes would appear as Čexov's fiancée and sometimes as his wife. At any rate, she strongly resented the presence of Ol'ga, to whom he wrote in 1900:

Thanks for your good wishes on the occasion of my marriage. I informed my bride of your intention to visit Yalta in order to deceive her a bit. To this she said that when "that bad woman" comes to Yalta, she will not let me out of her embraces. I observed that embracing for such a long time in hot weather was unhygienic. She took offense, turned pensive, as though wishing to guess in what circle I had acquired this *façon de parler*, and after a bit she said that the theater is evil and that my intention of not writing any more plays was praiseworthy. Then she asked me to kiss her. To this I responded that for me as an academician it is no longer proper to kiss frequently. She cried, and I left (XVIII, 329).

Quite frequently he would announce his latest literary efforts in a highly misleading way; consider this strangely uninformative description of

The Seagull: "A comedy with three female parts, six male, four acts, a landscape (view of a lake), much talk on literature, little action, and a heavy weight of love" (XVI, 271). But most often of all, Čexov depicts himself as an utterly ridiculous figure. He writes Ol'ga: "I bow down to you, bow low, so low that my forehead touches the bottom of my well, which thus far has been dug to a depth of fifty-six feet" (XVIII, 220). Thus, on the basis of the letters one can say that Čexov constantly viewed his own situation as comically absurd. To do so was part of his nature.[1]

There is one other aspect of Čexov's makeup which is at least touched upon in the letters and which may have a relevance to his perception of life. This is the role that medical training played in his literary development, a subject which has been neglected in Čexov scholarship.[2] In a letter to Grigorij Rossolimo, a friend on the medical faculty at Moscow University, he observes: "I do not doubt that my studies in the medical sciences had a serious influence on my literary activity..." (XVIII, 243). He then goes on to detail several ways in which medicine has aided him. In this connection he notes: "Familiarity with the natural sciences, with the scientific method, has always kept me on my guard..." (XVIII, 244). Although this may be pure speculation, there is the possibility that what 'familiarity with the scientific method' gave him was a heightened sense of the absurd; specialized training in the rational and logical processes of scientific work may have sharpened his awareness of the irrational in life.

The view of Čexov which emphasizes his conception of a world dominated by a state of flux, in which logical connections between phenomena give way to whimsical *non-sequiturs*, is one that has been given increasing emphasis in recent years. However, elements of this interpretation go back to one of the earliest major commentaries on Čexov, Lev Šestov's essay, "Creation from Nothing" (*Tvorčestvo iz ničego*, 1908). Šestov feels that the essence of Čexov's work was a striving to kill every kind of hope, to reduce man to absolute despair. It is out of this idea that he evolves his title. But during the course of his discussion Šestov apparently defines hope as belief in the operation of rational processes in life. It is in the realm of ideas that Čexov manipu-

[1] For some observations on and examples of the bizarre from Čexov's notebooks see: Charles B. Timmer, "The Bizarre Element in Čechov's Art" in *Anton Čechov, 1860-1960: Some Essays*, ed. T. Eekman (Leiden, 1960), pp. 278-279.
[2] I know only one important study of the relation between Čexov's literary development and his medical training: see A. Roskin, "Čexov i nauka" in *A. P. Čexov: Stati i očerki* (Moskva, 1959), pp. 220-233.

lates his destructive pen, according to this critic: "Finally, he frees himself entirely from ideas of every kind, and loses even the notion of connection between the happenings of life. ... Anticipating a little, I would here point to his comedy, *The Seagull*, where in defiance of all literary principles, the basis of action appears to be not the logical development of passions, or the inevitable connection between cause and effect, but naked accident, ostentatiously nude." [3] The view of Čexov which I am putting forth does not seem to me at all inconsistent with Šestov's interpretation; indeed, he offers a valuable insight into Čexov. The only possible area for disagreement would be in his definition of hope. There appears to be an implicit premise here that hope is dependent on the operation of logical processes. Čexov himself denies any such notion in "A Doctor's Visit" (*Slucaj iz praktiki*, 1898), as we shall see in the next chapter.

In more recent years proponents of Čexov the anti-rationalist, the portrayer of whimsical accident, have placed their emphasis on his literary devices. They have endeavored to make out a case for him as a rebel against the literary tradition of realism and prefer to see his role in literary history as that of a bridge between realism and symbolism. P. Bicilli, for example, emphasizes Čexov's impressionism, and in analyzing his style, speaks of his "impressionistic representation of actuality ... which hinders its direct perception". [4] I would suggest that the purpose here is to obliterate the perception rather than simply to hinder it. His impressionism serves to question the nature of actuality itself. Another commentator, Arnold Hauser, has compared Čexov's literary devices with the painting techniques of such impressionists as Degas. Here is how he defines Čexov's impressionism in the formal sphere:

... this feeling that nothing in life reaches an end and a goal has considerable formal consequences; it leads to stress being laid on the episodical nature and irrelevance of all external happenings, it ... prefers to express itself in an ex-centric form of composition in which the given framework is neglected and violated. ... He follows a formal principle that is in every respect opposed to "frontality," one in which everything is aimed at giving the representation the character of something overheard by chance, intimated by chance, something that has occurred by chance. [5]

[3] Lev Šestov, "Anton Tchekhov: Creation from the Void", *Chekhov and Other Essays* (Ann Arbor, Michigan, 1966), p. 13.
[4] P. Bicilli, *Tvorčestvo Čexova: Opyt stilističeskago analiza*, Godišnik na universiteta sv. Kliment Oxridski; istoriko-filologičeski fakultet, XXXVIII, 6 (Sofia, Bulgaria, 1942), p. 70.
[5] Arnold Hauser, *The Social History of Art* (New York, 1958), IV, 209.

If we compare this statement with that of Šestov, quoted above, it is easy to follow the tradition which would connect Čexov with the aftermath of realism: "... the given framework is neglected and violated" in favor of 'chance' amounts to much the same thing as Šestov's conclusion, that "... in defiance of all literary principles the basis of action appears to be... naked accident". Though he employs his formal analysis towards quite different ends, Šestov is clearly the progenitor of modern Čexov criticism in the West.

The most recent of Čexov's critics to expound such a view of his stylistic features is Dmitrij Čiževskij, who offers probably the most sustained analysis of the anti-realist tendencies in Čexov. He notes:

Čexov relinquishes to a great extent the external motivation for dialogue and plot in his works, so characteristic of realism. In his longer stories so much happens "without any reason," that we may say this anticipates the main tendencies of symbolist writing, or the tendency to explain events through blind coincidence. ... While the realistic tradition was searching for a strong connection between the experiences and behavior of men and the events in their lives, in Čexov's works there is almost always an abyss between the hero's experiences and events, as well as between experiences and plot. Čexov, like the realists, tends to follow reality in giving dates, place names, and other "realia." But this reality seems and acts on the hero's experience only in an unmotivated, distorted, inadequate form: between the "external causes" and experience there is a strange disparity.[6]

Čiževskij further notes that after 1890 the verb 'seems' and the family of words related to it occur all the more frequently, indicating a displacement of actuality by the character's distorted or totally unrecognizable perception of it.

Not only in the realm of stylistic analysis, but also in discussions of Čexov's themes there has been a recent interest in what Charles Timmer has called 'the bizarre element' in Čexov's writings. Timmer defines the bizarre as the sudden intrusion of the 'irrelevant' on a situation and observes that one's reaction is 'bewilderment'. He points to numerous examples of the bizarre in the early stories and then goes on to say that "... the bizarre gradually disappears in Čechov's later work, or rather, it loses its grotesque aspect and approaches more and more that particular attitude toward things, which we call the absurd".[7] He insists,

---

[6] Dmitrij Čiževskij, "Über die Stellung Čechovs innerhalb der russischen Literaturentwicklung" in *Anton Čechov, 1860-1960: Some Essays*, ed. T. Eekman (Leiden, 1960), pp. 304-305.

[7] Charles B. Timmer, "The Bizarre Element in Čechov's Art" in *Anton Čechov, 1860-1960: Some Essays*, ed. T. Eekman (Leiden, 1960), p. 280.

however, that Čexov treats the absurd only incidentally, that his treatment of it never becomes the expression of a philosophical program:
"For Čechov life as such (existence) is neither absurd nor intelligible.
The absurd elements in his stories should therefore not be confused with
the absurd as idea." [8] I feel that Timmer here understates his case. Indeed, the essay as a whole provokes uncertainty as to why he brought
up the issue: if the absurd is only incidental, is it important? I would
argue that it is much more than incidental, that it is a basic element in
Čexov's entire artistic vision. Timmer's point is considerably more telling
when he writes: "The long standing controversy, whether Čechov was
an optimist or a pessimist... loses its meaning, when we realize that
Čechov, like every sensitive artist, was torn between two contrary insights: that the world, or life as such, is unreasonable and at the same
time, that man cannot leave off trying to find a reasonable explanation
for this world...".[9] With this formulation Timmer goes on to interpret
Čexov's references to the expectation of a beautiful life in the future
not as optimism, but as expressions of man's search for a rational
pattern in human experience.

Two principal kinds of problems – time and ambiguity – emerge in a
number of the more salient Čexovian explorations of a world in which
the nature of existence itself becomes extremely precarious. The pre-
cariousness derives from the fact that one's relationship to himself and
to life outside him is constantly changing; precisely for this reason it
becomes impossible, or at least ludicrous, for man to stop and make any
kind of definite statement about the nature of his existence. Time, of
course, lies at the heart of this problem: because it never stops, man
can never pause to analyze the nature of his existence. In several stories
from this period Čexov directs his attention to the role of time itself in
this process. Time involves both change and continuity, or at least repetition, which may be the illusion of continuity. Thus, a number of late
stories evolve around the relation of the past to the present, and the
conflict between continuity and change. Finally, in the plays Čexov
imposes this conflict on the future as well. The remainder of this chapter
will be devoted to a closer look at stories in which Čexov treats the
concept of time programmatically.

There is a further result of this vision: if our existence is precarious,
if the nature of being is in a constant process of alteration, then at any
given moment one's identity is always uncertain, one's relationship to

---

8 Charles B. Timmer, "The Bizarre Element in Čechov's Art", p. 280.
9 Charles B. Timmer, "The Bizarre Element in Čechov's Art", pp. 280-281.

oneself and to the world at large is forever ambiguous. Many of the later stories explore varieties of this ambiguity, which is a double-headed monster; it can be either thematic or stylistic, or there can be a combination of the two: stylistic ambiguity may be simply a manifestation of its thematic counterpart. The problem of ambiguity is the central issue in the following chapter.

There is a further difficulty in that the stories which explore time relationships frequently cross over into the realm of ambiguity; indeed, the unresolved conflict between permanence and change in a story such as "My Life" (*Moja žizn'*, 1896) may itself be a variety of ambiguity. Similarly, many stories which are not programmatically concerned with time, such as "The Lady with the Dog" (*Dama s sobačkoj*, 1899), will nevertheless incidentally introduce the time theme. Finally, the problem of time lies at the heart of the last story, "Betrothed", where the ambiguity depends on whether we see the stages in the heroine's life as a continuous process of moral growth, or of moral disillusionment. Thus, the division of the stories into categories of time and ambiguity is rather arbitrary, though tenable if we keep in mind the fact that these two problems in Čexov actually converge more often than they diverge.

The first of the time stories is a very short piece from 1894, "The Student" (*Student*). Here the essential problem is an attempt to determine the relationship of the past to the present, and beyond that to find a meaningful pattern in human history. In a later story, "My Life", two of the characters arrive at formulations of the entire problem of time, and at least one of their formulas is relevant here. In her letter of parting to Misail, Marja Viktorovna writes: "King David had a ring with an inscription on it, 'All things pass.' . . . All things pass, life too will pass, therefore one needs nothing" (IX, 182). In his summation of his own experience Misail arrives at the opposite formulation: "If I had the inclination to order myself a ring, I would select this inscription: 'nothing passes'" (IX, 189). These contradictory inscriptions have their own special meanings, their own special ironies, in "My Life", but in general the two mottoes form a useful summary of the entire problem of time in Čexov. It might be said that "The Student" deals with only one of the formulations: nothing passes. The central conflict evolves out of the implications contained in that statement.

The story opens with a change of weather: "At first the weather had been fine, calm" (VIII, 345), but by the end of the first paragraph it has turned cold. This paragraph presents the process of a basic alternation in the phenomena of nature, just as the remainder of the story dramatizes a basic alternation in Ivan Velikopol'skij's interpretation of history. It is important to see the process as a whole; there is both good weather and bad, there is repetition of both good and evil in history, a combination which Ivan himself is not able to perceive.

When the weather grows cold, Ivan's mood turns sour: "The student thought about the fact that just such a wind blew in the times of Rurik and of Ivan the Terrible and of Peter, and that in their time there was just such cruel poverty, hunger, just such straw roofs full of holes, ignorance, misery, just such a wilderness around, darkness, a feeling of oppression – all these horrors have been, are and will be, and just because another thousand years will pass, life will not become better" (VIII, 346). Here is the motto 'nothing passes', but with the emphasis on the repetition of a seemingly endless cycle of misery and despair.

But there is another side to this coin; if nothing passes, then whatever goodness there is in man, whatever faculty for compassion and love, is also repeated. Ivan comes upon two women sitting by a fire. A theological student, he retells the story of how Peter betrayed Christ. One of the women is moved to tears by his account. As he leaves them, he thinks: ". . . if she cried, then everything that happened to Peter on that terrible night has some kind of relation to her. . . . The past, he thought, is connected with the present by an uninterrupted chain of events, which flow one from another. And he thought that he had just seen both ends of the chain: shake one end of it and the other quivers" (VIII, 348). Particularly in view of its religious overtones, Ivan's idea here is closely analogous to the notion of the still point in T. S. Eliot's later poetry:

> Time present and time past
> Are both perhaps present in time future,
> And time future contained in time past
> If all time is eternally present
> All time is unredeemable.[10]

And later:

> At the still point of the turning world. . . .
> Except for the point, the still point,
> There would be no dance, and there is only the dance.[11]

[10]   T. S. Eliot, "Burnt Norton" in *The Complete Poems and Plays, 1909-1950* (New York, 1952), p. 117.
[11]   T. S. Eliot, "Burnt Norton", p. 119. My remarks on 'the still point' are based on Louis Martz's interpretation of this idea in his essay, "The Wheel and the Point: Aspects of Imagery and Theme in Eliot's Later Poetry" in *T. S. Eliot: A Selected Critique*, ed. Leonard Unger (New York, 1948), pp. 444-463. I have in mind particularly this sentence: "In 'Triumphal March' the crowd is seeking desperately for 'light,' for a still point in the meaningless flux of life without faith . . ." (p. 452).

What Ivan believes he has found is precisely the still point in human history. In the seemingly purposeless movement of time, there is a meaningful thread in experience. The irony in the story is that at this moment Ivan has already forgotten that just a trifle earlier he had discovered another still point, the still point of evil in the world. Therefore, at any given moment Ivan only half realizes his idea. The story as a whole, however, does contain both ideas, the meaningless repetition of evil in time, and the meaningful thread of human compassion. It is a further irony that the story of betrayal which he relates is a product and an expression of his sense of meaningless repetition in history. And yet his ultimate sense of the permanence of good is derived from the experience of telling his story. Thus, as a whole, the story simply maintains a balance of the tension implicit in the idea that nothing passes.

One story from 1897, "At Home" (*V rodnom uglu*), further explores the implications of the motto 'nothing passes'. Vera Kardina, after ten years at boarding school, is returning to her home in the steppe. Vera has forgotten that nothing passes and herein lies her problem: she believes she has escaped her past, that the time when servants were flogged, her grandfather's time, has come to an end, and that such a past has no relationship to her life. In short, she carries an implicit faith in the belief that there are such things as change and progress.

The past itself is symbolized by the steppe. This past is dead, and symbols of death are both seen and felt on the broad plains: ". . . in the distance an ancient grave-mound or a windmill . . . Birds fly singly low over the plain and the monotonous beat of their wings induces a drowsiness. It is hot. An hour or two passes, and still the steppe, the steppe, and still in the distance the grave-mound" (IX, 232). Both literally and symbolically, Vera is driving back into the dead past to which she belongs. Ironically, she has no understanding of this whatsoever. ". . . Vera, too, yielded to the fascination of the steppe, forgot about the past and thought only of how spacious it was here, how free; healthy, intelligent, beautiful, young – she was only twenty-three – until this time she had lacked in her life just this spaciousness and freedom" (IX, 233). But the spaciousness becomes utterly confining and the freedom she thinks she has found also restricts her. The question of freedom in regard to the past is an important issue both here and in "My Life". In both stories Čexov arrives at the view that the more we believe we are free of the past, the more bound to it we are. The only way to escape its grasp is to acknowledge its power over us. This is at any rate Misail's experience in "My Life". In the present story, however, Čexov focuses only on the first half of this idea: to believe one is free of the past is to be trapped by it.

Vera discovers that the local inhabitants live in a dead past. Reflecting on her neighbors, she finds that: "They seemed to have no fatherland, no religion, no public interests. When they talked of literature or discussed some abstract problem, it was obvious from Dr. Neščapov's face that the matter was of no interest to him whatever..." (IX, 238). The absence of all interests is, after all, one variety of death. After further exposure to her native corner, Vera begins to see the steppe in a different light: "And at the same time the endless plain, monotonous, without a single living soul, frightened her, and at moments it was clear that this calm green monster would swallow up her life and turn it into nothing" (IX, 235).

Finally, in a moment of exasperation at her maid, she cries: "'Get out! The rods! Beat her!'" (IX, 242). The echo of her grandfather's impotent shouts is unmistakable; her bondage to the past is finally realized. As the story ends, the symbol of the dead past is repeated: "It is necessary not to live your separate life, but to become at one with this luxurious steppe, boundless and indifferent as eternity, with its flowers, its ancient grave-mounds..." (IX, 243). But now together with the deadness of the past appears a symbol of life: the steppe contains not only grave-mounds, but flowers as well. Vera apparently submits utterly to the past, but the point is not so much her submission to a living death as it is the unavoidable relationship between one's past and his present.

"Three Years" (*Tri goda*, 1895) is one of the two most extended and extensive treatments of the time problem. If Čexov managed to break out of the short-story genre and into a form closer to that of the novel, then it was in this story, where the theme unfolds and evolves through an elaborate span of events. Čexov also explores his theme in greater breadth than is normally possible in the short story: it is developed in far more manifestations through the large number of characters.

This story too focuses on the relationship of the past to the present, but here, as in the plays, there is some effort to project this relationship on the future. Like "The Student" and "At Home", "Three Years" offers no solution to the conflict between permanence and change; it places a greater emphasis on the element of change, but it maintains the tension between these opposed forces. The two protagonists are Laptev, the son of a Moscow merchant, and Julija, the daughter of a provincial doctor. Each is trying to escape his past, to alter the circumstances of his life in such a way that he can place his faith in the viability of progress, and yet each seeks also something permanent, unchanging on which to hang his faith. In short, they wish to have their cake and eat it too; they would like to change all that is undesirable in the past and to make permanent whatever suits them. Their desires are similar to Ivan Velikopol'skij's semiconscious formulations.

As in "At Home" there are spatial correlatives for the differences in time: the past from which Laptev has emerged is the Moscow of the merchants, a district which he hates to visit now, and when at the end of the story Julija suggests that they must return to live in that district, Laptev is overwhelmed by despair: " 'But now, when you said that we must move to Pjatnickaja, to that prison, then I began to feel that I already have no future' " (VIII, 468). Julija's past is a small town somewhere in the provinces, and she has a firm belief in her ability to cut herself off from her past by marrying Laptev and moving to Moscow. Uncertain whether she should accept the proposal of this man whom she does not love, Julija finally agrees when she realizes that the marriage will provide an opportunity to escape her past: "... and she thought about the fact that she could now, if she liked, change her life" (VIII, 404). Similarly, the theater and artists' district of Moscow comes to symbolize the route of Laptev's attempted escape from his past: it is in this district that he has found interests which seem to him a mark of progress in his life, a step up the ladder in the human condition, as it were.

Variations on the theme are embodied in the experience of the secondary characters. Laptev's sister, Nina, who appears only at the beginning of the story, sums up the central dilemmas rather well. She is slowly dying of tuberculosis, and the regular changes in her condition serve as a constant reminder of the process of change in life; her complexion, which had formerly been rosy, is now pale. One of the changes in her condition seems particularly revealing: by disposition she had been full of laughter; when she is slowly dying, she still often laughs, but now the merest trifle is enough to set her off. Through the simple device of intensifying one element in Nina's makeup, Čexov conveys the sense of change. As a symbol, her behavior is particularly effective: Čexov preserves the paradox of permanence and change by revealing each through the same detail at the same time.

Another of the minor characters, Panaurov, Nina's husband, functions as comic relief in his observations on the effects of time. Panaurov was a former landowner, now turned leech. When he had used up the money from the sale of his estate, he married Nina, a wealthy merchant's daughter, rapidly consumed the money from the dowry, and now in desperation has gone to work in a government office. His own financial collapse is, of course, a sign of social change, and in several respects, especially his comic role, he reminds one of Simeonov-Piščik in *The Cherry Orchard*. One of the major signs of change in the story is the falling off of religious faith, particularly as we see it in Julija when she marries Laptev, and in Laptev's own rejection of his father's austere religiosity. Panaurov's attitude toward this aspect of the theme is close to parody: he lights his cigarettes (a fairly recent invention) from the holy lamp. Panaurov's quasi-philosophical reflection on the nature of change is: " 'Yes, everything on this earth comes to an end' " (VIII, 395). But Panaurov uses this sentiment simply to justify the fact that he has deserted his wife for a mistress. Another of the comic variations on the theme is Panaurov's attempt to seduce Julija on a train. His argument is that he is now too old to make love – a ruse to throw Julija off her guard. In a sense, he is using the concept of change to assert the 'permanence' of his interest in love.

Laptev's brother, Fëdor, performs a role somewhat like that of Nina: at moments he personifies the paradox of permanence and change. Reflecting on Fëdor's recent activities, Laptev concludes that "his brother's character was changing for the worse" (VIII, 410). But the change that he observes in his brother is a reversion to the religious interests of their father. At another point it is Fëdor who performs the most symbolic action to be found in any of the stories of time: "Fëdor opened his watch and for a long time, a very long time, looked at it with strained attention as though he wanted to detect the movement of the hand . . ." (VIII, 437). Again we have the paradox of permanence and change as Fëdor 'stops' to observe time passing.

Indeed, each character in "Three Years" seems to be in transit; he is breaking away from at least a part of his past, he is constantly being forced to re-evaluate his own character, as he is compelled to adjust to the changes time brings; yet he can never wholly dispense with his past. Near the end Laptev decides that he can make a new life for himself only if he forsakes Moscow and family. Thus, he would avoid the fate which he fears: becoming a slave to the family business. Yet he finds himself unable to leave.

The change which Julija so desired in her marriage has been effected, but she has lost as much as she has gained. When she returns on a visit to her native town, she meets a funeral procession, symbolic of the deadness of this past for her. She finds she is no longer the 'single joy' in her father's life, and when she goes to church, the service has ceased to hold its meaning for her. She has lost more than she desired. A bit later she reproaches Laptev for having taken her religious faith from her. What she wants, of course, is to reject what she dislikes from the past, but to retain the sense of permanence which religion offers.

Laptev does not think he is troubled by his break with the religious faith of his fathers, as Fëdor and Julija are. He associates religion with the stifling life of the Moscow merchant – the life he endured as a boy in his father's house. And yet, though he makes this break with the past, he finds that he still yearns for permanent values. When Polina, his former mistress, begins living with a mutual friend, Laptev "felt sad that there were no lasting, permanent attachments. And he felt vexed that Polina Nikolaevna had gone to live with Jarcev, and vexed with himself that his feeling for his wife was not what it had been" (VIII, 459). In essence, this irritation is Laptev's religious longing. The value of the religious experience for the other characters lies precisely in its permanence. Its beliefs exist outside of time and as such they offer an escape from time and change. Thus, Laptev's dilemma is that he wishes both to escape from time and to enjoy the benefits of its transitory nature. As he reflects on the happier moments of his boyhood spent with Fëdor, he says to Julija: " '. . . it seems to me that losing him, I am once for all cut off from my past . . . But now, when you said that we must move to Pjatnickaja, to that prison, then I began to feel that I already have no future' " (VIII, 468). He has no future because he is being returned to his past, while at the same time he is denied everything which he would cherish. Like Vera in "At Home", he is driven back into his past by the attempt to escape it. Furthermore, permanent attachments, that element of experience which he seeks, are denied him: Nina has died, his baby has died, his friendship with Polina has ended, Fëdor has changed, his father has died, and Laptev's own love for Julija has turned into indifference. Time seemingly has attacked him with a vengeance.

This is not entirely accurate, however. If he has only partially escaped his past, he has at least escaped from the more stifling aspects of his father's religiosity, he has found new values for himself in art, and Julija's original dislike of him has turned gradually into a mellowed love. There is no real hope for the future at the end of the story, but neither is there despair. The force of time has not acted decisively in either direction. Obviously, Laptev has learned something about the nature of permanence and change when the story asks: "What awaits

us in the future?" and he replies, " 'Let us live a while and we'll see' "
(VIII, 473).

Like "Three Years", "My Life" presents a broader panorama than
the short story can encompass. It is a portrait of an entire provincial
town, and the theme is the exposure of the paradox that none of its
inhabitants has any real faith in his own beliefs. "My Life" also resembles "Ward No. 6" in its condemnation of an entire society, though, as
previously observed, 'savage indignation' has been replaced now by a
calmer, more thoughtful narrative approach. Čexov achieves this through
the first-person narrator Misail, who is trying to escape from the hypocrisy which infests the town and its inhabitants, but who is also aware
that the same inconsistencies appear in his own life as in the lives of
those around him.

Central to the theme of "My Life" is the paradoxical relationship of
past to present existence, though this is by no means the only form of
paradox in the story. There are four characters who are united by their
rejection of the provincial town, Marja Viktorovna and Dr. Blagogo,
Misail and his sister Kleopatra. The revolt of the first two is utterly
unsuccessful, while that of the latter pair achieves a certain measure of
success. The motto which Marja sets up for herself, referred to above,
formulates one possible attitude toward past and present, and sum-
marizes the plight of the unsuccessful rebels: "King David had a ring
with an inscription on it: 'All things pass.' When one is sad, those words
make one cheerful, and when one is cheerful, they make one sad. I have
got myself a ring like that with Hebrew letters on it, and this talisman
keeps me from infatuations. All things pass, life will pass, one wants
nothing. Or at least one wants nothing but a sense of freedom, for when
anyone is free, he wants nothing, nothing" (IX, 182). Marja argues that
the past has no relation to the present, nor does the present have any
relation to the future. Thus, she is free of the power of the past. And
yet every phrase in this statement is contradicted by the testimony of
the story. She claims her philosophy keeps her from infatuations, but all
experience becomes for her nothing but infatuation – her enthusiasm
for agriculture, her desire to help the peasants, her love for Misail, and
finally her flight to America.

But perhaps most ironic is her desire for absolute freedom; what she
actually reaches is a condition of never-ending, temporary escape. Because she is constantly using her freedom to avoid the past, she is
powerless to change anything, and though she keeps running, she will
encounter the same kind of society wherever she may go. Thus, her

motto, "all things pass", leads to her perpetual defeat by the past itself. Misail is aware of this paradox: "I remembered from my childhood how a green parrot, belonging to one of the rich men of the town had escaped from its cage, and how for quite a month afterwards the beautiful bird had haunted the town, flying from garden to garden, homeless and solitary. Marja Viktorovna reminded me of that bird" (IX, 146). Marja has escaped from her cage, but her freedom, like the parrot's, dooms her to a meaningless repetition of flights. This bird imagery recurs obsessively throughout the story.[12]

Like Marja, Dr. Blagogo eventually flees from the town. He holds a concept of progress which results in a kind of perpetual, meaningless motion, a counterpart to Marja's desire for freedom. When Misail and Blagogo discuss the question of human progress, the latter observes:

"I am going up a ladder which is called progress, civilization, culture; I go on and up without knowing definitely where I am going, but really it is worth living for the sake of that delightful ladder; while you know what you are living for, you live for the sake of some people's not enslaving others, that the artist and the man who rubs his paints may dine equally well. But you know that's the petty, bourgeois, kitchen, grey side of life, and surely it is revolting to live for that alone? If some insects do enslave others, bother them, let them devour each other! We need not think about them. You know they will die and decay just the same, however zealously you rescue them from slavery. We must think of that great millennium which awaits humanity in the remote future" (IX, 132).

Blagogo is actually arguing against progress: the image of mounting a ladder for the sake of the ladder suggests a treadmill rather than progression. Further, when he argues against the abolition of human slavery, he is ultimately denying the value of progress. If man is to die anyway, why is any change desirable? A bit later he contends: " 'Cultured life has not yet begun among us. There's the same savagery, the same uniform boorishness, the same triviality, as five hundred years ago' " (IX, 141). In spite of all this, the same Blagogo considers himself the exponent of progress.

Summing up the experience of the story, Misail says of Marja and

[12] At the beginning of the story the bird imagery has a significant and characteristic relation to Misail, who consistently rejects the illusory freedom of the bird. The story opens with Misail's losing another position. His superior assures him he would have been 'sent flying' long ago but for the respect with which he regards Misail's father. Misail makes a bad joke, but a valid point about his own conceptions when he replies: " 'You flatter me too much, your excellency, assuming that I know how to fly' " (IX, 104).

the doctor: "She has America and her ring with the inscription on it, I thought, while this fellow has his doctor's degree and a professor's chair to look forward to, and only my sister and I are left with the old things" (IX, 185).

In the sense that Misail and his sister remain in the provincial town, it is true that they are "left with the old things". But the other side of the time paradox lies in the fact that only these two actually manage to change their lives. Misail defines his attitude in these terms: "If I had the inclination to order myself a ring, I would select this inscription: 'nothing passes'. I believe that nothing passes without leaving a trace, and that every step we take, however small, has significance for our present and our future existence" (IX, 184). Thus, the past invariably alters the present, and it is in this sense impossible to escape the past. Misail is constantly reminded of this in ironic ways; his father continually reproaches him for disregarding his forefathers and the family heritage. Misail acknowledges this heritage through his love for his father – a feeling which the father is unable to reciprocate. Another way in which he acknowledges or is unable to escape the past is his inability to outgrow his childish response to his father. The following scene represents their apparently eternal relationship:

"Don't dare to talk to me like that, stupid!" he shouted in a thin, shrill voice. "Wastrel!" and with a rapid, skillful, and habitual movement he slapped me twice in the face. "You are forgetting yourself."
When my father beat me as a child, I had to stand up straight with my hands held stiffly to my trouser seams, and look him straight in the face. And now when he hit me I was utterly overwhelmed and, as though I were still a child, drew myself up and tried to look him in the face. My father was old and very thin, but his delicate muscles must have been as strong as leather, for his blow hurt a good deal (IX, 107).

Finally, only by acknowledging the existence of the past in the present can one hope to change the present. At the end of the story Misail is triumphant. It is he, not Marja or Blagogo, who has managed to change his life; he announces that through his persistence the community comes to accept the fact that he is a first-rate house painter in spite of his noble rank. Thus, the two mottoes contain implications which contradict their overt meanings: 'all things pass' means that nothing passes, that one can change nothing, while to acknowledge that 'nothing passes' means that some things, at any rate, do pass, that one can change his life.

In his last three plays Čexov makes a specialty of projecting this exploration of past and present onto the future. In regard to time, what Čexov does in *Uncle Vanja, Three Sisters*, and *The Cherry Orchard* is essentially to maintain the balance between degeneration and progress, as well as between permanence and change. Perhaps the clearest instance of this is the final scene in *Three Sisters*; after all the confident avowals of faith in a better future and all the doubts about the possibility of change, the dialogue between Čebutykin and Ol'ga preserves the possibility of both views. Ol'ga says: "Oh dear sisters, our life isn't over yet. We shall live! The music plays so gaily, so joyously, and it looks as if a little more and we shall know why we live, why we suffer. ... If we only knew, if we only knew!" Čebutykin unwittingly offers her his own answer: "It's all the same! It's all the same!" And equally unwittingly, Ol'ga refuses to accept it: "If we only knew, if we only knew!" (XI, 303). The exchange is all the more effective because Ol'ga and Čebutykin are not responding consciously each to the other's views.

Uncle Vanja comes the closest to upsetting the balance of forces, here contained in the difference between aspiration and realization. Dr. Astrov insists, when he is explaining his historical map of the neighborhood, that man ought to create but that instead he destroys. And on parting he tells Elena: "... you are a good, sincere person, but it seems there is also something strange in your whole nature. ... it's strange how I am convinced that if you should stay on, there would be an enormous devastation" (XI, 236-237). Ultimately, Sonja's final words of comfort sound more like delusion than the expression of a hope.

Francis Fergusson has called *The Cherry Orchard* "a theater-poem of the suffering of change".[13] Lopaxin continually reminds everyone in the play that 'time is passing'. One could look upon the entire work as a study in the extent to which each character understands this remark. To take only three of the most salient points of view: Lopaxin himself is perhaps the most sensitive to it because, like Misail, he is most aware of his past and his inability to escape it wholly: once a peasant, always a peasant is the view he expresses in the first moments of act one. Ljubov' Andreevna seems to be almost outside time. She is in the grip neither of the past nor of the present. When she arrives at home, the children's room looks exactly the same to her; she cannot see that without children it is now a useless room; and yet the selling of the estate means very little to her; she seems to comprehend it best as the occasion on which her aunt in Jaroslavl' sends her the money that will enable her to return

---

[13]   Francis Fergusson, *The Idea of a Theater* (New York, 1953), p. 175.

to Paris. Firs, of course, is the only character who fully comprehends what the sale of the estate means, for to him it is not a change but an end.

Finally, then, Čexov arrives at no solution to the problem of time. There can be no solution in the conflict between permanence and change, and yet his explorations of the paradoxes inherent in our concept of time offer an illumination of the way it affects our confused response to existence.

IX

STORIES OF AMBIGUITY

One could, with respect to terminology, talk about either ambiguity or paradox in describing that particular aspect of Čexov's work which involves the concept of meaning in the later stories. If the term 'ambiguity' ordinarily denotes situations in which two or more interpretations can coexist, then it refers to a "both-and" type of relationship. The term 'paradox' normally indicates contradictory meanings, and thus refers to an "either-or" situation. The difficulty in regard to Čexov is that the two or more meanings of a given story are ordinarily opposed to each other. However, there is some precedent for calling this relationship ambiguous: William Empson's last two categories of ambiguity involve contradictory meanings,[1] and Edmund Wilson's initial example of ambiguity in Henry James' work is *The Turn of the Screw*, where a choice of interpretations hinges on two opposed suppositions: the governess does see the ghosts; she does not see the ghosts.[2] On the other hand, as Cleanth Brooks defines paradox in "The Language of Paradox"[3] the contradictory situations which he cites are invariably reconciled. Thus, one could define the type of ambiguity we usually find in Čexov's later stories as unresolved paradox. In the following collection of alternative readings one interpretation may appear considerably more plausible than another for a given story; however, my primary intention is to indicate that no single reading will adequately account for the whole fabric in any of these stories. This in itself is sufficient to establish their ambiguity.

Inasmuch as Empson and Brooks confine their discussions to poetry, they are using ambiguity and paradox in reference to particular words and phrases. Assuming that the semantic unit is correspondingly larger

---

[1] William Empson, *Seven Types of Ambiguity* (New York, 1955), pp. 199-264.
[2] Edmund Wilson, *The Triple Thinkers* (New York, 1948), pp. 88-95.
[3] Cleanth Brooks, *The Well Wrought Urn* (New York, 1947), pp. 3-22.

in artistic prose, we shall ordinarily be talking about ambiguity engendered by what Tolstoj called 'the labyrinth of linkages' of prose fiction.[4] In short, Čexov's ambiguity frequently emerges from the reader's perception of contradictions in parallel passages throughout a given story.

One of the clearest examples of Čexov's ambiguity is his last short story, "Betrothed" (*Nevesta*, 1903). It is useful for two reasons to begin here – because the ambiguity is closely related to the problem of time discussed in the last chapter and because "Betrothed" offers the reader his only opportunity to watch Čexov in the process of constructing a story which can be equally well interpreted in several different ways. This is made possible through the existence of a different, earlier version of the manuscript.[5] The ambiguity is related to the question of human progress versus the monotonous appearance of constant change which moves mankind neither forward nor backward – the ladder versus the treadmill. Framed after the manner of the announcer in a radio soap opera, the question in "Betrothed" is this: does the heroine, Nadja, escape the confines of her parents' narrow provincialism and will she eventually find a better life, or is she condemned to a constant flitting from one passion to another, each of which is essentially meaningless in its relation to all the others? The commonly accepted interpretation of the story is the first one, both in the West and in the Soviet Union.[6] In this reading Nadja gradually becomes aware of the *pošlost'* in life at

---

[4] See Victor Erlich, *Russian Formalism* (The Hague, 1955), p. 209.

[5] There are actually three complete versions of the manuscript in existence: the rough draft (IX, 505-528), the fair copy submitted to Miroljubov, the editor of the *Journal for Everybody* (*Žurnal dlja vsex*), where it was first published, and the final version, which appeared in the 1906 edition of Čexov's collected works and also in the 1944-51 Soviet edition (IX, 432-453). The magazine version is available in *Literaturnoe nasledstvo: Čexov*, ed. V. V. Vinogradov *et al.* (Moskva, 1960), LXVIII, 87-109. Although most of the crucial changes had already been incorporated in the magazine version, for the sake of simplicity my references are limited to the rough draft and the story in its final form, as it appeared in the 1906 edition.

[6] See in particular, Ronald Hingley, *Chekhov: A Biographical and Critical Study* (London, 1950), pp. 170-171; V. Ermilov, *Čexov* (Moskva, 1949), p. 414; and Zinovij Papernyj, *A. P. Čexov: Očerk tvorčestva* (Moskva, 1960), pp. 280-291. From my own experience I should like to add that during the 1960 centennial celebrations of Čexov's birth, educational institutions in Moscow were deluged with posters describing what was purported to be Čexov's formula for a better life in the future, such as this quotation from "Betrothed": "Oh, if only that new, bright life would come more quickly – that life in which one will be able to face one's fate boldly and directly, to know that one is right, to be lighthearted and free! And sooner or later such a life will come" (IX, 449).

home, aware too of the fact that nothing in her family's way of life has changed during the past twenty years. Under the influence of a friend studying at the university, Saša, she realizes that her forthcoming marriage would condemn her to just such a life forever. Therefore, she takes Saša's advice, breaks off her engagement, and leaves her family to study. After a year at the university she returns home on a visit and finds that she has definitely outgrown her earlier life and confidently looks forward to a much better and more interesting one in the future. This interpretation starts running into difficulties when one notices that of all the Čexov characters who discuss the future only Nadja and possibly Trofimov in *The Cherry Orchard* are so unreservedly committed to their faith in a better future.

The second possible interpretation would see Nadja going through a series of awakenings and a process in which each new stage implies a rejection of the previous one. We see such a process in her disillusionment with the people who guide her. At the beginning of the story she believes that her mother is an extraordinary person, but as Saša comes to have more influence over Nadja, the mother becomes increasingly ordinary until finally Nadja can no longer understand why her mother ever struck her as remarkable.

Even before she leaves home, the process of disillusionment with Saša gets under way: " 'He is a strange, naïve man', thought Nadja, 'and in his dreams, in all these wonderful gardens, unusual fountains, one feels something absurd', but for some reason in his naïveté, even in this absurdity there was so much beauty that scarcely had she thought about going away to study when a cold feeling would pour through her heart and her bosom and she was filled with a feeling of joy and delight" (IX, 439).

When she tells Saša that she has made up her mind to leave, he is delighted: "But she looked at him, not blinking, with large, adoring eyes, as though spellbound, expecting him to say to her immediately something significant, limitless in its importance; he hadn't yet told her anything, but already it seemed to her that something new and broad was opening before her, something she hadn't known about earlier, and already she was looking at him full of expectation, ready for everything, even death" (IX, 444). But instead of saying something significant Saša immediately plunges into talking about the details of their departure.

These hints at disillusionment with Saša are not fully realized until she sees him again after a year of study, when he appears to her "grey, provincial" (IX, 446). As she sits in his room looking at him, "... for some reason Andrej Andreič rose up in her imagination and the naked lady with the vase [an earlier image of the *pošlost'* she associated with her prospective marriage to Andrej] and all her past which seemed to her now so far away, like childhood. And she started crying because Saša already seemed to her not so new, intellectual, interesting as he had been last year" (IX, 446-447). She comes to the conclusion that "from Saša, from his words, from his smile, and from his whole figure came something out of date, old fashioned, done with long ago, and, perhaps, already departed for the grave" (IX, 447). Saša is dying of tuberculosis, but in context obviously this speech points to something more than a premonition of his death.

In the final scene she is at home again on a visit. She reaffirms her faith in a better future and receives a telegram announcing Saša's death. The last paragraph reads: "She went up to her room to pack, and the next morning said goodbye to her own, and vibrant, joyful left the town – as she supposed, forever" (IX, 450). These words convey several facts about the present but say nothing really about the future. We know for certain only that Nadja thought she would never return. It is equally possible that she is right and that she is wrong. If we keep in mind the fact that we have twice observed her going through this process of excited expectation followed by disillusionment, the last phrase suggests the possibility that the whole process is beginning all over again. Therefore, the question remains: has Nadja escaped a narrowly provincial life and will she find some kind of more exalted existence, or is she condemned to an endless repetition of these awakenings and disillusionments? It seems to me both interpretations are equally tenable and this, of course, is at the heart of the story's ambiguity.

The original version was considerably less susceptible to the latter reading. In the rough draft there is no doubt that Nadja is moving forward to a better life; the concept of an endless series of illusions is simply not there. Probably the most important changes from this point of view concern the presentation of Saša's character, particularly as it appears in several of the scenes just discussed. When Nadja announces to Saša that she is going away to study, she does not await something significant from his lips. She has no expectation for him to disappoint; instead, he makes just the kind of speech that Nadja in the finished version hopes to hear:

"Listen to me. We will speak seriously," he began, frowning. "I am convinced, believe deeply that Russia needs only two sorts of people: the holy and the enlightened. I deeply believe in this and consider it my duty to convince others, such as you. We live in rude, ignorant times, we must go for a minority. I swear to you, you will not regret it, will not swerve, and you'll marry, and your bridegroom will be a remarkable man," again he started laughing. "Go away to study and there let fate carry you where it will. And so shall we go tomorrow?" (IX, 521).

In short, by dropping this speech Čexov reversed the conception of Saša's character in this scene. Indeed, Saša deteriorates at several points in the revision; thus, originally, when Nadja visits him after her year of study, she does not classify him with those elements of her old life which she had rejected.

When she returns home for a visit, she makes this observation on her life – an observation subsequently dropped: " 'I am satisfied, mama. Naturally, when I began my courses, I thought I would attain everything and that I'd want nothing more, but as I went to school and studied, new plans opened out, and then again new plans, and always broader and broader, and it seems there isn't and never will be an end to either work or anxiety' " (IX, 525). This speech causes the reader to set more store by Nadja's understanding of herself than he can in the finished story. The final paragraph was also rewritten. Here is first the original and then the revised version:

She went up to her room to pack and the next morning she left; before her she pictured a broad, pure life of labor (IX, 527).

"Goodbye, dear Saša!" she thought, and before her she pictured a new life, broad and vast, and this life, still not clear, full of mysteries, attracted her and beckoned her to it.
She went up to her room to pack, and the next morning she said goodbye to her own, and vibrant, joyful, left the town – as she supposed, forever (IX, 450).

This rearrangement of the elements obviously indicates, it seems to me, an effort to make Nadja's future considerably less certain, to cast a final doubt on her outcome.

If there is a deliberate effort to plant ambiguity at the very core of the story, then what is the significance of this effort? As in the great majority of the last stories, the point of the ambiguity is to highlight the precarious relationship between actuality and one's consciousness of it. Čexov's ambiguity is always a reflection of the ambiguity inherent in the character's relationship to his existence: he can never be certain just what that relationship is, and finally in one of the very last stories, "The Bishop", there is some doubt whether a relationship exists at all.[7]

"The Black Monk" (*Černyj monax,* 1894) is possibly the earliest story in this cycle. If there is ambiguity here it would seem to be of an accidental nature. Apparently, it is the story of a young scholar who deludes himself into believing that he is a man of genius rather than an ordinary person. His delusion destroys not only himself but his sweetheart and her father as well. There is no doubt that Čexov himself – if the author's intention makes any difference – did intend to convey this sort of pattern. In a letter to Suvorin, who had presumably accused Čexov of describing his own mental condition in the person of Kovrin, Čexov denies any suggestion that this might be a self-portrait, but goes on: "I wrote 'The Black Monk' without any despondent thoughts, in cold meditation. The desire to represent a megalomaniac simply came to me. This monk, wandering in a field, came in a dream, and when I woke up in the morning I told Miša [his brother] about him" (XVI, 118). Thus, Čexov apparently viewed Kovrin as the source of all the misfortunes in the story. But even if this is the case, the very fact that such delusions attracted Čexov at this time may be indicative of his interest in probing the question, what is real? If nothing else, we certainly have here a story in which the writer is studying the hero's distorted relationship to actuality.

There are, however, some indications that Kovrin's story may be simply an analogue to the story of his horticulturist friend Pesockij, or even that the force which destroys Kovrin and his friend may originate in Pesockij himself. It would be impossible to make out a fully developed case for this reading, but there are just enough hints to cast some doubt on the view that Kovrin's hallucinations are the first cause of the misfortunes. The view that he is the guilty one is expressed by Thomas Winner in his discussion of "The Black Monk": "The depiction of Kovrin is silhouetted against that of his friends, the family of the horticulturalist Pesockij. While there is something of the ridiculous about the

---

[7]   Dmitrij Merežkovskij wrote: "Čexov heroes have no life, there is only the daily routine without any event, or with only one event: death, the end of the daily routine, the end of being. Daily routine and death: these are the two fixed poles of Čexov's world." See "Čexov i Gor'kij" in *Grjaduščij xam* (St. Petersburg, 1906), p. 50. I would say rather that the first pole – daily routine – has ultimately a dubious kind of being, or at least one is never exactly certain just what the nature of it is.

old horticulturalist, his useful labor forms a contrast to the fruitless intellectual endeavors of Kovrin." [8]

There is a suggestion in the opening description of Pesockij's estate that the organization of the land itself may reflect the dual nature of its proprietor. One is lulled into a ballad-writing mood by what is called the English garden and by a snipe with its mournful chirp, while the other part of the garden exhibits nothing but health and the genius of Pesockij for growing things.

The relationship between the horticulturalist and Kovrin verges on the abnormal; to a certain extent the older man looks upon the younger as his own reincarnation. Kovrin was orphaned as a child and brought up by Pesockij. At one point his daughter Tanja tells Kovrin: " 'Surely you know that my father worships you. Sometimes I think he loves you more than me. He is proud of you. You are a scholar, an unusual person, you have made a brilliant career for yourself, and he is sure that you will turn out so because he brought you up' " (VIII, 266). (Is it coincidence that the black monk will praise Kovrin in the same way, assuring him that he is an unusual person?) One evening Pesockij confides his fondest hope, that Tanja and Kovrin will marry; in this way Pesockij could be assured that his marvellous achievements in horticulture would be preserved and that his efforts would be perpetuated. In short, he would like to sacrifice his spiritual son and only daughter to his work. Later in the story when Kovrin is in the clutches of his hallucinations, he thinks about the ideal with which the black monk presents him: "To give away everything for an idea – youth, strength, health, to be ready to die for the general welfare..." (VIII, 280). This is the essence of the vision which Kovrin finds in his hallucinations; it is considered by his friends madness, but is it any less healthy than the sacrifice which Pesockij would ask of his children?

Pesockij's split personality and his likeness to the young scholar are made explicit at one point. Kovrin is reading over some of the articles Pesockij has written on horticulture and he notes the strange contrast between the health of the man's creative activity in the garden and the deadly venom contained in his scholarly articles: " 'His work is beautiful, dear, healthy, but here [in the articles] there are passions and war,' thought Kovrin. 'It must be that in all phases of life people of ideas are nervous and are distinguished by exalted sensitivity. Probably, it has

---

[8]   Thomas Winner, "Čechov and Scientism: Observations on the Searching Stories" in *Anton Čechov, 1860-1960: Some Essays*, ed. Thomas Eekman (Leiden, 1960), p. 332.

to be so' " (VIII, 274). Thus, the disease characterized by nervousness and sensitivity is as typical of Pesockij as it is of Kovrin.

There is one other peculiarity in the relationship between the young scholar and his friend: not only is it on the latter's estate that the black monk first appears to him, but at least three of these appearances follow immediately after Tanja sings a song which Kovrin comes to associate with the estate. Just prior to the monk's first appearance Kovrin claims that he had been thinking all day about the legend of the black monk, but it is only in the evening after hearing the song that his first hallucination occurs. Furthermore, the manifestation bears a closer resemblance to the ghostly appearance described in the song than it does to the legend: the song depicts a girl with a disordered imagination who hears beautiful sounds, but according to the legend, the black monk appears to perfectly normal people. In addition, the girl in the song hears celestial music, a parallel to the unearthly ideas that Kovrin hears from the black monk, while in the legend no sound is associated with the vision.

Shortly before the monk's first appearance Kovrin had been walking through the garden with Tanja. They had discussed the 'black, thick, sour smoke' which hung just above the ground and which had been produced to prevent frost from killing the plants. They had observed the workmen who "wandered through the smoke like shadows" (VIII, 265). When the black monk appears, "his bare feet did not touch the ground", and he "disappeared like smoke" (VIII, 271). Thus, the monk's first appearance is associated with Tanja's singing, and the black smoke which had hovered just above the ground in Pesockij's garden. Certainly Čexov was aware of these associations as he worked through the story.

The black monk's second appearance also bears a strong emotional connection with the Pesockijs, for it is the joy this second hallucination evokes in Kovrin which induces him to propose to Tanja.

Ultimately, Kovrin accuses the Pesockijs of ruining his life by curing him, while Tanja accuses him of destroying her own happiness and driving her father to despair. Both accusations are justifiable; Kovrin had been considerably more productive as a scholar before the doctors cured him of his hallucinations, and Pesockij was driven to the grave by what he considered his son-in-law's madness.

At the black monk's last appearance, two years after Pesockij's death, the hallucination is preceded for the third time by Kovrin's overhearing the song. Dying, he cries out to Tanja and to Pesockij's garden. His cry could be equally a plea for help or a cry of accusation, or both.

In "Betrothed" and "The Black Monk" the ambiguity hinges on the question, what has happened to the characters? In "The Darling" (*Dušečka*, 1898) it hinges rather on the question, what does the central character herself represent? The traditional interpretation sees Olen'ka as completely passive. This is the view taken by Renato Poggioli,[9] for instance, when he quotes with approval and accepts as a proper summation of Olen'ka's character this line from the story: "She wanted a love that would absorb her whole being, her soul, her mind, that would give her ideas, a purpose in life, that would warm her aging blood" (IX, 323). But there is another side to Olen'ka's life; there are hints that it so dominates the loved one that it eventually destroys him. At any rate, she completely takes over the opinions of her first two husbands, Kukin and Pustovalov, both of whom die. Describing her absorption of Kukin's opinions, Čexov writes: "Olen'ka was filling out and beamed with satisfaction, but Kukin was getting thinner and more sallow..." (IX, 317). The syntactical arrangement of the sentence hints at a direct relationship between Olen'ka's vigor and Kukin's languor. Though it does not necessarily mean this, it could be taken to imply that as Olen'ka emotionally feeds on her husband, she saps him of his vitality. Her third attachment is with the veterinarian, Vladimir Platonič. Her relationship with him differs in two respects from that with Kukin and Pustovalov. In the first place, the veterinarian is the only man to resent her parroting his opinions: " 'I've asked you before not to talk about things you don't understand! When veterinarians are speaking among themselves, please don't butt in! It's really annoying' " (IX, 322). In the second place, the veterinarian does not die; he finally deserts Olen'ka to return to his wife. Now it could be more than coincidence that these two sets of conditions occur in just these combinations.

Olen'ka's final encounter is with Saša, a young boy. It is a mother's love she shows here, but like the veterinarian, Saša deeply resents her fondling attentions. The final lines read: "... she goes back to bed and thinks of Saša who is fast asleep in the next room and sometimes shouts in his sleep: 'I'll give it to you! Scram! No fighting!' " (IX, 327). Obviously, Saša is having a dream in which he is talking with his schoolmates, but in view of the pattern established in Olen'ka's relation to those she loves, and in view of Saša's open resistance to her attentions, the final line may apply to Olen'ka as well. If not, then the ending

---

[9] See Renato Poggioli, "Storytelling in a Double Key" in *The Phoenix and the Spider* (Cambridge, Massachusetts, 1957), pp. 109-131.

appears considerably less relevant to the story than Čexov's endings normally are.

Frequently Čexov's ambiguity hinges on his characters' social position. In several stories the plight of the socially displaced person creates the ambiguity – a man like Lopaxin in *The Cherry Orchard* who is both peasant and landowner, or neither, occupying a no man's land in between. In this case the ambiguity is apt to be considerably more all-pervading, inasmuch as the character is no more certain of his situation than the reader is. In "A Woman's Kingdom" (*Bab'e carstvo*, 1894) Anna Akimovna, the young lady who owns a factory, finds her position in society utterly confusing. She does not know who she is or how she is expected to act. Her dilemma is fairly well summed up in this passage: "Fate itself had flung her out of the simple working-class surroundings, in which, if she could trust her memory, she had felt so snug and at home, into these immense rooms, where she could never think what to do with herself and could not understand why so many people kept passing before her eyes. What was happening now seemed to her trivial and useless since it did not and could not give her happiness for one minute" (VIII, 315). She is in the absurd position of managing a factory whose workings are totally inexplicable to her.

One symptom of Anna's social displacement is the impossibility of deciding what sort of mate would be proper for her. She is constantly being advised by the other characters on what she ought to do about marriage, and each piece of advice conflicts with all the other suggestions. This too is, of course, a reflection of her ambiguous position. She is advised to marry a gentleman, to marry a merchant, to marry one of the factory hands, not to marry at all, but simply to have love affairs. Each of her counselors assures her that his course of action is best for a person in her position, but no two people can ever agree on what her position is. This aspect of Anna's dilemma is neatly evoked by the juxtaposition of two scenes involving her status in regard to marriage. At one point she wishes that her father were still alive so that he might select her prospective husband for her, thus relieving her of the decision. Her reflections are interrupted by the appearance of a servant who begs her to decide for him what he should do about his own marriage. She simultaneously occupies the positions of child and mistress. It is true that she needs guidance, and it is equally true that she must give guidance.

The setting suggests another dimension of her ambiguous position. The story covers a twenty-four-hour period from Christmas eve to

Christmas night. The parallel between the humble origins of Christ, the lord of men, and Anna Akimovna, the daughter of an ordinary workman, who has become herself the mistress of two thousand workers is inescapable. Further, the title, in Russian if not in English, suggests the major ambiguities of the story: *bab'e* (an adjective derived from a noun signifying a peasant wife) points to the incongruity of a person of humble origins who is the ruler of a kingdom, as well as to the problem of marriage.

The ambiguity of the simple working man turned factory owner crops up in another story, "A Doctor's Visit" (*Slučaj iz praktiki,* 1898), which is distinguished by its revelation of an absurd situation; both the content of the story and the treatment of that content defy any rational approach to the factory owner's problem. The story is filled with all kinds of incongruities. To begin with, a doctor, Korolëv, is called in to treat a physical ailment which is actually spiritual in nature. As Korolëv later rephrases his duty, he is being asked to cure an incurable disease. Finally, the man of medical science is forced to account for his patient's malady by conjuring up a devil, a red-eyed monster, who is held responsible for it.

Incongruity informs every detail in the lives of the Ljalikovs, the factory owners whose daughter, Liza, is the patient. Liza's mother wears a "black silk dress with fashionably styled sleeves, but, judging by her face, she was simple, poorly educated . . ." (IX, 305). When Korolëv looks at a portrait of the father, he finds that it accurately reflects the spiritual imbalance of the whole family. Ljalikov's "frock coat fits like a sack. ... His culture is meager, luxury accidental, stupid, uncomfortable, like this frock coat; the floors are irritating with their polish, the chandelier is irritating, and for some reason one is reminded of a story about a merchant who would go to the baths with his medal around his neck" (IX, 308).

Owing to her own sense of social inadequacy, the mother is forced to hand over the duties of mistress of the house to the governess, Xristina Dmitrievna. Thus, it is the latter who receives Korolëv and acts as hostess at dinner. This is an appropriate gesture, for as the story develops, Korolëv realizes that the governess is the only person in the entire household who enjoys any benefit whatsoever from the factory. After viewing the miserable conditions of the workers in its five plants and the unhappiness of the owners, Korolëv arrives at the conclusion that ". . . these five plants operate and poorly made cotton prints are sold at eastern markets only in order that Xristina Dmitrievna can eat sterlet and drink madeira" (IX, 310). In short, the entire system is absurd; the nominal master has become his servant's servant. Korolëv feels he can understand a system in which the strong exploit the weak, but it is "a logical absurdity when both strong and weak fall as a sacrifice to their mutual relations, involuntarily submitting to some controlling force, unknown, standing outside life, foreign to man" (IX, 311).

Mood is an extremely important factor in this story, and Korolëv's responses now become directed more by emotional stimuli than by reason. In the courtyard in front of the house he hears metallic sounds tolling the hour in the various plants: "And it was as though in the midst of the night silence a monster with crimson eyes had made these noises, the devil himself, who lorded it over both the masters and the workers here, and who deceived both them and others" (IX, 310). Thus, Korolëv is forced to conjure up a devil, or a monster with crimson eyes – another logical absurdity – to account for the absurdity of this life.

The story ends with a scene in which the doctor tries to 'treat' his patient by assuring her that the present is a very difficult time and that within a generation or two the problems and doubts which face those living now will have solved themselves. In one sense, his treatment is a purely emotional one, just as the disease is. But there is a difficulty here: logically, how can his reassurances that the problems of the present, which cannot even be understood – how can these reassurances carry any weight of conviction? The answer would seem to be that in a hopeless situation and one that is absurd, the only source of hope left is in the absurd itself. In other words, his hope for the future is at least no more irrational than the hopelessness of the present. And this might be Čexov's answer to Lev Šestov: to ignore logical processes does not necessarily mean to kill all hope. Although the ambiguity does not envelop the narrative so completely in "A Doctor's Visit" as in the other stories discussed, nevertheless the question of the Ljalikovs' status is central to the treatment of their absurd situation. This is one of the rare stories in which Čexov explicitly handles the absurd.

A consciousness of social displacement also pervades "The New Villa" (*Novaja dača*, 1899). The engineer Kučerov, who comes of wealthy and distinguished parentage, and his wife, the granddaughter of a peasant, wish to establish democratic relations with the peasants who inhabit the neighborhood. But they are attempting to establish a relationship which cannot exist. While the peasants may defiantly shout, " 'We're not serfs now' " (IX, 331), they will deride what seem to them Kučerov's false pretenses: " 'Landowners too-oo! ... They've built a house, brought in horses, but maybe they aren't much themselves. Land-owners too-oo!'" (IX, 330). Given these conflicting social conceptions, a barrage of mutual misunderstanding is inevitable: when Kučerov's wife promises the peasants that her husband will build a school for the village children, she is certain she has displayed her goodwill. The peasants, recalling previous attempts by well-meaning people to help them – attempts which ultimately produced new burdens for them – consider her promise much closer to a threat than a sign of goodwill. The result of such conflicting interpretations is to produce a long series of acts the significance of which is certainly ambiguous when the en-gineer's point of view is juxtaposed with that of the peasants. The tech-nique in "The New Villa" is reminiscent of the multiple points of view on a single incident in the Japanese film, *Rashomon*. Both works point toward the relativity of truth, the impossibility of accurately defining one's relationship to his surroundings.

In several of the major stories written during this period the ambi-guity crystallizes in the narrator's uncertain attitude toward the people and events he describes. In "The House with a Mezzanine" (*Dom s mezoninom*, 1896) the ambiguity in Lida's character becomes a reflec-tion of the narrator's personality. Soviet interpretation, for which there is solid evidence, sees the story as a melodrama in which Lida, the older sister, is the villainess, destroying the romance between her younger sister, Misjus', and the painter-narrator, as well as exerting her will in local government affairs at every turn.[10] Certainly she displays a des-potic nature: she tyrannizes over Misjus' and her mother; she seeks power in the local *zemstvo* organization; there are hints that her in-struction of peasants appeals to her mainly as an outlet for her tyrannical tendencies; and she crushes the beginnings of love in Misjus' and the narrator.

However, to view the narrator and Misjus' as innocent victims of Lida's cruelty leaves a number of incidents and remarks unexplained. We must keep in mind the fact that we see Lida only through the narrator's eyes and that he himself vacillates in his attitude toward her. He begins by describing his life in the country: "Condemned by destiny to perpetual idleness, I did absolutely nothing" (IX, 86). Describing his impression of the two sisters, he observes: "And everything seemed to me young and pure, thanks to the presence of Lida and Misjus', and there was an atmosphere of refinement over everything" (IX, 89). He

---

[10]   Once again, the 'model' Soviet interpretation is to be found in Ermilov, *Čexov*, pp. 266-277.

makes this remark at a time when he had already seen enough of Lida to know her character and interests. He continues: "As a rule I sat on the lower step of the terrace; I was tormented by dissatisfaction with myself, grieved by the thought that my life was passing so rapidly and uninterestingly . . ." (IX, 90). This observation could refer equally well to either the romance beginning to develop between him and Misjus', or, in view of the artist's indolent life, it could also refer to his frustration at the contrast between his own inactivity and Lida's absorption in her work. As a matter of fact, in a later scene when Lida and the artist attack one another's social ideas, she accuses him of criticizing her to cover his own indifference. And he himself confesses to a friend that: "From my earliest days I've been wrung by envy, self-dissatisfaction, and distrust in my work" (IX, 94). Viewed in this light, the relationship between Lida and the narrator is ambiguous through its vagueness.

Unlike her sister, Misjus' is an extremely passive personality. She does everything her sister tells her, and certainly one reason Lida resents the artist's presence is that she fears he will disrupt her influence over her sister. The artist accepts a peculiar role in his relationship with Misjus' also: he becomes her spiritual guide for a short time, only because she expects this of him. The possessor is also the possessed: "Ženja [Misjus'] thought that as an artist I must know a great deal and that I can accurately guess at what I don't know. She wished I would lead her into the region of the eternal and the beautiful, to that higher world in which, according to her, I was my own master, and she talked with me of God, eternal life, miracles. And I, who had not admitted that myself and my imagination would perish forever after death, answered, 'yes, man is immortal,' 'yes, eternal life awaits us,' while she listened, believed and did not demand proof" (IX, 92). He indicates his passive nature again when he bows before Lida's decision that the romance must come to an end. At the real center of the story, then, stands the narrator, who vacillates between the extreme character types of Misjus' and Lida, who leads and is led by Misjus', who admires and abhors the strength of Lida's personality.

Nikitin, the central character in "The Teacher of Literature" (*Učitel' slovesnosti*, 1894), if not ambivalent, is certainly shifty in his attitude toward his environment. D. S. Mirsky is the spokesman for the standard interpretation of the story:

Chekhov excels in the art of tracing the first stages of an emotional process; in indicating those first symptoms of a deviation when to the general eye, and to the conscious eye of the subject in question, the nascent curve still seems to coincide with a straight line. An infinitesimal touch, which at first hardly arrests the reader's attention, gives a hint at the direction the story is going to take. It is then repeated as a leit-motiv, and at each repetition the true equation of the curve becomes more apparent, and it ends by shooting away in a direction very different from that of the original straight line. ... In "The Teacher of Literature" the straight line is again the hero's love; the curve, his dormant dissatisfaction with selfish happiness and his intellectual ambition.[11]

Mirsky assumes that Nikitin comes to a real awareness of the false values in his life, but there remains a nagging doubt about whether such an awareness ever actually occurs. Nikitin's peculiarity is that mood alone governs his reactions to the world. His inner attitude determines the nature of the external world, as if the latter were dependent on the former. We are introduced to a man whose emotional response bears no direct relationship to the stimulus. Therefore, we have no means of knowing whether his feelings are in any way permanent or simply the result of a combination of factors which make up his mood: "Since Nikitin had been in love with Maša, everything at the Šelestovs pleased him: the house, the garden, and the evening tea, and the wickerwork chairs and the old nurse, and even the word 'loutishness' which the old man was fond of using" (VIII, 352). Here he is clearly reacting not to the Šelestov family, but to his love for Maša.

After their marriage he tells Maša: " 'But I don't look upon my happiness as on something that has come to me by accident, as if from heaven. This happiness is a perfectly natural, consistent, logically probable occurrence. I believe that man is the creator of his own happiness and I am now taking precisely that which I have created' " (VIII, 367). Nikitin is probably right in what he says, but ironically for the wrong reason. He believes his happiness is something real which he has created, but it exists only in his own imagination. It cannot operate independently of his mood; thus it has no real foundation.

Here is Nikitin's 'awakening': in bed one night he thinks that there is "another world. ... And he had a passionate poignant longing to be in that other world, to work himself at some factory or big workshop, to speak with authority, to write, to publish, to raise a stir, to exhaust himself, to suffer..." (VIII, 369-370). But this other world is another product of Nikitin's imagination; it bears no direct relation to his experience.

[11]   D. S. Mirsky, *A History of Russian Literature* (New York, 1949), p. 362.

The weather, a detail from actual experience, is a revealing reference point in the story. Just after his marriage Nikitin writes in his diary: "I recalled our first meetings, our rides into the country, my declaration of love, and the weather, which as though on purpose had been exquisitely fine all summer" (VIII, 364). But the weather which Nikitin thought so delightful when it fitted his own concept of the world, has no influence over him when his mood changes. One year later, "Spring was beginning as exquisitely as last year, and it promised the same joys..." (VIII, 371). But now Nikitin notes in his diary: "There is nothing more terrible than vulgarity. I must escape from here, I must escape today, or I shall go out of my mind!" (VIII, 372). Frequently during the course of the story Čexov permits us to read passages from Nikitin's diary. Certainly this device increases our sense of direct contact with Nikitin, but as a way of representing the world to which he responds it is far from direct. It blurs our perception of external reality to a point where we have no basis for judging the appropriateness of Nikitin's responses. Thus, we are left not quite certain whether this is an awakening to the actual world around him, or whether it is another of his moods, no more accurate a reflection of actuality than his previous one. Čexov offers us no way of knowing for sure, and herein lies the ambiguity.

By way of contrast, James Joyce's "Araby" is another story of disillusionment, but it contains no ambiguity whatsoever. The hero's romantic concept of a village fair is violently shattered by the conventionality and crudeness of the real thing, but in Joyce the hero's realization is of secondary importance. His preconception and the stark reality are the two focuses for the story. The reader knows what the hero thought the fair would be like and he knows what it is actually like, while Čexov limits our perception of the real to Nikitin's impressions of it.

In the trilogy of stories from 1898, "The Man in a Case" (*Čelovek v futljare*), "Gooseberries" (*Kryžovnik*), and "About Love" (*O ljubvi*), there is a problem in the way the narrator understands his own story and in the extent of his commitment to the principles he espouses. In this series the 'labyrinth of linkages' extends from one story into the next. In the first there are two central characters, Burkin and Ivan Ivanyč, who are joined by a third figure in the next two, Alexin. All three stories focus on the theme of *futljarnost'*,[12] as the title of the first pointedly reminds us. In "The Man in a Case" Burkin, the narrator, apparently

---

[12] See Chapter IV, footnote 2 and Chapter VII above for some further remarks on the concept of *futljarnost'* in Čexov's work.

comprehends that *futljarnost'*, retreat and escape from life, is not a peculiarity of Belikov alone. He observes at the end of his narrative that within a week of Belikov's death life in the town had slipped back into its familiar pattern and he asks how many "such men in shells were left, how many more of them there will be" (IX, 264). Then Burkin and Ivan Ivanyč step outside to look at the night:

It was already midnight. On the right could be seen the whole village, a long street stretching far away for some three miles. Everything was sunk in deep, silent slumber; not a movement, not a sound; one could hardly believe that nature could be so still. When on a moonlit night you see a wide village street, with its cottages, its haystacks, and its willows that have dropped off to sleep, a feeling of serenity comes over the soul; as it rests thus, hidden from toil, care, and sorrow by the nocturnal shadows, the street is gentle, sad, beautiful, and it seems as though the stars look down upon it kindly and tenderly, and as if there were no more evil on earth, and all were well. On the left, where the village ended, the open country began; the fields could be seen stretching far away to the horizon, and there was no movement, no sound in that whole expanse drenched with moonlight (IX, 264).

The earth itself is enveloped in a shell which lulls one; the spirit of *futljarnost'* spreads over the entire world. Burkin apparently succumbs to its spell as he falls asleep. Ivan Ivanyč, on the other hand, becomes extremely agitated and extends the implications of his friend's story: "'And isn't the fact that we live in the stifling, crowded city, write useless documents, play whist – isn't this a shell? And that we spend our whole life among loafers, petty quarrelers, stupid, lazy women, speak and hear various inanities – isn't this a shell? Now if you like, I'll tell you a very instructive story'" (IX, 265).

When Ivan Ivanyč does tell his story in "Gooseberries" the confusions multiply because his behavior and even his words contradict his narrative. The two friends visit Alexin's estate in the country, where their first action is to bathe. Ivan Ivanyč is especially taken with his bath in the open air and continues to splash about rapturously long after his companions have finished. The image that emerges is of a man who deeply loves the country from which he has long been cut off by life in the city. But his story concerns his brother, who retreats from city to country, to retire in the shell of a small estate. When Ivan Ivanyč observes, "'... I never sympathized with his desire to lock himself up for his whole life on his own country estate'" (IX, 269), his words fail to jibe with his obvious delight in the country life.

After explaining that his brother's cramped style of living made him realize that his own life was no less shell-like, Ivan Ivanyč says: " 'I then left my brother's place early in the morning, and since then living in the city has become unendurable for me. Peace and quiet oppress me...' " (IX, 274). It is unclear whether Ivan Ivanyč realizes that at this point he is talking about both city and country. There is also the possibility that his behavior in the bath contradicts these words.

There is a further contradiction in his statement that his brother's way of life showed him the inadequacy of his own behavior: he subsequently rejects the implications of this awareness for his own life when he pleads that he is now old, and instead implores Alexin, who is younger, to live in a way which he himself refuses to do. Alexin, incidentally, is unmoved, seeing no connection between Ivan Ivanyč's story and his own life.

When the three men retire for the night, Ivan Ivanyč falls asleep instantly, as if he is no longer troubled by his own agitation. This time it is Burkin who cannot fall asleep, irritated by the smell of tobacco still burning in Ivan Ivanyč's last pipe. It may be that Burkin is aware of the implications in the tale and that the smell of the pipe is a vague reminder of Ivan Ivanyč's plea, or it may be that Burkin is aroused, ironically, by the irritating smell to a far greater degree than he was by Ivan Ivanyč's stirring message, or it may be, as Mark Schorer has suggested, that the smell of the pipe is "the smell of some lingering falsehood, of Ivan's story, in fact, which tried at once to prove and disprove its point".[13]

"About Love" is Alexin's story of how he and a young woman sacrificed their love for the happiness of others; the young woman already had a husband and children. His point is that he and the woman made a mistake, that now he feels everything should have been sacrificed for the only real love he would ever know. Alexin's story is a protest against the concealment of real feeling under the protective cloak of social convention. It is also an answer to Ivan Ivanyč's appeal at the end of "Gooseberries": " 'There is no happiness and there shouldn't be, but if there is a meaning and purpose in life, then this meaning and purpose lie not in our happiness but in something more rational and greater. Do good!' " (IX, 274). In effect this is what Alexin has done, and the result is his own brand of *futljarnost'*.

The story ends on an irrelevance as Burkin and Ivan Ivanyč recall having met the woman whom Alexin loved: "Burkin was even ac-

[13] *The Story: A Critical Anthology*, ed. Mark Schorer (Englewood Cliffs, New Jersey, 1950), p. 64.

quainted with her and found her beautiful" (IX, 285). The irrelevance points up the failure of both men to comprehend the correlation between Alexin's experience and theirs. The series of stories possesses its own inner intensity as it moves from Burkin's account of an acquaintance to Ivan Ivanyč's account of his brother to Alexin's account of himself, while at the same time the sense of the characters' commitment to their principles becomes increasingly hazy. There is a final parallel between Burkin in the first tale and Alexin in the last. Each man's *futljarnost'* has taken the form of a rejection of love, and there may be a further hint at Alexin's resemblance to Belikov in the image of a squirrel in its cage which is used twice to describe Alexin in "About Love". Thus, for all the intensity of conviction which these characters exhibit there is a strong sense that they fail to comprehend the nature of their own commitment – a sense which is reinforced by the disparity between their convictions and their acts.

In "The Lady with the Dog" (*Dama s sobačkoj*, 1899) the hero's inability to understand his own feelings infects the entire story to a point where the reader is unsure what has happened. Perhaps in Anna, Gurov has found the only real love of his entire life. As they wonder what they should do about their love, the story ends: "And it seemed that it would be a little while longer – and the solution would be found, and then would begin a new beautiful life" (IX, 372). It *seemed* that way, but on the other hand we know that Gurov has had a long history of self-deception:

Oft-repeated experience, actually bitter experience, had taught him long ago that every intimacy which at the beginning so pleasantly diversifies life and seems to be a sweet and easy adventure, among decent people, especially among Muscovites, who are sluggish and indecisive, inevitably grows into a real problem, extraordinarily complicated, and the situation finally becomes painful. But at every new meeting with an interesting woman this experience somehow slipped from his memory, and he felt a desire to live, and everything seemed simple and amusing (IX, 358).

The fundamental question which lies before Gurov at the end of the story is not what he and Anna will do in the future, but rather precisely what kind of relationship exists between them. Is this a new experience for Gurov, or is it merely a repetition of the emotional tangle he has been in so often before? Gurov himself is unable to answer and thus the narrative which describes their relationship is itself ambiguous.

The final story to be considered here, "The Bishop" (*Arxierej*, 1902), casts some doubt on the central character's mode of existence. The bishop is himself so uncertain that what he sees and feels in the present really exists, or that his past ever really existed, that his own actuality becomes tenuous at best. It is in this story, incidentally, that the word 'seems' comes close to replacing the verb 'to be'. It 'seems' to the bishop "as though in a dream or delirium" that he sees his mother for the first time in nine years standing among the crowd in church (IX, 416). Thinking on his younger days, he is confused, ". . . and all the past had left for somewhere far away into the mist, as if it had been dreamed" (IX, 423) ". . . and now that past rose up before him – living, fair, and joyful, as in all likelihood it had never been" (IX, 425). Curiously, he thinks of his life in the past in a foreign country as more real than his present life in his native country. The bishop does exist and he accurately perceives reality (his mother was standing there in church), but there is a serious disparity between reality and the bishop's perception of it, and this disparity becomes most acute when he is faced with those to whom he should be closest. We stand in a peculiar relationship to reality when we refuse to accept our principal means of confirming that reality – the evidence of our own senses.

At one point there is a kind of double doubting as to the bishop's existence. Katja, his niece, "gazed without blinking at her uncle, his holiness, as though trying to discover what sort of a person he was" (IX, 421). We are not told that Katja tried to discover what sort of person he was; rather, it is *as though* she tried to discover this. One possible implication is that if he does not really exist, then there is nothing to discover.

The bishop dies and his existence is quickly forgotten by everyone except his mother, who would sometimes tell acquaintances "about her children, her grandchildren, and about how she had had a bishop son (*syn arxierej*), and here she would speak timidly, fearing that they wouldn't believe her. . . . And as a matter of fact not everyone did believe her" (IX, 431). For sheer vague suggestiveness this is one of Čexov's finest passages. It may mean that some did not believe that one of her sons became a bishop, though the existence of a hypothetical son is not doubted; but the odd coupling of *syn arxierej* could carry a lingering doubt about the existence of the son himself, even of a hypothetical one. Her timid speech when referring to the bishop may imply her own doubt about his existence (either as son or bishop); even if she is sure she had a son and that son was a bishop, she has no faith in her ability to attest to such a reality before others. In short, an aura of doubt about existence itself hangs over the ending of "The Bishop".

Ambiguity is a concomitant of Čexov's impressionism; whenever our focus shifts from what is to what it seems to us to be, we have opened the floodgates to a deluge of possibilities, none of which can ever be certainties. In addition, Čexov's ambiguity forms one of the literary paths which move distinctly away from realism toward symbolism. His splintering of meaning within a character's perception of the external world forms a bridge between the realist's single-plane view of actuality and the symbolist's conception of heterogenous levels of actuality encompassed by a single image.[14] "The Bishop" is an appropriate story with which to end an account of Čexov's studies in the tenuous and uncertain nature of man's existence in a world whose exact proportions he is incapable of ascertaining, and where all truths are relative. Although this vision of life was not a consciously thought out and formulated philosophic conception, nevertheless it is a fundamental theme, which both in its presence and in the attempt at its denial, runs from the very earliest through the final stories that Čexov wrote. The last ten years represent the ultimate, though subdued, triumph of the chameleon over the dream.

[14] For an excellent discussion of the homogeneous nature of the realist's conception of reality versus the symbolist's renovation of heterogeneous, intertwining layers see Dmitrij Čiževskij, *Outline of Comparative Slavic Literatures*, Survey of Slavic Civilization, I (Boston, 1952), pp. 104-130, esp. pp. 105 and 123-124.

SELECTED BIBLIOGRAPHY

Aleksandrov, B. I., *Seminarii po Čexovu: Posobie dlja vuzov* (Moskva, 1957).
Belčikov, N. F., ed., *Čexov i ego sreda* (Leningrad, 1930).
Bentley, Eric, *The Life of the Drama* (New York, 1965).
Bicilli, P., *Tvorčestvo Čexova: Opyt stilističeskago analiza*, Godišnik na universiteta sv. Kliment Oxridski, istoriko-filologičeski fakultet, XXXVIII, 6 (Sofia, Bulgaria, 1942).
Booth, Wayne C., *The Rhetoric of Fiction* (Chicago, 1961).
Brewster, Dorothy and Angus Burrell, *Dead Reckonings in Fiction* (New York, 1924).
——, *Modern Fiction* (New York, 1934).
Brodskij, N. L., ed., *Čexov v vospominanijax sovremennikov* (Moskva, 1952).
Brooks, Cleanth, *The Well Wrought Urn* (New York, 1947).
Bruford, William H., *Chekhov and His Russia: A Sociological Study* (London, 1948).
——, *Anton Chekhov* (New Haven, Connecticut, 1957).
Bunin, Ivan, *O Čexove. Nezakončennaja rukopis'* (New York, 1955).
Cerf, Bennett and Henry C. Moriarty, eds., *An Anthology of Famous British Stories* (New York, 1952).
Čexov, Anton Pavlovič, *Polnoe sobranie sočinenij i pisem*, eds. A. M. Egolin and N. S. Tixonov, 20 vols. (Moskva, 1944-51).
——, *Ward Six and Other Stories*, trans. Ann Dunnigan (New York, 1965).
Čexov, Mixail P., *Anton Čexov i ego sjužety* (Moskva, 1923).
——, *Vokrug Čexova* (Moskva, 1959).
Čiževskij, Dmitrij, "Gogol: Artist and Thinker", *Annals of the Ukrainian Academy of Arts and Sciences in the U. S.*, II (Summer 1952), 261-279.
——, *Outline of Comparative Slavic Literatures*, Survey of Slavic Civilization, I (Boston, 1952).
Cross, Ethan Allen, *The Short Story* (Chicago, 1917).
Curtin, Constance, "Čexov's *Sleepy*: An Interpretation", *Slavic and East European Journal*, IX (Winter 1965), 390-400.
Derman, Avram B., *Anton Pavlovič Čexov: Kritiko-biografičeskij očerk* (Moskva, 1939).
——, *Moskva v žizni i tvorčestve A. P. Čexova* (Moskva, 1948).
——, *O masterstve Čexova* (Moskva, 1959).
——, *Tvorčeskij portret Čexova* (Moskva, 1929).
Eekman, Thomas, ed., *Anton Čechov, 1860-1960: Some Essays* (Leiden, 1960).
Èjxenbaum, Boris, *Literatura: Teorija, kritika, polemika* (Leningrad, 1927).
Eliot, T. S., *The Complete Poems and Plays, 1909-1950* (New York, 1950).
Elizarova, M. E., *Tvorčestvo Čexova i voprosy realizma konca XIX veka* (Moskva, 1958).

Elton, Oliver, *Chekhov* (Oxford, 1929).

Empson, William, *Seven Types of Ambiguity* (New York, 1955).

Erenburg, Il'ja, *Perečityvaja Čexova* (Moskva, 1960).

Erlich, Victor, *Russian Formalism. History – Doctrine* (The Hague, 1955).

Ermilov, Vladimir, *Anton Pavlovič Čexov* (Moskva, 1949).

Fergusson, Francis, *The Idea of a Theater* (New York, 1953).

Flores, Angel, ed., *Nineteenth Century German Tales* (New York, 1959).

Florinsky, Michael T., *Russia: A History and an Interpretation*, 2 vols. (New York, 1959).

Frye, Northrup, *Anatomy of Criticism* (Princeton, New Jersey, 1957).

Garnett, Edward, *Chekhov and His Art* (London, 1929).

Garšin, Vsevolod M., *Sočinenija* (Moskva, 1960).

Gerhardi, W., *Anton Chekhov: A Critical Study* (New York, 1923).

Gitovič, N. I., *Letopis' žizni i tvorčestva Čexova* (Moskva, 1955).

Gitovič, N. I. and I. V. Fedorova, eds., *A. P. Čexov v vospominanijax sovremennikov* (Moskva, 1960).

Givens, Seon, ed., *James Joyce: Two Decades of Criticism* (New York, 1948).

Gogol', Nikolaj V., *Sobranie sočinenij*, 6 vols. (Moskva, 1952).

Golubkov, V. V., *Masterstvo A. P. Čexova* (Moskva, 1958).

Gordon, Caroline and Allen Tate, *The House of Fiction* (New York, 1960).

Hagan, John, "Chekhov's Fiction and the Ideal of 'Objectivity' ", *PMLA*, LXXXI (October 1966), 409-418.

——, "The Tragic Sense in Chekhov's Earliest Stories", *Criticism*, VII (Winter 1965), 52-81.

Harrison, John William, "Symbolic Action in Chekhov's 'Peasants' and 'In the Ravine' ", *Modern Fiction Studies*, VII, 369-372.

Hauser, Arnold, *The Social History of Art*, 4 vols. (New York, 1958).

Hawthorne, Nathaniel, *Hawthorne's Short Stories*, ed. Newton Arvin (New York, 1955).

Hemingway, Ernest, *The Short Stories of Ernest Hemingway* (New York, 1938).

Hingley, Ronald, *Chekhov: A Biographical and Critical Study* (London, 1950).

James, Henry, *The Future of the Novel*, ed. Leon Edel (New York, 1956).

——, *The Short Stories of Henry James*, ed. Clifton Fadiman (New York, 1948).

Joyce, James, *The Portable James Joyce*, ed. Harry Levin (New York, 1952).

Kantemir, Antiox, *Sobranie stixotvorenij* (Leningrad, 1956).

Konšina, E. N., ed., *Iz arxiva A. P. Čexova* (Moskva, 1960).

Lermontov, Mixail, *Polnoe sobranie sočinenij*, ed. Boris Èjxenbaum, 5 vols. (Moskva, 1936).

Magarshack, David, *Chekhov: A Life* (New York, 1955).

——, *Chekhov the Dramatist* (London, 1952).

Mann, Thomas, *Last Essays* (New York, 1959).

Mansfield, Katherine, *Stories* (New York, 1956).

Maupassant, Guy De, *The Best Stories of Guy De Maupassant*, ed. Saxe Commins (New York, 1945).

Melville, Herman, *The Portable Melville*, ed. Jay Leyda (New York, 1952).

Merežkovskij, Dmitrij, *Grjaduščij xam* (St. Petersburg, 1906).

Mirsky, D. S., *A History of Russian Literature* (New York, 1949).

Mudrick, Marvin, "Character and Event in Fiction", *The Yale Review*, L (Winter 1961), 202-219.

Murry, John Middleton, *John Clare and Other Studies* (New York, 1950).

——, *Selected Criticism 1916-1957* (London, 1960).

Newman, Frances, *The Short Story's Mutations* (New York, 1925).

O'Connor, Frank, *The Lonely Voice: A Study of the Short Story* (New York, 1962).

O'Faolain, Sean, *The Short Story* (New York, 1951).
Papernyj, Zinovij, *A. P. Čexov: Očerk tvorčestva* (Moskva, 1960).
Poggioli, Renato, *The Phoenix and the Spider* (Cambridge, Massachusetts, 1957).
Rahv, Philip, *Image and Idea* (New York, 1957).
Reeve, F. D., "Tension in Prose: Čexov's 'Three Years' ", *Slavic and East European Journal*, XVI (Summer 1958), 99-108.
Roskin, A., *A. P. Čexov: Stat'i očerki* (Moskva, 1959).
——, *Stat'i o literature i teatre – Antoša Čexonte* (Moskva, 1959).
Saak'jan, Ju. A., ed., *Velikij xudožnik: Sbornik statej* (Rostov-na-Donu, 1959).
Schorer, Mark, ed., *The Story: A Critical Anthology* (Englewood Cliffs, New Jersey, 1950).
Šestov, Lev, *Anton Tchekhov and Other Essays* (Ann Arbor, Michigan, 1966).
Simmons, Ernest J., *Chekhov: A Biography* (Boston, 1962).
Šklovskij, Viktor, *O teorii prozy* (Moskva, 1925).
——, *Xudožestvennaja proza: Razmyšlenija i razbory* (Moskva, 1959).
——, *Zametki o proze russkix klassikov* (Moskva, 1953).
Sobolev, Jurij, *Čexov* (Moskva, 1930).
Struve, Gleb, "Chekhov in Communist Censorship", *The Slavonic and East European Review*, XXXIII (June 1955), 327-341.
——, "On Chekhov's Craftsmanship: The Anatomy of a Story", *The Slavic Review*, XX (October 1961), 467-477.
Tolstoj, Lev, *The Kingdom of God*, trans. Aylmer Maude (New York, 1951).
——, *Polnoe sobranie xudožestvennyx proizvedenij*, 15 vols. (Moskva, 1929).
Toumanova, N. N., *Anton Chekhov: The Voice of Twilight Russia* (New York, 1937).
Trilling, Lionel, *The Liberal Imagination* (New York, 1950).
Trofimov, I. I., ed., *Tvorčestvo Čexova. Sbornik statej* (Moskva, 1956).
Turgenev, Ivan, *The Borzoi Turgenev*, trans. Harry Stevens (New York, 1950).
Unger, Leonard, ed., *T. S. Eliot: A Selected Critique* (New York, 1948).
Vinogradov, V. V., *et al.*, eds., *Literaturnoe nasledstvo: Čexov*, LXVIII (Moskva, 1960).
Wellek, René and Austin Warren, *Theory of Literature* (New York, 1956).
West, Jr., Ray B., *The Short Story in America* (New York, 1952).
Wilson, Edmund, *The Triple Thinkers* (New York, 1948).
Winner, Thomas G., *Chekhov and His Prose* (New York, 1966).
——, "Čexov's *Ward No. 6* and Tolstoyan Ethics", *Slavic and East European Journal*, XVII (Winter 1959), 321-335.
Woodcock, George, "The Elusive Ideal: Notes on Turgenev", *The Sewanee Review*, LXIX (Winter 1961), 34-48.
Zajcev, Boris, *Čexov: Literaturnaja biografija* (New York, 1954).

INDEX

"Abolished!" (*Uprazdnili!*), 53, 58
"About Love" (*O ljubvi*), 168, 170-171
Absurd, the, 139-140, 163-164
"Affair That Fell Through, An" (*Propaščee delo*), 50
Alarm Clock, The (*Budil'nik*), 31
Al'bom. See "Album, The"
"Album, The" (*Al'bom*), 53, 55
Allegory, 20, 130n.
"Anonymous Story, An" (*Rasskaz neizvestnogo čeloveka*), 39, 43-46, 105, 117, 128-129
"Antoša Č's Office of Announcements" (*Kontora ob"javlenij Antoši Č . . .*), 30
Apuleius, 11
Arxierej. See "Bishop, The"
"At Home" (*Doma*), 77-78
"At Home" (*V rodnum uglu*), 143-144, 145, 147
Avilova, Lidija, 113

Bab'e carstvo. See "Woman's Kingdom, A"
Baby. See "Peasant Wives"
"Bad Story, A" (*Skvernaja istorija*), 50
"Because of Little Apples" (*Za jabločki*), 60, 61
Begičev, V. P., 33
"Belated Blossoms" (*Cvety zapozdalye*), 37-40, 43
Bentley, Eric, 109, 117, 124
"Bet, The" (*Pari*), 20
"Betrothed" (*Nevesta*), 38, 73, 134, 141, 154-157, 160
Bicilli, Petr, 104n., 138
Bierce, Ambrose, 15
"Bishop, The" (*Arxierej*), 157-158, 171-173
Bjalyj, G., 104n.

"Black Monk, The" (*Čërnyj monax*), 134, 158-161
Boccaccio, Giovanni, 11, 12
Booth, Wayne C., 96n., 98n.
"Boys, The" (*Mal'čiki*), 78-79
Brooks, Cleanth, 153
Brothers Karamazov, The, 22
Bruford, W. H., 60n.
"Burbot, The" (*Nalim*), 70-71
"Burnt Norton" (T. S. Eliot), 142

Čajka. See Seagull, The
Čelovek v futljare. See "Man in a Case, The"
Čërnyj monax. See "Black Monk, The"
"Certificate, A" (*Spravka*), 53, 55
Cervantes, 11, 12
Čexov, Aleksandr, 89n., 136
"Chameleon, The" (*Xameleon*), 53-54, 57, 97
Character, Character type: rote of in short story, 22-23; writer as, 28-29; hero modelled on literary types, 39-46; villain as victim, 61-62, 66-67, 70; indifference as mark of villain, 62-63, 70, 124-125, 128; dreamer as, 76-77, 81-82, 94-95, 97-98; reformer as, 117, 124, 127, 128; villain as hero, 119, 122-123
Cherry Orchard, The (*Višnëvyj sad*), 37, 75, 122, 135, 146, 151-152, 155, 162
"Chorus Girl, The" (*Xoristka*), 63, 105
Christie, Agatha, 36
Čiževskij, Dmitrij, 31, 33n., 139, 173n.
Coleridge, Samuel Taylor, 17
"Comic Advertisements and Announcements" (*Komičeskie reklamy i ob"javlenija*), 30

"Common Trifle, A" (*Žitejskaja meloč*), 78
"Confession, or Olja, Ženja, Zoja, A" (*Ispoved', ili Olja, Ženja, Zoja*), 50-53
Čto čašče vsego vstrečaetsja v romanax, povestjax i t. p. See "What Is Most Often Met in Novels, Stories, and So Forth?"
Curtin, Constance, 91n.
Cvety zapozdalye. See "Belated Blossoms"

Dal', Vladimir, 15
Dama s sobačkoj. See "Lady with the Dog, The"
"Darling, The" (*Dušečka*), 15, 161-162
"Daughter of Albion, A" (*Doč' Al'biona*), 60
"Death of a Government Clerk, The" (*Smert' činovnika*), 32-34
Decameron, The, 12
Degas, Edgar, 138
Derman, Avram, 26, 41n., 124n.
Dickens, Charles, 19
Djadja Vanja. See Uncle Vanja
Doč' Al'biona. See "Daughter of Albion, A"
"Doctor's Visit, A" (*Slučaj iz praktiki*), 138, 163-164
Doma. See "At Home"
Dom s mezaninom. See "House with a Mezzanine, The"
Dopolnitel'nye voprosy k ličnym kartam statističeskoj perepisi, predlagaemye Antošej Čexonte. See "Questionnaire to Be Filled Out for the Census, Composed by Antoša Čexonte"
Dostoevskij, Fëdor, 89
Drama na oxote. See "Shooting Party, The"
"Dreams" (*Mečty*), 80-82, 91
"Dreary Story, A" (*Skučnaja istorija*), 13, 59, 73, 97, 98, 99, 106-112, 113, 114, 129, 133n., 134
Duèl'. See "Duel, The"
"Duel, The" (*Duèl'*), 15-16, 40-43, 44n., 46, 73n., 116, 117, 122-125
Dušečka. See "Darling, The"

Dvoe v odnom. See "Two in One"
"Easter Eve" (*Svjatoju noč'ju*), 64-65, 70
Eger'. See "Huntsman, The"
Èjxenbaum, Boris, 21
Elegy. *See* Short story genre
Eliot, T. S., 142
Empson, William, 153
"Enemies" (*Vragi*), 63n.
Erlich, Victor, 77n., 154n.
Ermilov, Vladimir, 106, 127n., 130n., 154n., 165n.

"Fall of the House of Usher, The" (Poe), 18
"Fat and Thin" (*Tolstyj i tonkij*), 53, 55-56, 57-58, 59, 97
Fergusson, Francis, 74-75, 151
"Flying Islands, The" (*Letajuščie ostrova*), 29
Frye, Northrup, 13-14, 62, 63, 65
Futljarnost': defined, 62n.; emotional timidity in, 70, 124-125, 127; as evil, 117, 121; in "Thieves", 118-119; despotism of, 120, 125, 129-131; in "Ward No. 6", 129-132; and order, 130-131; in "The Man in a Case", 168-169; in "Gooseberries", 169-170; in "About Love", 170-171

Gardner, Erle Stanley, 36
Garšin, Vsevolod, 93, 103, 133n.; "An Occurrence" (*Proisšestvie*), 104-105
Gitovič, N. I., 33n., 109n., 133n.
Gogol', Nikolaj, 15, 17, 80, 89; "The Overcoat", 33-34; "Nevskij Prospect", 104
Golubkov, V. V., 127n.
Gončarov, Ivan, 89
"Gooseberries" (*Kryžovnik*), 168-171
Gordon, Caroline, 74-75
Gor'kij, Maksim, 60n., 72
Gothic revival, 17
"Grasshopper, The" (*Poprygunja*), 116, 117, 126-127
Grešnik iz Toledo. See "Sinner from Toledo, A"
Grigorovič, Dmitrij, 29, 70, 89, 103
"Griša", 77, 91
"Gusev", 114

Hagan, John, 106n.
"Happiness" (*Ščast'e*), 85-86
Hauser, Arnold, 138-139
Hawthorne, Nathaniel, 15, 17
"Head of the Family, The" (*Otec semejstva*), 60-61
Hemingway, Ernest, 23, 24
Hendry, Irene, 12
Hingley, Ronald, 154n.
Hoffmann, E. T. A., 17
"House with a Mezzanine, The" (*Dom s mezoninom*), 16, 49, 52, 105, 165-166
Huckleberry Finn, 90
Hugo, Victor, 29, 31
"Huntsman, The" (*Eger'*), 70-71

Imeniny. See "Name Day"
Impressionism, Impressionist: perception of reality, 53, 59, 77-78, 88, 90-92, 135, 137, 138; absence of tendentiousness in, 98-99; accident as causal principle in, 137-139; concept of time in, 140-141, 152; ambiguity in, 140-141, 153-154, 173
"In Exile" (*V ssylke*), 114, 117, 127
"In Hotel Rooms" (*V nomerax*), 56-57
"In Our Practical Age, When, and So Forth" (*V naš praktičeskij vek, kogda, i t. d.*), 50
"In the Ravine" (*V ovrage*), 16, 134
Intrigi. See "Intrigues"
"Intrigues" (*Intrigi*), 79
"Ionyč", 24-27, 28, 37, 52
Irving, Washington, 15
Ispoved', ili Olja, Ženje, Zoja. See "Confession, or Olja, Ženja, Zoja, A"
I to i se. See "This and That"
Ivanov, 95, 96, 98-99, 106-109
Ivask, George, 88n.

James, Henry: "The Beast in the Jungle", 21; "The Art of Fiction", 22; "The Turn of the Screw", 35, 153; "The Aspern Papers", 96n.; *The Ambassadors*, 127
Jokaj, Mor, 29
Journal for Everybody (*Žurnal dlja vsex*), 154n.

Joyce, James, 17, 18, 21; *Dubliners*, 12; "Araby", 24, 168

Kantemir, Antiox, 30
"Kaštanka", 77
"Killers, The" (Hemingway), 23-24
"Kiss, The" (*Poceluj*), 82-85, 86
Knipper, Ol'ga, 136, 137
Knjaginja. See "Princess, The"
Komičeskie reklamy i ob"javlenija. See "Comic Advertisements and Announcements"
Kontora ob"javlenij Antoši Č ... See "Antoša Č's Office of Announcements"
Korolenko, Vladimir, 16, 116
Kryžovnik. See "Gooseberries"

"Lady with the Dog, The" (*Dama s sobačkoj*), 15, 52, 72, 141, 171
Leontev-Ščeglov, I. L., 95, 114
Lermontov, Mixail, 74; *A Hero of Our Time*, 40; "The Rock", (*Utës*), 71-72
Letajuščie ostrova. See "Flying Islands, The"
"Letter to a Learned Friend" (*Pis'mo k učënomu sosedu*), 30
"Live Merchandise" (*Živoj tovar*), 31-32
Lošadinaja familija. See "Name Like a Horse's, A"
Lyric poem. *See* Short story genre

Magarshack, David, 32, 113
Mal'čiki. See "Boys, The"
Malkiel', Marija, 136
"Man in a Case, The" (*Čelovek v futljare*), 23, 168-169, 171
Mansfield, Katharine, 14, 17, 18
Martz, Louis, 142n.
Mathewson, Rufus, 40n., 102n.
Matlaw, Ralph, 16, 36-37, 40n., 123
Maupassant, Guy de, 12, 18, 19
Mečty. See "Dreams"
"Meeting, Though It Took Place, Nevertheless ..., The" (*Svidanie xotja i sostojalos', no ...*), 52
Melville, Herman, 15
Merežkovskij, Dmitrij, 88n., 158n.
Miroljubov, V. S., 154n.

Mirsky, D. S., 166-167
"Misery" (*Toska*), 65-67, 70, 71
Mizinova, Lidija, 136
Moja žizn'. See "My Life"
Moj jubilej. See "My Anniversary"
Mudrick, Marvin, 22
"Murder, The" (*Ubijstvo*), 114
Murder of Roger Ackroyd, The, 36
Mužiki. See "Peasants"
"My Anniversary" (*Moj jubilej*), 28-29
"My Life" (*Moja žizn'*), 16, 105, 133n.,
    141, 148-150

Nalim. See "Burbot, The"
"Name Day" (*Imeniny*), 93, 94-96, 98,
    99, 100-102, 110
"Name Like a Horse's, A" (*Lošadinaja
    familija*), 61
Na puti. See "On the Road"
Nature: storm as reflection of inner
    turmoil, 42-43, 47, 72-73, 118-119;
    parody of romantic setting in, 51-
    52; as indicator of emotional mood,
    54, 57, 70-73, 103, 164, 168; audi-
    tory and visual images in, 87-89; as
    reflection of theme, 141-142; as
    death symbol, 143-144
"Neighbors" (*Sosedi*), 127-128
Nenužnaja pobeda. See "Unnecessary
    Victory, The"
Neprijatnost'. See "Unpleasantness,
    An"
"Nervous Breakdown, A" (*Pripadok*).
    63n., 94, 98, 99, 102-105, 133n.
Nevesta. See "Betrothed"
New Times (*Novoe vremja*), 119
"New Villa, The" (*Novaja dača*), 164-
    165
Northern Messenger, The (*Severnyj
    vestnik*), 93, 94
"Notes from Underground", 15
Novaja dača. See "New Villa, The"
Novel: short story and, 11-12, 19;
    distinguished from short story, 13-
    14, 18, 19-22; Čexov's attempts at,
    46, 89-90, 93, 144

Objectivity, 95-97, 106, 108-109
O'Connor, Frank, 13-14
O'Faolain, Sean, 19n., 22
O ljubvi. See "About Love"

"On Official Business" (*Po delam
    služby*), 28, 46-47, 72, 73n.
"On the Road" (*Na puti*), 60, 71-74
Ostranenie, 77
Ostrov Saxalin. See Saxalin Island
Otec semejstva. See "Head of the
    Family, The"
Othello, 108
Oxford English Dictionary, 15
"Oysters" (*Ustricy*), 62-63

Palata No. 6. See "Ward No. 6"
Panixida. See "Requiem"
Papernyj, Zinovij, 88, 154n.
Parable, 20
Paradox, 72, 73-74, 153-154
Pari. See "Bet, The"
Pathetic fallacy, 72
"Peasants" (*Mužiki*), 134
"Peasant Wives" (*Baby*), 117, 120-121,
    130
Piazza Tales, The (Melville), 15
Pis'mo k učěnomu sosedu. See "Letter
    to a Learned Friend"
Pleščeev, Aleksej, 93, 98, 99, 103,
    109n.
Plot: analogues for, 12; as distinguish-
    ing trait of *povest'*, 16; in Romantic
    fiction, 17-18; concept of suspense
    in short story, 18, 21-22, 27; use of
    detective story as basis of, 18, 20n.,
    22, 34-37, 46-47; role of event in,
    23; theme of fiction versus reality
    in, 24, 36-37, 39-40, 42-43; as love
    triangle parodied, 31-32; Čexov's
    parody of in Gogol's "The Over-
    coat", 32-34; moral viewpoint of
    pathos used in, 60; use of melo-
    dramatic devices in, 117, 118, 120,
    122, 124, 126
Poceluj. See "Kiss, The"
Po delam služby. See "On Official
    Business"
Poe, Edgar Allan, 14, 15, 17, 18
Poggioli, Renato, 63, 64, 66, 70, 161
Point of view, 27, 95-96
Poprygunja. See "Grasshopper, The"
Povest'. See Plot; *Rasskaz*
"Princess, The" (*Knjaginja*), 98, 105
Pripadok. See "Nervous Breakdown,
    A"

Propaščee delo. *See* "Affair That Fell Through, An"

Puškin, Aleksandr, 15, 16n., 17; "The Queen of Spades", 18; "Remembrance" (*Vospominanie*), 42

"Questionnaire to Be Filled Out for the Census, Composed by Antoša Čexonte" (*Dopolnitel'nye voprosy k ličnym kartam statističeskoj perepisi, predlagaemye Antošej Čexonte*), 30

Rashomon (Japanese film), 165

Rasskaz: distinguished from *povest'*, 15-17; Čexov's attitude toward *povest'* and, 15-16. *See also* Plot

Rasskaz neiznestnogo čeloveka. *See* "Anonymous Story, An".

Realism: tradition of in short story, 15, 18, 31; influence of on short story, 20; concept of Čexov deviating from, 138-139, 173

Repetitor. *See* "Tutor, The"

"Requiem" (*Panixida*), 63-64, 70

Romantic: concept of love parodied, 37-40, 49-51; setting parodied, 51-52

Romanticism, Romantic movement: influence of on short story, 17-19, 31

Roskin, A., 137n.

Rossolimo, Grigorij, 137

Saltykov-Ščedrin, Mixail, 93

Satire, 33, 41-42, 54, 57-59

Saxalin, 94, 112, 113-116, 127, 133n., 135

Saxalin Island (*Ostrov Saxalin*), 114

Ščast'e. *See* "Happiness"

Schorer, Mark, 21, 170

Seagull, The (*Čajka*), 137

"Sergeant Prišibeev" (*Unter Prišibeev*), 61-62, 67

Šestov, Lev, 133n., 137-139, 164

"Shooting Party, The" (*Drama na oxote*), 29, 34-37

Short story genre: elegy and, 11; concept of time in, 11, 13, 24-27; revelation in, 11, 13, 21-23, 27; lyric poem and, 12-13, 17; distinguished from tale, 14-15; Čexov's attitude toward, 15-16; tone as ordering principle in, 17-18, 19; importance of technique in, 19-20. *See also* Character; Novel; Plot; *Rasskaz*; Realism; Romanticism

Simmons, Ernest, 113, 114

"Sinner from Toledo, A" (*Grešnik iz Toledo*), 29

"Sire de Malétroit's Door" (R. L. Stevenson), 23, 24

Šklovskij, Viktor, 12, 34, 57, 77

Skučnaja istorija. *See* "Dreary Story, A"

Skvernaja istorija. *See* "Bad Story, A"

"Sleepy" (*Spat' xočetsja*), 91

Slučaj iz praktiki. *See* "Doctor's Visit, A"

Smert' činovnika. *See* "Death of a Government Clerk, The"

Sosedi. *See* "Neighbors"

Spat' xočetsja. *See* "Sleepy"

Spravka. *See* "Certificate, A"

Step'. *See* "Steppe, The"

"Steppe, The" (*Step'*), 16, 85, 86-92, 93, 114

Stevenson, Robert Louis, 23

Struve, Gleb, 91n., 106n.

Student. *See* "Student, The"

"Student, The" (*Student*), 141-143, 144

"Surgery" (*Xirurgija*), 56

Suvorin, Aleksej: mentioned as Čexov's correspondent, 44n., 89n., 93, 94, 98n., 103n., 107n., 114, 116, 133n., 135, 136, 158; as traveling companion, 115; criticism by of Čexov story, 119

Švedskaja spička. *See* "Swedish Match, The"

Svidanie xotja i sostojalos', no . . . See "Meeting, Though It Took Place, Nevertheless . . . , The"

Svjatoju noč'ju. *See* "Easter Eve"

"Swedish Match, The" (*Švedskaja spička*), 29, 34

Symbolism, Symbolist (Russian), 31, 138, 173

Talant. *See* "Talent"

"Talent" (*Talant*), 80

Tales of a Traveller (Irving), 15
Tales of Soldiers and Civilians (Bierce), 15
Tales of the Grotesque and Arabesque (Poe), 15
Tate, Allan, 74-75
"Teacher of Literature, The" (*Učiteľ slovesnosti*), 166-168
Thackeray, William, 19
"Thieves" (*Vory*), 118-119, 120, 121
"This and That" (*I to i se*), 49-50, 51
"Thousand and One Passions, or the Terrible Night, A" (*Tysjača odna strasť, ili strašnaja noč*), 29
Three Sisters (*Tri sestry*), 151
"Three Years" (*Tri goda*), 16, 144-148
Tif. See "Typhus"
Timmer, Charles B., 137n., 139-140
Tolstoj, Lev, 20, 89, 104, 115-116, 132-133, 154; "The Death of Ivan Il'ič", 15; "The Kreuzer Sonata", 40, 133n.; *Anna Karenina*, 40; "The Cossacks", 40; "Family Happiness", 51; *War and Peace*, 51; Sevastopol stories, 51, 104n.; *The Kingdom of God*, 132; *Resurrection*, 132
Tolstyj i tonkij. See "Fat and Thin"
Tom Jones, 90
Toska. See "Misery"
Tri goda. See "Three Years"
Trilling, Lionel, 18
Tri sestry. See Three Sisters
Turgenev, Ivan, 89, 129; *Rudin*, 39, 44n.; *On the Eve*, 39, 41, 43-45, 129; *Fathers and Sons*, 40
"Tutor, The" (*Repetitor*), 61, 62, 67
Twice-Told Tales (Hawthorne), 15
"Two in One" (*Dvoe v odnom*), 53, 54-55, 97
"Typhus" (*Tif*), 91
Tysjača odna strasť, ili strašnaja noč. See "Thousand and One Passions, or the Terrible Night, A"

Ubijstvo. See "Murder, The"
Učiteľ slovesnosti. See "Teacher of Literature, The"
Uncle Tom's Cabin, 60
Uncle Vanja (*Djadja Vanja*), 151
"Unnecessary Victory, The" (*Nenužnaja pobeda*), 29

"Unpleasantness, An" (*Neprijatnosť*), 98, 99-100
Unter Prišibeev. See "Sergeant Prišibeev"
Uprazdnili! See "Abolished!"
Ustricy. See "Oysters"

Vereščagin, V. V., 40
Verne, Jules, 29
"Veročka", 60, 67-70, 71
"Vint", 53, 58-59
Višnëvyj sad. See Cherry Orchard, The
V naš praktičeskij vek, kogda, i t. d. See "In Our Practical Age, When, and So Forth"
V nomerax. See "In Hotel Rooms"
Vory. See "Thieves"
V ovrage. See "In the Ravine"
Vragi. See "Enemies"
V rodnom uglu. See "At Home"
V ssylke. See "In Exile"

"Ward No. 6" (*Palata No. 6*), 16, 122, 129-133, 134, 135, 148
Warren, Austin, 21
Wellek, René, 21
West, Jr., Ray B., 19n., 20
"What Is Most Often Met in Novels, Stories, and So Forth?" (*Čto čašče vsego vstrečaetsja v romanax, povestjax i t. p.*), 29
"Wife, The" (*Žena*), 116, 124-126, 127
Wilson, Edmund, 153
Winner, Thomas, 30n., 40n., 90n., 116-117, 120n., 132n., 158-159
"Woman's Kingdom, A" (*Bab'e carstvo*), 162-163
Woodcock, George, 129
Wordsworth, William, 17

Xameleon. See "Chameleon, The"
Xirurgia. See "Surgery"
Xoristka. See "Chorus Girl, The"

Za jabločki. See "Because of Little Apples"
Zajcev, Boris, 106
Žena. See "Wife, The"
Žitejskaja meloč. See "Common Trifle, A"
Živoj tovar. See "Live Merchandise"